Policy Implementation and Bureaucracy

Policy Implementation and Bureaucracy

Second Edition

Randall B. Ripley
Professor and Chairperson
Department of Political Science
Senior Faculty Associate, Mershon Center

Grace A. Franklin
Research Associate
Mershon Center

both of
The Ohio State University

The Dorsey Press
Chicago, Illinois 60600

Cover photo by Tim Kaage

THE DORSEY PRESS, 1982 and 1986

ISBN 0-256-03393-5
Library of Congress Catalog Card No. 82–72855

Printed in the United States of America

1 2 3 4 5 6 7 8 9 0 DO 3 2 1 0 9 8 7 6

PREFACE

National policy gets made for the most part through an interaction of Congress, the bureaucracy, the presidency, and various interest groups. In an earlier volume, *Congress, the Bureaucracy, and Public Policy* (which The Dorsey Press published in 1984), we analyzed the *formulation and legitimation* of national policy by those institutions.

That book dealt with a bread-and-butter area for political scientists in the United States: how a bill becomes a law. In the present book we tackle the next logical topic of interest to people who follow the interaction of institutions and policies: what happens after a bill becomes a law? How does *implementation* of policies and programs authorized in statutes occur? What institutions play important roles? What promotes rapid and successful implementation? What works against speed and success? Does implementation activity vary for different types of policy? An understanding of implementation is critical to any grasp of what it is that American governments do.

Because bureaucracy—at several geographical (and governmental) levels—is the primary governmental agent involved in implementation of policies and the programs designed to pursue those policies, this volume also focuses considerable attention on the nature and behavior of bureaucratic actors.

This volume, then, focuses on twin themes: bureaucratic activity and the implementation of public policy. The analysis of bureaucratic activity will not cover all aspects of such activity but will concentrate on that portion related to implementation. We advance a number of general propositions about impleme but our central focus is not on theory for its own sake. W to analyze implementation—and particularly the role of bureaucracies in it—on the basis of empirical reality. Above all, as students of American politics we are interested in implementation as part of the chain of activities that leads to patterns of allocation of scarce benefits and values for individuals and groups in society and for society as a whole. (And, in recent years, general awareness of the reality of scarce resources instead of an assumption of unlimited resources has intensified political conflict over many policies and programs.)

Our central interest is politics, not the content of policies. We are political scientists looking at institutions dealing with policies, not policy analysts trying to judge the relative success or failure of those policies.

To give the book a manageable empirical focus we have limited ourselves to questions about the implementation of policies within the confines of the United States. Primarily these are policies that are usually described as domestic, but they also include some foreign and defense policies with domestic aspects (for example, procurement of weapons for either the U.S. armed forces or for sale to foreign governments). What we have excluded is study of programs such as the deployment of U.S. troops and weapons abroad and the dispersal of tangible benefits such as arms aid, technical assistance, and food aid in foreign countries. Such implementation activities outside the United States are very important to U.S. national security, but we are looking for general patterns of supports and constraints in which implementation is set, and the conditions abroad are often so different in kind—and involve largely non-American bureaucracies—that we have chosen to exclude nondomestic policy implementation.

We will, however, deal with multiple bureaucracies. Unlike the formulation and legitimation of national policy—which takes place primarily in Washington with the principal participants almost all being Washington-based actors and institutions—implementation of domestic policy takes place throughout the United States. The federal bureaucracy in Washington is only one actor. Federal bureaucrats scattered all over the country, state bureaucrats, local bureaucrats, and a host of nonbureaucratic actors at all geographical levels also get involved. The very real impact of the federal nature of our governing system is apparent in a study of implementation.

We have chosen concrete examples throughout the book to illustrate the processes we are analyzing, not simply to tell interesting stories. These examples involve broad policies, specific programs, and a variety of governmental agencies. Some of the examples took place some years ago; some are current, with further actions clearly yet to be taken. The Reagan period provides a particularly interesting challenge in finding apposite examples, both because new programs were, for the most part, not created and because Reagan appointees in some instances sought to change the previous implementation practices of their agencies.

As is the case with all of our research and writing, our location at the Mershon Center of The Ohio State University has facilitated this enterprise through providing both intellectual stimulation and tangible support.

Helpful comments from Robert T. Daland, Carl E. Van Horn, and Samuel C. Patterson on the manuscript for the first edition of this book were put to what we hope was good use. In preparing this second edition we had the benefit of reviews of the first edition by Gayle Avant, Department of Political Science, Baylor University; Michael Johnson, Department of Political Science, University of Pittsburgh; Robert Stein, Department of Political Science, Rice University; Paul Dommel, Department of Political Science, Cleveland State University; John Wooley, Department of Political Science, Washington University; and William N. Dunn, Department of Political Science, University of Pittsburgh.

Randall B. Ripley
Grace A. Franklin

CONTENTS

List of Figures

List of Tables

CHAPTER 1

Program Implementation in the United States

What happens after a bill becomes a law? Only recently have political scientists begun to pay systematic attention to that question. It is a question that requires careful analysis in order to understand government, politics, and public policy in the United States.

Earlier students of administration treated implementation processes as if they were sterile—that is, not "infected" with politics. It seems clear to us, however, that program implementation is, above all, a political process and should be analyzed as such. Bargaining—at the heart of American politics—occurs during implementation. Implementation activities are not fixed in number, content, or duration. Rather they vary among different policies and change during the lifetime of any specific policy or program.

We hope to provide an empirically rich analysis of some of the realities of implementation politics. We also want to contribute to the development of conceptual frameworks in order to understand the realities that we will analyze. Specifically, we want to develop further a scheme we derived from Lowi and used in the analysis of policy formulation and legitimation (Ripley and Franklin, 1984) and apply that scheme to implementation.

PRELIMINARY OBSERVATIONS

In most books authors withhold their generalizations until the final chapter. We want to reverse that convention and offer a few generalizations about public policy and its implementation at the outset of this book. These will serve as guideposts to help sort out the plentiful individual policies considered in later chapters. They also serve as an indication that rationality and objectivity are not the dominant features of policy implementation. Any observer viewing the implementation of public policy in the United States and expecting to find order, timely performance, and achievement of clearly stated goals would be severely disappointed.

Two conclusions are constantly reinforced whenever public program implementation is subjected to scrutiny:

1. *No one is clearly in charge of implementation.*
2. *Domestic programs virtually never achieve all that is expected of them.*

Some observers, upon encountering these two truths, go on to conclude that the governing structures in the United States are hopelessly inept, or corrupt, or both. Those with a very conservative or right-wing orientation argue that since the programs seem to proceed haphazardly this is a compelling reason for cutting the scope of government activity dramatically. Those with a radical left-wing perspective argue that implementation is mired down because selfish capitalist interests are in charge of all policy activities in the country and, by nature, proceed in a corrupt and inefficient way, particularly in terms of denying the poorer classes in society their just share of national wealth. Both points of view are understandable expressions of frustration at a system that doesn't seem to work as efficiently as it "ought to."

We want to investigate the implementation of public programs in the United States without falling into an ideological camp by looking at the nature of implementation in general, its relation to bureaucratic behavior, and a number of real-world cases of implementation of different types of policy. We begin this analysis with some beliefs accumulated during years of analyzing bureaucratic behavior and public policy performance, and we want to examine empirical evidence related to those beliefs to see the degree to which they are accurate or the degree to which they need to be altered because they are not supported by evidence. These beliefs can be stated in a series of generalizations.

1. No one, in the sense of a single institution or a small, coordinated set of actors, is in charge of the implementation of domestic programs in the United States. In a very real sense there is no single government in the United States to promote, oversee, or conduct implementation (see F.C. Mosher, 1980). Rather, there are many governments and, in some cases, government is often indistinguishable from nongovernment. The contracting out of much public business has increased in recent years and further complicated an already complex situation.

2. Domestic programs virtually never achieve all that is expected of them in a straightforward and timely manner. This is the case in part because the expectations are numerous, diffuse, and often unrealistic.

3. The first two generalizations are true in part because of a series of complexities arising from the structure of American governments and the conflicting values, interests, and beliefs of key actors in the implementation process.

4. The most important set of actors in implementation processes are in various bureaucracies. They do not *control* implementation, but their influence is central.

5. Patterns of implementation vary depending on the different major social purposes of policies being implemented.

6. The decentralized (federalistic) nature of policy implementation has a series of critical effects on how that implementation occurs.

7. *Effective implementation* may have different meanings in different situations.

8. Even if implementation of a specific program is judged to be effective, that does not guarantee that the program will necessarily achieve its desired impact.

The first three chapters of this book examine a variety of general matters that address these eight beginning generalizations. The remainder of the present chapter looks at the first three generalizations by examining the place of implementation in the policy process and the nature of implementation in general.

Chapter 2 focuses on the fourth generalization by examining American bureaucracy. Specifically, Chapter 2 addresses the general character and importance of bureaucracy, the growth of American bureaucracy, the political nature of American bureaucracy, and the place of bureaucrats in the implementation process.

Chapter 3 develops material related to the last four generalizations in that it will address the impact of federalism in the implementation process and the different types of domestic policy that can be implemented.

Chapters 4 through 7 will take the four major policy types developed in Chapter 3 individually and examine empirical evidence about the implementation patterns within each type to investigate the expectations laid out at the end of Chapter 3. We will pay special attention to the role of bureaucracy and bureaucrats in each type because they are, in fact, central actors across all types.

The final chapter of the book (Chapter 8) reviews the variations in political patterns surrounding implementation of different types of policies presented in the earlier chapters and elaborates and amends (as the evidence warrants) the expectations about implementation patterns presented in Chapter 3.

IMPLEMENTATION IN THE POLICY PROCESS

How can we study a set of activities that no one controls and that fails to achieve expectations? The favorite device of analysis is to develop a model that reduces the complexities and apparent chaos enough to allow comprehension without overly distorting and simplifying reality. To understand implementation, we need to understand what it is and where it fits in the overall flow of activities called the policy process.

Implementation is what happens after laws are passed authorizing a program, a policy, a benefit, or some kind of tangible output. The term refers to the set of activities that follow statements of intent about program goals and desired results by government officials. Implementation encompasses actions (and nonactions) by a variety of actors, especially bureaucrats, designed to put programs into effect, ostensibly in such a way as to achieve goals.

Implementation encompasses many kinds of actions. Agencies charged by law with responsibility for administering programs must *acquire resources* needed to move ahead. These resources include personnel, equipment, land, raw materials, and—above all—money. Second, agencies engage in *interpretation and planning*. They expand the language of statutes into concrete directives, regulations, and program plans and designs. Third, agencies must *organize* their activities by creating bureaucratic units and routines for attacking their workload. Finally, agencies *extend benefits or restrictions* to their clientele or target groups. They provide the services or payments or limits on activity or whatever else represents the tangible output of a program.

Where do these activities fit in the overall flow of activities we refer to as a policy process? In answering this question, two general points need to be remembered. First, any portrayal of the policy process in the United States represents an enormous simplification of an extremely complex set of phenomena. Second, the policy process can be conceived of as a mix of *activities* (with political, technical, and intellectual activities all prominent and also all intermingled) and *products* (the results of those activities).

Figure 1–1 presents an overview of the flow of policy activities and products. Figure 1–1 drastically simplifies reality. Readers should be aware that the rationality and orderliness that the diagram implies only rarely appear in the real world of policy. The diagram represents the *logical* flow of activities and resulting products; it does not always represent the actual *chronological* flow. However, many chronologies of individual policies approximate the flow portrayed in Figure 1–1. The figure constitutes a good, but rough, guide to reality.

Policy formulation is the development of alternatives for what should be done in general to attack various items on the agenda of government. *Policy legitimation* is the ratification or adoption of some specific alternative or set of alternatives. The formulation of programs involves detailing alternatives about the precise means (the program) for achieving goals. Legitimation of programs involves ratification of the specific alternative chosen. In all of these formulation and legitimation activities there is a constant interplay of actors each pursuing his or her own interests and forming, dissolving, and reforming into a constantly changing pattern of coalitions. The executive branch, Congress, and a myriad of interest groups all get into the debate and decision making in many ways (see Ripley and Franklin, 1984, for a detailed account of the patterns that emerge in the course of policy formulation and legitimation).

FIGURE 1–1   The Flow of Policy Activities and Products

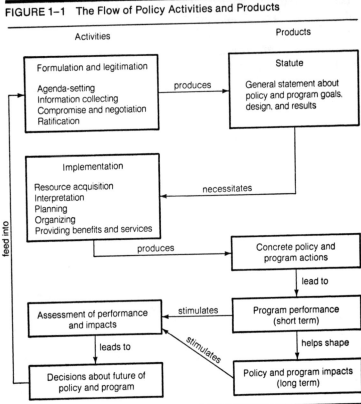

Activities | Products

Formulation and legitimation

Agenda-setting
Information collecting
Compromise and negotiation
Ratification

produces →

Statute

General statement about
policy and program goals,
design, and results

Implementation

Resource acquisition
Interpretation
Planning
Organizing
Providing benefits and services

← necessitates

produces →

**Concrete policy and
program actions**

↓ lead to

**Assessment of performance
and impacts** ← stimulates — **Program performance
(short term)**

↓ leads to   ↓ helps shape

stimulates

**Decisions about future of
policy and program**

**Policy and program impacts
(long term)**

feed into

Statutes resulting from policy and program formulation and legitimation contain general statements about goals, design, and desired results. Policy statements contain the intentions of the government in relation to a particular substantive area. There is no single definitive source for all policy statements of the federal government in the United States. However, a major source of statements is the statutes passed by Congress and signed by the president. Additional sources are statements of the president, statements of other major executive branch officials such as departmental secretaries, and written regulations promulgated by federal agencies and published in the *Federal Register*. Program designs lay out the details of the contents of a program plus the plans for administering it.

The formal adoption of program proposals in legislation logically necessitates *implementation*. Logic is sometimes defied in that there are cases in which implementation simply never occurs. Implementation has been characterized briefly above as involving acquisition of resources, interpreting and planning specific program designs derived from broad mandates in the legislation, organizing, and providing benefits. All of these implementation activities result in *concrete policies and programs*. We again underscore that implementation is no less political than any other set of policy activities. The politics differ from the politics of other stages and the actors may vary somewhat, but there are also numerous similarities. The rest of this book is an attempt to describe, analyze, and explain those politics of implementation.

Policy actions lead to short-term policy results, which we have called *program performance*. The exact components of program performance vary depending on the exact nature of each individual program. The central feature is that they are the immediate, tangible results of the program. For example, one important study of three major federal programs (Van Horn, 1979b) poses three central performance questions: Who governs?, How are funds spent?, and Who benefits? *Short-run* does not have a fixed time span attached to it, but it is reasonable to suggest that in the case of most programs at least the first several years' results can fairly be considered as falling in that category.

Short-term program performance helps shape *policy and program impacts*. These impacts are the longer-run results of policies and programs. They occur at both the societal and individual level. They relate to the ultimate and most important question: so what? What difference does it make, to whom, and in what way that the program or policy was enacted and implemented? Do the targeted beneficiaries of a medical care program have better health as a result? Does federal aid to education produce more learning on the part of the students whose schools and teachers have been aided? Do those who learn more therefore get better jobs afterwards? Is there less social violence among the young because they are in better educational settings and get employed more quickly after completing their formal schooling?

Questions about impact can be generated almost endlessly. These questions can come in layers, such as:

Do the intended beneficiaries benefit in the ways they were expected to?

Did they benefit in additional ways?

Were they harmed in some unexpected ways?

Did others not intended to benefit also benefit?

Were there planned benefits for society as a whole beyond simply adding up the benefits of the individuals?

Were there unplanned benefits for society as a whole?

Were there unplanned detriments for society as a whole?

Interesting and important questions are fairly easy to pose about any program of at least moderate size. Answers are much more difficult to produce. However, questions about both short-term results (program performance) and longer-term results (policy and program impacts) stimulate the *assessment of performance and impacts.* Persons making policy and program decisions in the White House, the rest of the federal bureaucracy, and Congress want to find out what happens, in a general way, as a result of the programs they create for the nation. Policy actors have a number of different sources for making assessments and a number of different criteria and values for measuring what they see. If they are members of Congress they may rely, for example, on the reactions of their constituents; if they are bureaucrats they may rely on client groups; and policy actors of any sort may rely on organized interest groups. They also rely in part on their own assessment of political gains to be made and costs to be paid on the basis of keeping a program, changing it, or dropping it. They look for help in making assessments from their own professional staff. From time to time, they also commission research and evaluation on program performance and/or program impact by outsiders—both those in private research companies and those based in universities. The instinct to assess is strong, even though the nature of the assessment will not fully meet the criteria of any one perspective. Some academic types are likely to be unhappy that political criteria are often weighed so heavily. By the same token, an interest group may be quite displeased that systematic studies, replete with statistically based assertions, are undertaken at all or are accorded any weight.

Assessment takes place constantly, even if it is only carried out on the basis of the intuitive feel of policymakers and even if the criteria are exclusively political in the narrowest sense of "what's in it for me?" Assessment of implementation produces constantly shifting results because the implementation activities themselves typically undergo constant change.

Based on whatever kind of assessment occurs, *decisions on the future* of the policy and programs are made, and will be carried into subsequent rounds of formulation and legitimation.

The policy process in the United States (in all countries for that matter) is complicated. The cycle so tidily described in the few preceding pages is not, in fact, tidy at all. It stops and starts in unusual and unique ways at unexpected times. It can begin again at the beginning or at any one of a number of midpoints on short notice. (See Jones, 1984, for an excellent introduction to this general point.) The central point that should emerge in these introductory considerations is that in the midst of this complex and only partially predictable process implementation occupies a key location. It is literally in the middle of the flow of activities and products. Implementation determines what happens to policy statements as they are translated into concrete actions that attempt to bring about desired results both for individuals and for the nation as a whole. Assessments of implementation experience by policymakers help shape decisions about subsequent policy and program ventures.

THE NATURE OF IMPLEMENTATION

In recent years social scientists interested in implementation have generated numerous discussions of the phenomenon. Central to many of these discussions is some sort of checklist of both the numerous factors influencing implementation and the barriers to progress toward goals or success imbedded in the implementation process itself. Some of the discussions also contain examples of the general points drawn from the real world, although more frequently the focus is on refining theory or concepts.

Our central interest is in conveying a sense of reality about implementation politics in an orderly fashion. The phrase *orderly fashion* implies that we take conceptual, abstract, theoretical discussions of implementation seriously. However, we do not seek to refine theory or concepts for their own sake. We want to use the theoretical literature on implementation to help inform our discussion of empirical reality. We hope our discussion advances the cause of understanding implementation at an abstract level. Inevitably, however, the complex nature of implementation when looked at empirically makes satisfying abstract discussion particularly difficult.

The best of the literature that includes at least some conceptual or theoretical discussion of implementation (for good examples, see Berman, 1978; Bullock and Lamb, 1984; Chase, 1979; Elmore, 1978; Hargrove, 1975; Mazmaniam and Sabatier, 1983; Montjoy and O'Toole, 1979; O'Toole and Montjoy, 1984; Pressman and Wildavsky, 1984; Rein and Rabinovitz, 1978; Van Horn and Van Meter, 1976; Van Meter and Van Horn, 1975; and Van Horn, 1979b) strongly underscores several generalizations about implementation:

1. There are a very large number of external factors that can influence implementation.

2. For implementation to proceed without any major hitches, all or virtually all of these external factors must be supportive or at least neutral. Any one or few that push in a nonsupportive direction can derail the entire implementation process in a variety of ways.

3. There are also a large number of factors internal to implementation processes that inevitably provide obstacles to smooth implementation.

In the rest of this chapter we will focus on what we consider the five most salient features surrounding implementation that help make it confusing, complex, and frustrating both to those who participate in implementation and those who study it—*if* they expect simple, straightforward, and easy success in implementing programs. These five features encompass what we consider the most important external and internal factors dealt with in the general literature on implementation. Our aim is to make manageable the diversity of perspectives represented in the literature and to focus on the most important factors; we will delete or mention only in passing the factors of lesser importance. The five features we think are most important can be summarized in a single long sentence:

> Implementation processes involve *many important actors* holding *diffuse and competing goals and expectations* who work within a *context of an increasingly large and complex mix of government programs* that require *participation from numerous layers and units of government* and who are affected by *powerful factors beyond their control.*

There are two principal ways of assessing implementation (see Ripley, 1985:134–138). One approach focuses on compliance. It asks whether implementers *comply with* prescribed procedures, timetables, and restrictions. The compliance perspective sets up a preexisting model of correct implementation behavior and measures actual behavior against it. The second approach to assessing implementation is to ask how implementation is proceeding. What is it achieving? Why? This perspective can be characterized as *inductive* or *empirical.* Less elegantly, the central questions are *what's happening?* and *why?* There are general references in this approach to what was expected or hoped for by different participants and observers, but there is no rigid preexisting model against which behavior is measured.

This volume is written from the second perspective. Our interest is constantly in what's happening (regardless of whether it is in compliance with somebody's standards or not) and explaining what is observed. The five most important features discussed in the remainder of this chapter—the profusion of actors, the multiplicity and vagueness of goals, the proliferation and complexity of government programs, the participation of governmental units at all territorial levels, and the uncontrollable factors that all affect implementation—are offered as general factors that help explain implementation patterns found in major domestic programs.

MANY ACTORS

Number and Identity

Just about anyone can get into the implementation game, although there are often tussles between those seeking entry and those seeking to prevent it. Jerseys for players are abundant, and numbers often would have to run into three digits in order to accommodate all of those participating with regard to any given

TABLE 1-1 Actors in Implementation Processes

Level	Executive Officials and Organizations	Legislative Officials and Organizations	Bureaucratic Officials and Organizations	Nongovernmental Individuals and Organizations	Judicial Officials and Organizations
Federal	President Executive Office of the president Staff	Congress (committees and individual members) Congressional staff and support agencies	Department and agency heads Staff-civil servants (in Washington and in federal regional offices)	Corporations Labor unions Interest groups Advisory bodies Media (with national focus and impact)	Federal judges (3 levels) Law clerks Marshals Masters, experts Federal attorneys
State	Governor Governor's staff	State legislature (committees and members) Staff and support agencies	Department and agency heads Staff-civil servants (in state capitol) (in field offices)	(Same as above with state focus and impact)	State judges Law clerks Miscellaneous state judicial officials
Local	Mayor County commissioners Other local elected executives Staff	City councils, boards of commissioners, other local elected officials Staff	Department and agency heads Staff-civil servants (in central office) (in field offices)	Same as above (with local focus and impact)	Local judges Law clerks Miscellaneous local judicial officials

policy. The game does not resemble some nicely ordered sport with small team size and well-defined rules like basketball. Rather it resembles lacrosse in its original form—played between two tribes with the number of players, the boundaries, the duration, and other important aspects of the game all somewhat nebulous.

There are at least 15 major clusters of potential implementers for any given policy over time. Each of these clusters contains its own subgroups, and the subgroups are likely to change. Table 1–1 summarizes this rich array of implementers. *The basic point is that executives, legislatures, bureaucrats, a variety of private or nongovernmental groups and individuals, and courts at all of the three major territorial levels in the United States (federal, state, and local) can and do get involved in the implementation of domestic policies.*

As already noted, the roles of the three layers of bureaucrats (especially the civil servants) are the most persistent and are often dominant. Various private, nongovernmental groups—especially interest groups—are generally the second most important set of actors in implementation. Executives, legislatures, and courts are sporadically—although sometimes importantly—involved. The presence of a large variety of nongovernmental individuals and organizations and of judicial officials and organizations is perhaps the most unexpected feature of Table 1–1. The following two sections highlight their potential for impact.

The Role of Private Actors

Interest groups. That organized interest groups are important in relation to public policy in the United States is hardly news to anyone with even a cursory knowledge of how policy is shaped. However, most of the empirical investigations of interest groups' role in policy end after the stage of legitimation and formulation. Little is known about their role in implementation. We expect that role to be a strong one, and we will look at a number of cases involving interest groups in Chapters 4 through 7.

By way of introduction it is important to note that the dominant academic model (the pluralist view) of the role of interest groups in American politics may not apply to implementation. The pluralist model (see Truman, 1951, for the classic statement) suggests that there is an array of preexisting groups that mobilize to push for or against the enactment of specific legislation. New groups also come into being specifically to help struggle for or against some new legislative creation.

Already existing groups—at all territorial levels—get involved in trying to influence implementation decisions in ways favorable to their interests. The activity of interest groups does not cease after legislation is enacted. In fact, new interest groups are often created or existing interest groups often reshape their activities after and as a result of the passage of legislation and establishment of programs. Not only can interests help create policies, but the existence of policies can also create interests around which groups form.

That new programs will create new groups based on the interests that are created or revealed by the existence of the program itself makes sense, although the pluralist model of the place of interest groups in American politics obscures this simple, but important, fact. What is less self-evident is that bureaucracies charged with implementing programs will, in fact, sometimes take the initiative in helping create and fund the existence and activities of interest groups that will then subsequently lobby for decisions favorable to their interests.

The motivations of bureaucracies undertaking these activities is not always clear. To some extent they want to create bodies of supporters for their own interests. They aspire to have allies that will show Congress, the Office of Management and Budget, and the White House how important and vital their programs are to the well-being of the nation. To some extent, however, they also encourage and even fund groups that will compete with each other and that will also put conflicting pressures, sometimes severe, on the bureaucracy to move in different directions simultaneously and, possibly, to move in directions not necessarily favored by the bureaucracy. To the extent that this behavior occurs it may well be based on the widespread acceptance by the bureaucrats of the legitimacy and even desirability of active interest groups. There is good evidence that all of the major actors involved in the formulation and legitimation of policy in the United States hold such beliefs (see Aberbach and Rockman, 1977, 1978). As Lowi (1979:51) has summarized so convincingly, most actors act on their acceptance of "interest-group liberalism:"

> It is liberalism because it is optimistic about government, expects to use government in a positive and expansive role, is motivated by the

highest sentiments, and possesses a strong faith that what is good for government is good for the society. It is interest-group liberalism because it sees as both necessary and good a policy agenda that is accessible to all organized interests and makes no independent judgment of their claims. It is interest-group liberalism because it defines the public interest as a result of the amalgamation of various claims. A brief sketch of the working model of interest-group liberalism turns out to be a vulgarized version of the pluralist model of modern political science: (1) Organized interests are homogeneous and easy to define. Any duly elected representative of any interest is taken as an accurate representative of each and every member. (2) Organized interests emerge in every sector of our lives and adequately represent most of those sectors, so that one organized group can be found effectively answering and checking some other organized group as it seeks to prosecute its claims against society. And (3) the role of government is one of insuring access to the most effectively organized, and of ratifying the agreements and adjustments worked out among the competing leaders.

To Lowi's discussion we should add the observation that bureaucracies also, in some instances, seem to feel it part of their job to make sure that there are strong, relatively well-funded, functioning interest groups active in their policy bailiwicks.

The Department of Labor's Employment and Training Administration (ETA) serves as a good example of a bureaucracy dedicated to sustaining, creating, and funding a large number of interest groups that will both put pressure on ETA itself as well as on Congress for a variety of actions affecting not just statutes but also the details of implementation. These groups also complete with each other. And, local branches of the groups put pressures on state and local implementers.

ETA was particularly generous in funding a large variety of groups in the 1960s and 1970s. Even during the Reagan administration in the 1980s most of the same groups received funding, although they got a good deal less. ETA began funding with the passage of the Manpower Development and Training Act of 1962 and continued after the passage of the Comprehensive Employment and Training Act (CETA) in 1973 and the Job Training Partnership Act (JTPA) in 1982. Activities supported include special programs that presumably achieve some programmatic ends important to ETA and also provide a stable institutional base for the group involved; general institutional activities (such as in-house training of staff); research and evaluation activities (ETA funds both presumably neutral researchers in companies and based in universities but also funds occasional research by formally organized interest groups themselves); and various kinds of supportive activities for the entire employment and training system (for example, technical assistance for local affiliates of a national group; nationwide publicity and marketing of some ETA funded program).

ETA has funded five major kinds of interest group organizations in some or all of the above activity categories for the last several decades:

1. Organized labor. A variety of individual unions and the national AFL–CIO have received support. These, of course, were existing organizations. ETA played a direct role in creating the Human Resources Development Institute of the AFL–CIO.

2. Business. Some existing groups, such as the Business Roundtable (an organization of the chief executive officers of the largest corporations in the country), have received support. ETA has played a direct role in creating other groups, such as the National Alliance of Business (NAB) and the National Association of Private Industry Councils.

3. State and local governments. The employment and training-related activities of four national organizations have been funded in a variety of ways. These are the National Association of Counties, the National Governors Association, the United States Conference of Mayors, and the National League of Cities. They function as lobbies for other units of government in their dealings with the federal government.

4. Service provider organizations. During the 1960s two new national organizations and one already established group began to play a major role in employment and training implementation: the National Urban League and its affiliates (it was the preexisting group), Opportunities Industrialization Centers (both its national organization and local centers) and SER-Jobs for Progress (its national organizations and local affiliates). ETA helped nurture the new Urban League role with national contracts as well as providing contracts for local affiliates. It played a critical role in sustaining and expanding the strength of OIC and SER as those new organizations became part of the employment and training

landscape. This support also showed ETA expressing particular concern for the two largest ethnic minorities in the nation, minorities that were particularly targeted for help in the employment and training field: blacks (the major concern of the Urban League and OIC) and hispanics (the major concern of SER).

In addition, ETA also funded a variety of groups dealing with other target populations: women, the handicapped, and youth, for example.

5. Researchers. Researchers and their organizations also function as interest groups part of the time. Some companies came into being to work primarily or partially in the employment and training arena. They obviously developed a strong interest in not going out of business. Individuals in existing universities who assembled competent staff to work on questions of employment and training research also developed an interest in continuing to fund their staffs as well as providing institutional benefits to their universities.

ETA also created some new groups that had research as a central part of their reason for existing. These included a nonprofit company that both managed demonstration projects and did the research on their impact (Manpower Demonstration Research Corporation) and a council, composed mainly of academics, that both took positions on pending employment and training policy questions and commissioned and managed some research (the National Council on Employment Policy).

The case of the National Association of Private Industry Councils (NAPIC), mentioned above, provides a glimpse of one way ETA can help create and sustain a new interest group. The group sprang directly from a statutory addition to the basic employment and training statute (CETA at that time) in 1978. This Title created a Private Sector Initiatives Program (PSIP) and mandated the creation of a Private Industry Council (PIC) in each of the more than 450 political jurisdictions in states and localities charged with implementing it. PICs had to concur in the local plans for spending the money allocated to PSIP. The idea for NAPIC was generated by some of the individuals who were most active in the creation of some big city PICs. ETA quickly joined in support of the idea by making the critical decision that CETA administrative funds could be used to pay the membership dues in the association. The dues ranged between $500 and $5,000 for each PIC that wished to join, depending on the size of the PSIP allocation. Without this decision NAPIC—which quickly became firmly ensconced in Washington offices with a paid professional staff, national meetings, and the other trappings of permanent interest-group status—clearly would have folded almost immediately. PIC members at the local level had no source of public funds other than their CETA allocation. They certainly would not have paid the membership fee from personal resources. Nor would cities, counties, and states, most of which are in some sort of perpetual fiscal crisis, have authorized other public funds to pay the fee.

What's public? What's private?   In many important ways the distinction between public actors and private actors and between public purposes and private purposes breaks down in practice (see Dahl and Lindblom, 1953: chapter 1). Private actors make decisions about what are surely pieces of the public's business. Public actors also make decisions about what traditionally were thought of as private matters.

The fuzziness of the boundaries (see Clark, 1980) is often the subject of ideological dispute. For example, private businesspersons and their allies often allege that government, through regulation, is making decisions that business ought to be making for itself. Consumer-oriented groups allege that government has sold out to the private sector and that private interests are pursued at the expense of the public good. There is some truth in both sets of allegations.

A dramatic case of private interests conducting the public's business came to light in mid-1980 when the *Washington Post* (June 25, 1980) reported that the Department of Energy (DOE) was spending about seven eighths of its total budget of $11 billion for contractors and consultants. While DOE was an agency with 21,000 employees, it conducted most of the public's business by relying on the services of 200,000 contract workers employed under various auspices through about 4,000 contracts.

Another interesting case of thorough mixing of public and private occurred in 1980 as the Chrysler Corporation took advantage of the federal loan guarantee program enacted by Congress in 1979 to save the company from collapse. (See *The Wall Street Journal,* May 28, 1980, and June 27, 1980). The government and Chrysler signed a 55-page memorandum of understanding that specified the kind of daily government official involvement in corporate decisions that was activated as soon as the loan guarantees were first used. Prior governmental approval was required for a whole variety of Chrysler actions. Goals that must be met by the company were established for such matters as pricing decisions, volume of vehicle shipments, and cost-reduction programs.

Advisory groups. Cases of quasi-public/quasi-private actors being created by federal statute and federal regulations involve myriads of advisory groups and councils. For example, in 1983 every locality implementing a CETA program, more than 450 in number, had to have three advisory councils involved in its program: PIC (discussed above) for its PSIP programs, a youth council for youth-related programs, and a general planning council for all programs. Every locality also had to have three additional councils in the education field—one tied to vocational education and two tied to Title I of the Elementary and Secondary Education Act, the basic vehicle for providing federal aid to education to localities. Still other councils in both the employment and education fields existed at the state level—one in employment and training and four in some area of education; vocational education, disadvantaged children, education-training linkage, and basic skills.

The Role of Courts

Courts often get deeply involved in implementation questions, not just in the sense of making decisions that limit or channel or mandate certain kinds of implementation, but in the sense that judges and their appointees literally become program administrators (see Horowitz, 1977, for numerous examples and a general discussion). In the area of redistricting of legislative districts, for example, a number of federal district judges in the 1960s and 1970s simply drew the lines themselves and in effect, state and local bureaucrats became subordinate to the judges and their staffs on that matter. In the 1970s and 1980s judges and their appointees became particularly active in the area of school desegregation plans, particularly in northern cities in which de facto racial segregation existed even though legal segregation had never existed. Thus, for example, the experts appointed by the federal district judge overseeing desegregation in Boston beginning in the mid-1970s had to approve the school assignment of virtually every student in Boston's public schools.

Federal judges have a good deal of discretion in making judgments about implementation questions. For example, in the mid-1980s judges were often still upholding affirmative action quotas despite the argument by the Reagan administration that the Supreme Court had ruled against all such plans in June 1984 (*New York Times,* February 10, 1985).

Judicial involvement in recent years has been particularly important in the implementation of the provisions of the 1977 Surface Mining Control and Reclamation Act. Some rulings favored enforcers and some rulings favored coal companies eager to weaken the impact of the law. Judges again had considerable discretion. (See Chapter 6 of this volume for a lengthy discussion of the implementation of the 1977 strip-mining law.)

Lack of Hierarchy

The absence of a hierarchy or a "chain of command" among implementers causes even more complexity than does the bewildering number of actors. Ponder the clusters of actors in Table 1–1. Most of them are not in any formal hierarchical arrangement with each other at all. Pick any two sets of actors. They are likely to be independent of each other in the sense of having different institutional homes and different political bases of election or selection and support. Thus they deal with each other as equals—and potential allies or adversaries—not as superiors and subordinates. This situation promotes competition, bargaining, and compromise among actors.

Even in those cases in which actors involved in implementation are formally set in a hierarchical relationship the formal superior often finds his or her will frustrated by the response and behavior of the formal subordinates. Bargaining and compromise are still present to an important degree (see Lindblom, 1965). There is good evidence that the president-department secretary-civil servant bureaucrat relationship—formally the most hierarchical configuration in the federal government—is not really hierarchical (see Neustadt, 1973; Heclo, 1977). Commanders don't command; they bargain with the troops. The personal values and preferences of individuals—be they commanders or in the ranks—are important influences on implementation.

Conflict and Compromise

Policy formulation and legitimation activities are typically characterized by some conflict over both goals and means to attain those goals. This conflict is based on differing sets of values, interests, and beliefs on the parts of different actors. The conflict is resolved or at least reduced through a series of compromises in order to allow legislation to result. Lack of compromise almost always means lack of legislation. But even in the context of compromise there are individuals and groups who perceive themselves to be, on balance, winners or losers—at least on some specific points. The nature of the policy process in the United States is such that the losers do not have to abandon hope and the winners cannot relax after their formulation and legitimation victories. As Bardach (1977:38) puts it:

> the bargaining and maneuvering, the pulling and hauling, of the policy-adoption process carries over into the policy-implementation process. Die-hard opponents of the policy who lost out in the adoption stage seek and find means to continue their opposition when, say, administrative regulations and guidelines are being written. Many who supported the original policy proposal did so only because they expected to be able to twist it in the implementation phase to suit purposes never contemplated or desired by others who formed part of the original coalition. They too seek a role in the administrative process.

In short, the policy process is continuous and it offers continuous opportunities for raising both old and new issues. It also offers numerous points of access to many different actors for influencing outcomes. In a very real sense no decisions are ever final. All are appealable, amendable, and reversible.

To take a simple example: legislative fights over antiracial discrimination provisions in housing and education legislation do not really settle the question of how much the weight of government will be brought to bear against such discrimination. Even if the legislation is intended to prevent discrimination, there must be decisions over how the regulations are worded, what sanctions are specified, how they are used, their timing, their extent, and hundreds of other questions of detail. Compliance is not guaranteed by the legislation. Those with differing views struggle for language in the regulations favorable to their respective views. They also struggle for certain kinds of bureaucratic behavior along some scale from tough to lax.

New issues and conflicting opinions that were papered over or did not have to be faced in the formulation and legitimation process arise during implementation. For example, as housing legislation aimed at aiding the poor is implemented, differing values, interests, and beliefs lead different actors to stress different aspects of the law and to work for different ends. Those in the Department of Housing and Urban Development at the national level and their congressional supporters are most likely to be concerned with keeping the mortgage market supported and with keeping the homebuilding industry prosperous. Local elected officials may well be concerned with maximizing the number of federal dollars coming to their areas for supporting housing but, simultaneously, with maximizing their own control over the location of housing projects so as to keep the projects and their poor inhabitants isolated from the "better" neighborhoods. Groups representing individual beneficiaries, such as a local welfare rights organization or public housing tenants association, are most likely to have low rents as a major objective and are most likely to be concerned with locating the projects near jobs, health care facilities, and schools.

GOALS AND EXPECTATIONS

Goals embedded in programs are diffuse, numerous, and usually fuzzy. There is virtually never a single, clear goal on which all parties agree. At best there are many—not always consistent—goals that, in a sense, compete. In some cases no goals at all may be readily identifiable. In some cases there may be goals that are flatly contradictory tied to the same program. The nature of the formulation and legitimation process—with its built-in necessity for compromise—creates this situation. The easiest form of compromise at the goal level is to give everyone part of what they want—even if logically it sets up goals that are not compatible with each other, goals that in practice create immediate and unavoidable tensions when implementation decisions are faced.

A good example of competing goals contained in the same program is provided by the Model Cities program created in 1966 (see Ripley, 1972: chapter 5). This program contained at least the following major goals:

1. To help inner city residents with a variety of services.
2. To strengthen the authority of mayors over social program decision-making in their cities.
3. To bring efficiency and economy to a whole set of pre-existing overlapping programs.
4. To strengthen local neighborhood leaders by encouraging self-sufficiency, including providing training that would lead them to challenge mayors and other city officials efficiently.

Goals 2 and 4 clash head-on. Goals 1 and 3 clash in that they point in different directions in terms of arriving at a level of funding and service provision.

To take another example: during its lifetime the Comprehensive Employment and Training Act (1974–83) had at least the following major goals:

1. To help the economically disadvantaged with jobs.
2. To help the economically disadvantaged with income maintenance.
3. To help temporarily unemployed people with jobs or income maintenance regardless of whether they are disadvantaged in any other way.
4. To serve various target population groups—youth, veterans, hispanics, blacks, women, welfare recipients—as if they were *all* the highest priority.
5. To subsidize private business to induce it to hire the disadvantaged.
6. To subsidize local governments' ability to provide basic services such as police and fire protection, park maintenance, and garbage collection.

There are all sorts of inbuilt contradictions lurking in this mix of goals. Choices inevitably had to be made in concrete fashion at the point of implementation.

Aside from costs of competition and confusion, lack of goal clarity sometimes has additional unexpected costs. For example, in 1978 Congress passed a statute creating a national federally funded program to provide free meals to elderly persons. As passed, Congress presumably thought it had left room for volunteer programs providing such meals to the elderly in their homes to continue side-by-side with local, centrally served, group meal programs authorized under the Older Americans Act of 1972. However, as interpreted by the Administration on Aging, the

TABLE 1–2   Budget Outlays of the United States Government, 1792–1986

Fiscal Year	Outlays ($ Millions)
1792	5
1839	27
1889	299
1909	694
1929	2,900
1939	9,400
1949	40,600
1959	92,100
1969	184,500
1974	268,400
1979	493,700
1984	851,800
1986 (estimated)	973,700

SOURCES: *Historical Statistics of the United States, 1975:* 1104–5, for 1789–1969; *Statistical Abstract of the United States, 1975:* 314, for 1974; *Special Analyses, Budget of the United States Government, Fiscal Year 1981:* 77, for 1979, and *Special Analyses, Budget of the United States Government, Fiscal Year 1986,* C–2 for 1984 and 1986.

regulations that provided details on the new 1978 program made the continued existence of volunteer programs serving meals in the homes virtually impossible (Balzano, 1979). Congress was ambiguous in the language of the statute. Therefore, there was room for a federal agency to wipe out its volunteer competition. Congress finally intervened to save volunteer programs but only after some had died and just as money was vanishing (Ranii, 1980).

In their zeal to pass programs, supporters often claim too much, thus inflating expectations of what the program can accomplish. These claims foreordain program "failure" if accomplishments are measured against exaggerated goal statements.

GROWTH OF GOVERNMENT AND COMPLEXITY OF PROGRAMS

Governments in the United States have been growing larger and more complex over time. This growth, much of which has occurred

TABLE 1-3   Government Expenditures, 1950–1980

Fiscal Year	Total Expenditures All Governments ($ Billions)	Percent Federal	Percent of GNP
1950	70	60.3	24.4
1960	151	59.7	29.8
1970	333	55.5	33.5
1980	959	54.8	36.4

SOURCE: *Statistical Abstract of the United States,* 1984: 272, 448.

at the state and local levels in recent years, has helped spawn increased interest in implementation.

Table 1–2 shows a very crude index of the growth of the federal government: dollars spent, uncorrected for inflation.

Table 1–3 summarizes data on the expenditures of all governments in the United States from 1950 through 1980. Total spending has, of course, increased considerably. That spending has also represented an increasing percentage of the gross national product (GNP). However, the percent of total spending attributable to the federal government went down over this period of three decades.

Table 1–4 reports on civilian employment at all levels of government for the three decades from 1954 through 1984. During that period federal employment has grown quite slowly and, in fact, represents a declining percentage of the population. The dramatic growth has come at the state and local level.

Table 1–5 underscores that much of recent governmental growth has come at the state and local level by summarizing information about federal grants-in-aid to state and local governments. These grants have grown enormously (although Ronald Reagan has tried to reverse this situation, with limited success). This means that some of the growth in federal spending is, in fact, really targeted at increasing state and local spending and is federal only in a partial sense.

These four tables, taken together, show the governing enterprise in general to be growing, regardless of whether it is measured in terms of spending, employment, or spending as a percentage of the GNP. In Chapter 2 we will briefly address the related questions of why government programs have grown and why bureaucracy

TABLE 1-4 Government Civilian Employment, 1954-1984

Fiscal Year	Federal Executive Branch (Thousands)	State and Local Governments (Thousands)	Total (Thousands)	Federal as Percent of Total	Federal Employment per 1,000 Population
1954	2,382	4,552	6,934	34.4	14.6
1964	2,469	7,236	9,705	25.4	12.9
1974	2,847	11,713	14,560	19.6	13.3
1984	2,854	13,440	16,294	17.5	12.0

SOURCE: *Special Analyses, Budget of the United States Government, Fiscal Year 1986:* I-11.

has grown. Naturally, the two phenomena are closely linked, since bureaucrats are usually necessary to implement programs.

THE INTERGOVERNMENTAL CONTEXT

Almost no national or federal programs are implemented wholly or directly by the national government in Washington. Virtually all of them rely on some mix of federal field offices, state governments, local governments, and local nongovernmental actors. The latter contract to become front-line implementers through providing services to beneficiaries. For example, some programs to compensate unemployed people are implemented by a network including the United States Employment Service, 50 separate state employment security agencies, and numerous local offices of those 50 state agencies. Other employment and training programs authorized by the Job Training Partnership Act are implemented by a large number of actors, including the national office of the Employment and Training Administration (ETA) of the U.S. Department of Labor, 10 regional ETA offices, 50 state offices, between 500 and 600 local service delivery areas (usually cities or counties or consortia of cities and counties), and thousands of local nongovernmental contractors who provide various programmatic services. Aid to elementary and secondary education is implemented by a mix of the national office of the Department of Education, the Department of Education's field structure, 50 state departments of education, and thousands of local school districts and boards of education.

Ronald Reagan has sought, as president, to shift the balance toward states and away from the federal government (and also

TABLE 1-5 Federal Grants-In-Aid to State and Local Governments, 1950–1985

Fiscal Year	Amount ($ Millions)	Federal Grants as a Percent of	
		Domestic Federal Outlays	State-Local Expenditures
1950	2,253	9.3	10.4
1960	7,019	17.1	14.7
1970	24,065	22.0	19.2
1980	91,451	20.6	26.3
1985 (estimated)	107,016	15.6	n.a.

n.a.=not available

SOURCE: *Special Analyses, Budget of the United States Government, Fiscal Year 1986:* H-19.

away from cities) but has had only limited success. Even an altered balance leaves all of the same parties as important players. And the intergovernmental setting underscores the centrality of bargaining and negotiations in implementation (see Derthick, 1972; Ingram, 1977; Kettl, 1983; and Pressman and Wildavsky, 1984).

EXTERNAL UNCONTROLLABLE FACTORS

As if implementation were not already complicated enough, implementers also have to contend with external factors about which they can do nothing at all except react and/or hope. Perfect implementation in the sense of planning and execution might have no impact if offset by such factors. In late 1979 and early 1980, for example, the whole set of government programs designed to sustain the housing market were rendered ineffective because other pressures caused interest rates on loans for home mortgages to skyrocket out of the reach of all people but those with very high incomes. The programs did not create the pressures, but there was nothing program managers could do in the short run to offset them. To take another example with a longer history: the vast array of federal programs designed to pump some life into the family farm to make it a viable economic enterprise and keep population in rural areas was ineffectual against an even vaster array of forces that could not be affected by the programs themselves. These forces included changes in agricultural technology, food marketing and processing patterns, and the amount of capital required for profitable farming.

SUMMARY

Implementation activities are those tasks and activities undertaken after a law is passed. They translate the often broad, vague, and multiple statements about goals, program outlines, and policies in the statute into concrete actions, programs, and policies. Implementation activities occupy a central and essential place in the policy process.

Implementation activities include amassing resources needed to mobilize and carry out responsibilities, planning specific program designs using the legislation as a starting outline, interpreting broad instructions in the legislation and translating them into specific regulations, organizing staff and creating or amending appropriate operating routines, and providing the benefits and services to intended recipients. The actual flow of activities depicted in such a concise listing, with separate steps and nicely divided functions, is only an approximation of reality, which is much less tidy. Like the policy process of which it is part, implementation is a continuous process, with no clearcut endpoint.

Five characteristics of implementation stand out as being most significant. The *multiplicity of actors* involved in implementation includes individuals and organizations from all territorial levels of government (federal, state, and local) as well as from all branches of government (executive, legislative, judicial, bureaucracy) and from outside the governments. Overall, the role of bureaucrats, especially civil servants, is the most important in implementation, but the role of private, nongovernment actors is also quite prominent. The influence of any group of actors in implementation varies depending on the individual program or policy, and it will shift over time even for the same policy. These shifts, and the absence of hierarchical relationships among most of the actors, underscore one of the major themes of this book: no one is in clear control of the implementation of any specific program.

The proliferation of governmental programs and the increasing size of governmental expenditures make the challenge of management and coordination difficult if not impossible to accomplish, even if the multiplicity of actors were not a factor in implementation. Implementation of domestic policies and programs is powerfully affected by *the federal context* in which programs are set. Intergovernmental coordination has become a standard feature of program implementation in the 20th century, and the government in Washington regularly relies on the state and local governments to use federal funds to implement federal programs.

Goals and expectations for domestic programs and policies are nowhere authoritatively defined, nor are they agreed upon by the actors involved in implementation. *Diffuse, multiple, and competing goal statements* are the normal condition, a deliberate product of the conflict, compromise, and negotiation that characterize the formulation and legitimation processes necessary to produce legislation. Goals are vague in order to accommodate multiple points of view, and translating that vagueness into specific concrete implementation actions renews the potential for conflict and compromise. The nature of program goals means that no program can ever accomplish all that is expected of it—which is a second major theme in this book—because so many differing results are expected by different implementers and formulators.

The final significant feature of implementation is *the uncontrollable factors* that can intrude to thwart even technically perfect implementation activities. Unpredictable external conditions beyond the control of implementers can and do derail programs and policies.

Our intent in this book is to examine a variety of real-world examples of implementation and to explain why implementation occurred the way it did or didn't, using these five major features as principal explanatory factors, tracking their influence and importance, as well as introducing additional features that occur systematically.

CHAPTER 2

Bureaucracy, Bureaucrats, and Implementation

Our objective in this chapter is to present the background on bureaucracy in the United States necessary for understanding its general role in the implementation process discussed in Chapter 1. Remember throughout your reading of the chapter that bureaucrats are more numerous among implementers than anyone else, although there is no reason to expect that most of them think analytically about implementation. We do not intend to say everything worth saying about bureaucracy in general. That would fill, and already has filled, many volumes. We do want to sketch some major features of bureaucracy. Specifically, we will first explore some introductory generalizations about the character and importance of bureaucracy. Second, we will look at the growth of American bureaucracy. Bureaucracies are inherently political, and in the third section of the chapter, we will illustrate that point. Finally, we will briefly characterize the nature of the bureaucrats themselves and what they bring to the implementation process.

THE GENERAL CHARACTER AND IMPORTANCE OF BUREAUCRACY

The essential features of governmental bureaucracy in the United States can be summarized in six propositions.

1. Bureaucracies are everywhere; they are the chosen social instrument for addressing matters defined to be part of the public's business.
2. Bureaucracies are dominant in the implementation of programs and policies and have varying degrees of importance at other stages in the policy process.
3. Bureaucracies have a number of different social purposes.
4. Bureaucracies function in a context of large and complex governmental programs.
5. Bureaucracies rarely die; their instinct for survival is virtually inextinguishable.
6. Bureaucrats are not neutral in their policy preferences; nor are they fully controlled by any outside forces. Their autonomy allows them to bargain—successfully—in order to attain a sizeable share of their preferences.

We will elaborate each of these propositions in the following sections.

Pervasiveness

Bureaucracies are everywhere; they are the chosen social instruments for addressing matters that are defined to be part of the public's business.

Bureaucracies have evolved—partially consciously, partially unconsciously—as the chosen form of organization for dealing with collective problems in all modern societies. Governmental bureaucracies, often called agencies, deal with the business brought before governments both by constitutional mandate and by legislative interpretation of that mandate through the passage of statutes creating programs. Bureaucracy is not unique to government as a form of organization. Corporations, unions, universities, churches, charities, and virtually every kind of organization imaginable create and use some form of bureaucracy to carry out their missions.

Governmental bureaucracies are created by statutes and ordinances at the national, state, and local levels. Executives and legislatures create bureaucracies. Often the creation of a new bureaucracy takes place simultaneously with the creation of a new program. Sometimes a new bureaucracy is created to handle a rearrangement of programs.

The Constitution of the United States makes provision for bureaucracy only obliquely. It would be foolish, however, to take the claim seriously that the founders did not understand that effective government required organizations. They were students of history and were well aware that the governments of classic antiquity as well as the modern governments with which they were familiar all had organizations of public officials and employees of one kind or another to conduct the public business. The only bounds set on the size and mandate of bureaucracy in the Constitution are those set on the size and scope of government itself. Those limits are very broad and are more political than legal in character. Bureaucracy, like the rest of government, is also constrained by guarantees of constitutional liberties for citizens such as free speech, equal protection of the laws, and protection from self-incrimination.

Bureaucracy is inevitable in any society with characteristics we would recognize as modern. The size and mandate of the bureaucracy—as well as the details of its organization—are not inevitable, however. Over time a society decides how much government it wants and for what purposes. Those decisions are almost never fixed or final but rather are continually evolving. Basic political decisions shape the kind of bureaucracy that a society will have. It is interesting to note that as the 1980s opened, bureaucrats at all levels of government in the United States were a greater percentage of the total labor force (15.2 percent) than bureaucrats at all levels in France (14.3 percent), West Germany (13.5 percent), Japan (9.1 percent), or the United Kingdom (6.2 percent) (McGregor, 1982:318).

Governmental bureaucracy is neither good nor evil in and of itself. Individual pieces of the bureaucracy can function relatively well, or they can function badly. At the most general level a bureaucratic unit that serves the public well will:

1. Process its work at a steady and brisk pace.
2. Treat all individuals with whom it deals fairly and equally.
3. Hire and retain a staff of qualified professionals who care about the quality of the unit's programs.
4. Promote individual staff members on the basis of merit and proven worth.
5. Maintain records that can be recovered quickly when the need arises.

A bureaucratic unit that serves the public badly will:

1. Process its work at an unpredictable and often very slow pace.
2. Show favoritism in the treatment of some clients and discriminate against others.
3. Hire and retain a staff that shows little interest in professional standards or quality services in programs.
4. Promote individuals on the basis of political favoritism or nonprofessional criteria.
5. Create mountains of paper pointlessly and be unable to recover relevant file material in a timely fashion.

Selective Importance

Bureaucracies are dominant in the implementation of programs and policies and have varying degrees of importance in other stages of the policy process.

In policy and program *formulation and legitimation* activities, bureaucratic units play a large role, although they are not dominant. They share decision-making influence with Congress, the presidency, and interest groups at the federal level.

In agenda setting, bureaucratic units play only a very modest direct role. Very rarely will they join the debate over what the government should or should not address at the broadest level. Individual bureaucrats might participate in this process as individual citizens, but bureaucratic units rarely have the luxury to look ahead collectively and pose questions about what government should ponder. The pressures of conducting daily business generally preclude such philosophizing.

Bureaucratic units are the most important actors in collecting, analyzing, and disseminating information at the opening stages of formulation activities for both policies and programs. They also play a large role in developing and selecting specific alternative proposals—more so at the more concrete and specific level of programs than at the vaguer and more general level of policies. Likewise, bureaucratic units are important, along with other actors, in advocating the adoption of specific policies and programs.

At the time of final, formal decisions, however, bureaucratic units have almost no role. At the national level that role is reserved for Congress and the presidency. However, if agencies have been influential in the activities preceding formal ratification, they may well have helped foreordain the final outcome.

It is in the realm of *implementation* that agencies dominate. They are not without competitors, they are not impervious to outside influences, and they are not automatically obeyed. But implementation is their major activity and it is the arena in which they clearly claim preeminence.

Assessment of performance and impacts again relegates bureaucratic units back to a supporting rather than a starring role. In fact, there are no stars in this activity. It is carried out largely as a political function by all of the actors with something at stake—that is, by virtually everyone. Bureaucratic units certainly have something at stake (the health and continued existence of their programs and organizations) and so they participate too.

There is also a narrower, more formal kind of assessment that takes place on a sporadic basis. Such assessment involves formal study (policy analysis) of a program and its results. Bureaucratic units undertake some such studies themselves and commission others by persons based both in private research organizations and in universities. Formal policy analyses are done only sporadically and may have little or no influence even when done. We report this as a matter of fact and imply neither that most formal analyses are poorly done and deserve to be ignored nor that most such analyses are well done but are condemned to be ignored only because of the "irrationality" of politics.

Decisions on the future of policy and programs again involve the whole stable of actors with interests at stake. Bureaucratic units are involved but are not automatically successful in obtaining their first preferences. They must argue and bargain to obtain some of those preferences.

Social Purposes

Bureaucracies have a number of different social purposes.

Throughout our national history, bureaucracies have been created to achieve four major social purposes. Chapter 3 will deal in detail with types of policy. The following paragraphs briefly link examples of bureaucratic units with broad policy types.

1. Bureaucracies have been created to provide certain services that are the natural province of governmental responsibility. For some services, the government is commonly agreed to be the best (or in some cases to be the only) possible provider. In the United States these services include national defense, the conduct of

diplomatic relations with foreign nations, the provision of central banking and financial services, and the provision of a minimal apparatus to represent the government in legal matters. George Washington's first cabinet contained four members; the secretaries of state (diplomacy), treasury (financial services), and war (national defense), and the attorney general (legal services). The earliest additions to the president's cabinet were in the general services area; the post office and the Navy Department. Until recently there was probably general agreement that the government was the best provider of mail services and should be the exclusive provider. Problems with the U.S. Postal Service and the rise of competition from private delivery agencies suggest that the post office is no longer regarded as a sacred preserve of the federal government.

2. Bureaucratic units have been created to promote the interests of specific economic sectors in society such as farmers, organized labor, or segments of private business. Shortly after the new government was established it began to be involved in these kinds of activities, what we will call *distribution* in the scheme of policy types we use. The next additions to the roster of cabinet-level agencies had their central activities in this domain. These included the Department of the Interior, the Department of Agriculture, the Department of Commerce, and the Department of Labor.

3. Bureaucratic units have been created to regulate the conditions under which different kinds of private activity can take place. Some of this regulation involves competition between private sector units for permission to undertake certain activities— for example, the operation of radio or television stations or, until recently, the provision of air, truck, or rail service between pairs of destinations. In the late 19th century and throughout the 20th century, Congress created bodies—typically independent of the cabinet-level departments—to administer this kind of *competitive regulation*. These include the Interstate Commerce Commission, the Civil Aeronautics Board (CAB), and the Federal Communications Commission. Moves toward deregulation in the late 1970s and early 1980s reduced the functions of some of these agencies, particularly in the transportation area. The CAB went out of business altogether at the end of 1984.

Another form of regulation is aimed at protecting the public from some sort of undesirable practice or activity: uncontrolled strip-mining, unclean food, unsafe drugs, price fixing, fraudulent stock, unsafe aircraft, hazardous working conditions, polluted air, polluted water, unsafe automobiles, and so on. A host of agencies—some independent of cabinet-level departments and some embedded in them—were created to administer programs of *protective regulation:* the Food and Drug Administration (in the Department of Health and Human Services), the Occupational Safety and Health Administration (in the Department of Labor), the Securities and Exchange Commission, and the Federal Aviation Administration (in the Department of Transportation) are examples.

4. Bureaucracies have been created to redistribute various benefits, such as income, rights, and medical care, so that the less fortunate and less well-off in society get more of these benefits than they ordinarily would. Such *redistribution* promotes greater equality or at least less disparity between the most well-off and the least well-off. Some of the newest federal agencies are centrally concerned with programs promoting such redistribution, at least in part. These include the Department of Health and Human Services, the Department of Education, and the Department of Housing and Urban Development. The programs and agencies in this area were created for the most part beginning as a response to the Great Depression of the 1930s. They continued after World War II, with a particularly large infusion of new activity during the mid-1960s as President Lyndon Johnson tried to create a "Great Society."

Size and Complexity
Bureaucracies function in a context of large and complex governmental programs.

All governmental bureaucracies in the United States are set in the context of a large agenda of public business. Governments are expected to do a lot. Each separate piece of the agenda—what we call programs in this book—can be quite complex. American governmental bureaucracies have developed as relatively independent and autonomous fiefdoms. Theoretically, the bureaucracy as a single entity is responsible to and controlled by the president and his cabinet and central executive branch agencies such as the Office of Management and Budget. In fact, the relationship virtually never approaches such a hierarchical model. In addition, public bureaucracy has farmed out a good deal of public business to various private organizations and bureaucracies. Thus, to understand public programs in the United States, one needs to pay attention not only to federal, state, and local governmental units but also to a whole host of private organizations.

The growth and complexity of governments and the federal agenda were described briefly in Chapter 1. The complexity of any given program and the complexity of the agenda of any single sizable agency can be illustrated with several examples.

Joseph Califano (1978), when he was secretary of the Department of Health, Education and Welfare, provides a vivid description:

> Beyond the size of its budget and the number of its employees, HEW challenges those who would manage it by the sheer complexity—and volatility—of the responsibilities Congress has placed there. It is our responsibility to determine whether saccharin is carcinogenic, whether laetrile is efficacious, and how dangerous marijuana is. We confront tangled social problems like poverty that do not yield to quick, technical fixes. We cope with controversial problems that defy simple definition, much less solution, like discrimination on the basis of race, religion, ethnic origin, sex, handicaps, and...age.
>
> We struggle with deeply troubling ethical issues in biomedical research, issues that would confound a Socrates. We are dealing with searing social issues like abortion, teenage pregnancy, psychosurgery and sterilization.
>
> We must deal with problems such as these in ways that are acceptable to an array of competing, and often conflicting interests: pharmaceutical companies and Nader public interest groups; business and labor; rich and poor; black and white; Hispanics, Eskimos and Indians; women and handicapped citizens; big computer manufacturers and American Civil Liberties Union privacy lawyers; retired people on social security and active workers angry about payroll taxes.
>
> And, most importantly today, we must deal with these problems in the new world of molecular politics.

Califano's reference to "molecular politics" encapsulates the agency's political environment, in which there are numerous programs that spawn numerous interests and also interests that spawn programs. The interests establish relationships of mutual support with interested parties both in Congress and in the bureaucracy.

Any given program is likely to have many subparts and involve a number of bureaucratic units. Programs are deliberately designed in this way.

The point that public bureaucracy creates additional private bureaucracy to conduct part of the public business needs to be underscored. In part, private actors have a role because Congress creates a place for them in the statutes it passes. Congress also allows public bureaucracy great latitude in contracting out for work. Both nonprofit and for-profit firms receive such contracts. This contracting creates theoretically private bureaucracies that, in many ways, behave like public bureaucracies as they play their own roles in implementation of programs. They must interact with many of the same actors with which public bureaucracies interact. They have the same concern for survival and their own health as an organization as public bureaucracies. And, *if* they function well, they may also have genuine commitments to the public welfare, but there is nothing automatic about such a commitment.

The Defense Department, for example, sustains a number of private for-profit companies that are 100 percent dependent on defense contracts. The local political jurisdictions that receive Job Training Partnership Act (JTPA) funds from the Department of Labor sustain a large number of local nonprofit organizations to provide, under contract, services to individual clients. And as noted in Chapter 1, the Department of Energy was conducting about seven eighths of its total business through private, nongovernmental contractors. This pattern has been called by an Office of Management and Budget official in the Carter administration "third-party government" (Salamon, 1980). The Reagan administration has encouraged further growth of this phenomenon.

Survival
Bureaucracies rarely die; their instinct for survival is virtually inextinguishable.

Bureaucracies rarely die. For example, despite the enormous social changes in the United States in the 50 years between 1923 and 1973—a half century that saw the Great Depression, World War II, an epic struggle over racial equality, the Vietnam War, and the reactions to all of these events—85 percent of the federal government agencies in existence in 1923 still existed in 1973 (Kaufman, 1976). Over 60 percent had not changed even their organizational status very much. They were in the same position in the federal hierarchy and organizational structure throughout the entire period. And even those that had moved were still doing some of the same tasks; and the other tasks, for the most part, were not terminated but were instead transferred to other agencies.

Lambasting the size of governmental bureaucracy has been a perennial favorite topic for presidential candidates. When Jimmy Carter campaigned in the 1976 election, he promised to whittle the federal bureaucracy if he was elected. But Carter went further than most candidates—further than either prudent or feasible—and attached numerical goals to his promise: he would cut the number of federal agencies from an alleged 1,900 to about 200.

His pledge was naive from the outset because it badly exaggerated the number of administrative agencies in existence. When his staff began the actual count, they could find fewer than 500 agencies and about 1,200 advisory committees that administered nothing. It was also naive because no president—even one much more skillful than Carter—could have overcome the political realities of bureaucratic staying power.

By the end of his single term, Carter's administration had made a few adjustments in the organization of the boxes on the federal organizational chart. The Civil Service Commission was abolished, the Department of Energy was born, and the Department of Health, Education and Welfare was reorganized to create two departments: Education and Health and Human Services. The number of advisory commissions was reduced, but mostly by merging them rather than by outright elimination. A few fairly insignificant agencies, such as the American Revolution Bicentennial Commission, were abolished. But the basic picture of the federal bureaucracy in January 1981 when Carter left office was pretty much unchanged. The more ambitious goals— the impossible dream of reducing the number of agencies to 200, a reorganization of the Departments of Agriculture, Interior, and Commerce to create new departments (of Food and Agriculture, Natural Resources, and Community and Economic Development)— all faded and died because there was too much controversy surrounding the proposals for change and too much resistance from well-organized interest groups that had collected over the years around the departments' programs. There was also little political support from the public or any other source that might make the fight winnable. In short, the agencies that Carter had targeted were too well entrenched to be affected by the president's attempts at reorganization and reduction.

President Reagan's efforts to cut agencies also met with general lack of success. His most ambitious goals were the elimination of the Departments of Education and Energy, both announced in the 1980 campaign and pursued early in the first term. Both survived. And the Secretary of Education in Reagan's first term became a staunch and effective defender of his department.

In early 1985 Reagan announced a number of new targets. Even the most puny were likely to survive. For example, the United States Travel and Tourism Administration in the Department of Commerce was on the "hit list," just as it had been five times in the preceding 24 years. There was little reason to expect Reagan to succeed where others had failed.

Stronger agencies scheduled for elimination by Reagan rallied their supporters. Any president is likely to come out second best in such direct confrontations. A report in the *New York Times* (January 31, 1985) about the efforts of the Small Business Administration to survive an administration demolition attempt tells a typical story:

> Ever since it was created in the Eisenhower years, the Small Business Administration has been a favorite target of budget cutters, an almost perennial candidate for absorption by the Department of Commerce.
>
> Always it has survived, creating in the process a huge constituency for its ever-expanding programs, which are meant to promote free enterprise by aiding small companies with counseling, loan guarantees and loans, including of late low-interest disaster loans for such "nonphysical" losses as the ski operator who passes a winter without snow or the fisherman who has a bad season.
>
> Although the Administration's budget for the coming year is not yet unveiled, the defenders of the Small Business Administration have been mobilizing.
>
> Those benefiting from its programs have joined to plot strategy and issue statements to support the agency....
>
> On Capitol Hill, the heads of the various committees with jurisdiction over small business have begun to declare abolition an almost unthinkably bad idea. And the head of the agency, James C. Sanders, has been conducting a discreet campaign to keep the agency alive even as he acknowledges the importance of the Administration's efforts to cut the budget deficit....

In short, the famous "iron triangle" of Washington, the alliance of program beneficiaries, Congressional overseers and administrators, remains alive and well as President Reagan's revolution begins its fifth year.

Neutrality and Control

Bureaucrats are not neutral in their policy preferences, nor are they fully controlled by any outside forces.

Governmental bureaucracies are not fully controlled by any superior. The structure of the Constitution—both written and unwritten—is such that they are free to bargain over their own preferences. They have some accountability to Congress and to the president, but it is not final (Woll, 1977:64–65). This is not a fact to be unthinkingly deplored or applauded. But it is a fact that is central to understanding the behavior of bureaucracy in the United States. (For one argument that bureaucratic autonomy can promote the public interest, see Rourke, 1979).

Bureaucratic actors in the implementation process must certainly take account of the preferences of other important actors such as the president, Congress, presidential agencies such as Office of Management and Budget, departmental superiors, and interest groups. But they have considerable latitude to define and then work for their own substantive, procedural, and organizational preferences.

In short, bureaucracies are not neutral—simply waiting to be told by higher authorities what their goals are; nor are they fully accountable to anyone for their actions. Like the rest of the policy actors, they have latitude to bargain for what they want; and like the other actors, their latitude is not unlimited. Thus bargaining and compromise must take place *when* conflict arises. Some of the time, however, there is very little conflict, and the major actors can quickly agree on what they want. *The central point is that bureaucrats' personal and organizational attitudes toward the content and goals of programs are important factors that have a major impact on implementation.*

THE GROWTH OF AMERICAN BUREAUCRACY

Bureaucracy, contrary to some popular fantasies, does not just increase for no reason at all. Its growth is tied to the growing demands on government and the response of government to those demands in the form of new and expanded programs and agencies. To be sure, already existing bureaucracies help create part of the demand for their own services and their own expansion. And they work in league with Congress and interest groups in the formulation of new programs that tend to keep bureaucracy growing (see Fiorina, 1977; Ripley and Franklin, 1984).

Table 1–4 in the first chapter presented some descriptive figures on the growth of both federal and state and local bureaucracy in the three decades between 1954 and 1984. During that period civilian employment in the federal executive branch grew from just under 2.4 million to over 2.8 million. Federal employment in relation to the population of the country went down. About seven eighths of those employees are stationed in field offices, not in Washington, D.C. The major growth in government employment was at the state and local level, which went from about 4.5 million to almost 13.5 million. These figures are a bit misleading, however, as some of the growth in state and local government employment was stimulated by and funded by the federal government. In many instances it is very difficult to identify a governmental employee as definitively local or state or federal. An individual wearing a title bestowed by local government, for example, may be running a locally based program funded wholly with a combination of federal and state funds.

Table 2–1 puts the growth of the federal executive branch (civilians only) in a longer-term perspective. Complete figures are available since 1816. The figures are presented for every 20 years from 1831 through 1981, with a figure for 1984 completing the table. The table shows that two major bursts of increase in federal civilian employment have occurred. The first burst, between 1871 and 1911, was largely a response to the industrialization of the country after the Civil War and the ensuing increase in federal regulatory activity. The second burst, between 1931 and 1951, was a response both to the Great Depression and to World War II and the cold war. The growth after 1954 is probably understated by this table because the federal government in effect delegated many programs to states and localities, which administered them by hiring their own employees, and to private or public-private institutions such as the Communications Satellite Corporation.

TABLE 2-1 Civilian Employment in the Federal Executive Branch, 1816–1984

Year	Number of Employees	Number of Employees as a Percent of U.S. Population
1816	4,479	0.06
1831	11,067	0.08
1851	25,713	0.11
1871	50,155	0.13
1891	150,844	0.24
1911	387,673	0.42
1931	596,745	0.49
1951	2,455,901	1.62
1971	2,823,000	1.39
1981	2,806,000	1.22
1984	2,854,000	1.20

SOURCES: *Historical Statistics of the United States,* 1102–3, for 1816–1951; *Special Analyses, Budget of the United States, Fiscal Year 1986:* I–11 for 1971–1984 data.

In Chapter 1 we sketched the growth of government and its programs. Why did programs and the size of American bureaucracy grow? While competing theories exist, none offers a simple single-cause explanation (see Seitz, 1978). In fact, bureaucracy seemed to grow in this country through a combination of pushes and pulls (see Wilson, 1975). The pushes included specific external events or trends focused around war and violence (foreign or domestic) and economic development, a term that includes growing complexity, opportunities, and problems. The pull is, in a sense, the desire of bureaucrats working for agencies much of the time (although not all of the time) to enhance the importance of their own agency's work. Such efforts usually resulted in expanded bureaucracy.

The Advisory Commission on Intergovernmental Relations, in a major study of growth of government programs concluded that all actors pushed for growth in some areas, and that Congress (especially individual policy entrepreneurs sitting in Congress) was the uniformly most active source of support for new programs and growth (Colella, 1979; Beam, 1979).

THE POLITICAL NATURE OF AMERICAN BUREAUCRACY

Because implementation of policies ultimately determines who receives (or is denied) benefits and services and because bureaucracy is so important in implementation, this entire book is about the political nature of American bureaucracy as it implements programs. Already a number of examples and generalizations have illustrated the marriage of politics and bureaucracy. In this section we want to emphasize three critical political aspects of bureaucracy: (1) Decisions about organization and reorganization of bureaucratic units are simultaneously decisions about policies and programs. As such, they are political, not just managerial and not just aimed at efficiency. (2) Bureaucratic agencies have a number of resources they can use in their attempts to engineer situations in which their own policy and program preferences will prevail. (3) Every bureaucratic agency is involved in a web of relationships with other important actors, and the configuration of those relationships helps determine its implementation performance. Primary relationships in the implementation realm are those among bureaucratic units and those with clients. Secondary relationships for purposes of determining implementation performance on the part of agencies are with Congress, the president, and the institutional presidency (especially the White House Office and the Office of Management and Budget).

Organizational Decisions

The federal executive establishment is large and complex. In 1985 there were 13 cabinet-level departments. The *United States Government Manual* listed 9 separate units in the Executive office of the President and 56 independent establishments and government corporations. In the latter group, agencies range from large and important units, such as the Veterans Administration or the U.S. Postal Service, to those of middling importance, such as the Appalachian Regional Commission or the National Labor Relations Board, to those on whose actions the health of the Republic does not depend, such as the American Battle Monuments Commission.

Each unit within the executive branch is subdivided a number of times into various offices, divisions, administrations, bureaus, branches, and sections all arranged on stylish organization charts that imply a clear flow of policy from the top down and a clear flow of accountability from the bottom up.

These seemingly sterile charts, however, encapsulate a lot of political history. There are almost always political reasons for the location or relocation of agencies at different places. Organization charts represent the bare bones of treaties that are reached between contending political forces. A long-time observer of and participant in organization and reorganization struggles, Harold Seidman (1980:15), offers an insightful and accurate assessment:

> Organizational arrangements are not neutral. We do not organize in a vacuum. Organization is one way of expressing national commitment, influencing program direction, and ordering priorities. Organizational arrangements tend to give some interests and perspectives more effective access to those with decision-making authority, whether they be in the Congress or in the executive branch.

Bureaucratic Resources

Bureaucracies are powerful decision makers in the implementation arena largely because they are delegated the task of implementation by statute and those delegations are reinforced by various orders issued by the president and other high administrative officials. In part, then, bureaucracies are powerful because they are both legally empowered and required to undertake certain activities and because they are necessary in the context of modern government.

But bureaucracies can also enhance their importance and impact by skillful use of three sets of resources that can vary. First, bureaucrats are important because they have technical expertise in the substantive policy and program areas they administer. In general, the more complex the expertise required, the more important bureaucracies will become in terms of realizing their implementation objectives.

Second, a bureaucracy's constituencies are valuable resources. Client groups' stability, prestige, status, and political power all contribute to an agency's implementation performance (see Meier, 1979:57–62).

Third, bureaucracies have considerable latitude and discretion in making decisions about the dispersal of tangible benefits. For example, they usually have some choice where they locate or relocate or close their field facilities. They can shape the exact clientele receiving benefits by the wording of the regulations covering eligibility. They can shape the extent and nature of the benefits themselves through additional regulations. Through some of these decisions they strengthen their alliances with parts of Congress and important constituent groups.

Bureaucratic Relationships

It is well established that bureaucratic agencies are tied up with a variety of other actors in influencing the shaping of policy (see Ripley and Franklin, 1984, or virtually any politically aware treatment of bureaucracy). Less is known about bureaucratic relationships in shaping implementation. We start with the view that the most important relationships involving bureaucratic units during implementation are those among the bureaucratic units themselves and between bureaucratic units and clients and clientele groups. Less consistently important in relation to implementation (although central in policy formulation and legitimation activities) are relations with Congress and with the president and institutional presidency. These latter actors intervene only sporadically in implementation matters. We will describe those interventions with some care in Chapters 4 through 7.

Relations among bureaucratic units. Bureaucracies are constantly dealing with each other in a variety of ways. These relationships can involve nominal superiors and subordinates in a single large agency (the secretary of a department dealing with the chief of a bureau in that department, for example). They can involve a unit in the Washington office of a federal bureaucracy with counterpart units in regional or field offices. They can involve bureaucratic units in different settings working on the same or related problems. They can involve a federal bureaucracy dealing with a state or local bureaucracy.

The rank-and-file bureaucrats in a federal agency typically resist and resent two kinds of interference in their normal way of proceeding (see Heclo, 1977): intrusions from the temporary political appointees nominally in charge of them (secretaries of departments, for example) and intrusions from central control or management agencies such as the Office of Management and Budget or the General Accounting Office (nominally a congressional agency—but often marching to its own drummer).

Line bureaucracies—those agencies and units that are involved directly in program operations—interact in a variety of ways, both cooperative and antagonistic. Often, however, agencies that should logically know about each other's programs proceed in ignorance of them. In part such ignorance is simply a result of the complexity and proliferation of governmental programs and bureaus. Sometimes bureaucrats deliberately choose to ignore each other because of competitive motivations.

Relations with clients. *Clients as individuals.* Unorganized individuals are the primary clients of a number of bureaucratic programs. Agencies may approach these clients in a variety of ways. In some instances they seek to co-opt them as staunch supporters of the agencies' purposes and programs. In other cases they are genuinely interested in hearing what the clients want in the way of services and in hearing their ideas on how to improve service delivery. In still other cases the agency functions self-assuredly, even arrogantly, to pursue its own ends regardless of what the clients want. The agency, in an extreme case, appears as a juggernaut simply rolling over the clients presumably in their own best interest.

These relationships are not pure types. Any single agency may display aspects of each type of behavior, and an agency may shift styles over time. For example, the Tennessee Valley Authority has undergone periods in which it has emphasized each of the three styles most strongly (see Selznick, 1949, and Shabecoff, 1980).

Clients as groups. Clients that organize into formal interest groups are likely to be taken more seriously than clients that remain unorganized. In organized status they have some resources of their own (for example, access to Congress) that they can use to influence implementation decisions. And groups need not have a national membership to have impact, especially in programs that rely heavily on state and local bureaucracy or on federal field offices or on some combination of non-Washington-based bureaucracies for implementation. Most programs fit this description.

Citizen participation. Some programs have various requirements for citizen participation. These requirements can influence implementation. Bureaucrats tend to like participation they can control. They tend to oppose what they view as intrusive, limiting participation.

As of early 1978 there were 226 different requirements in federal programs for citizen participation, almost 85 percent of which had been enacted since 1964. One study (Rosenbaum, 1979) judged that 42 percent of these requirements confined participation primarily or completely to an advisory committee; 17 percent confined participation primarily or completely to public meetings and public notice; 27 percent permitted a broad range of modes, locations, and publics to be used; 13 percent had only vague references to participation with no concrete requirements.

Citizen participation rarely makes a dramatic black-and-white difference in the overall implementation of a program nationally, but such participation may make important differences at individual local levels (for evidence on the Comprehensive Employment and Training Act, for example, see Franklin and Ripley, 1984).

Relations with Congress. Congress is vital in setting the stage for the scope of bureaucratic implementation because statutes create the programs that are to be implemented. Bureaucracies that want to perpetuate programs must at least avoid angering Congress—or, more accurately, important individuals in Congress—with specific implementation decisions. And it doesn't hurt to curry support that gains favorable notice from important parts of Congress.

In general, Congress as a whole does not engage in detailed oversight of implementation. Rather, the standard practice is for the relevant parts of Congress to gain a general impression of the competence of a unit of the bureaucracy (department, bureau or office) and then to make decisions about the future of program renewal, organizational location for new programs, and possible relocation for existing programs on the basis of that general impression. Thus a bureaucratic unit interested in protecting or expanding its place in the policy world will behave in such a way as to increase the generally favorable perceptions in Congress about its basic competence. Such a strategy often involves publicizing the success of programs through self-serving publicity about how well things are going based on a few anecdotes, some nice pictures, and some hopeful rhetoric—often disseminated before a program could possibly have had much impact at all because it is too new.

Even though Congress does not oversee implementation of programs systematically, federal bureaucrats in Washington are extremely sensitive to the real and imagined implementation preferences of key representatives and senators. There is also constant interaction between bureaucrats and Congress—through hearings, reports, and personal conversation—that allows congressional preferences to be transmitted (or imagined) with ease.

Relations with the president and presidency. The president, even when he is considered along with his immediate supporting staff, has to work at intervening in bureaucratic implementation if he wants to have any impact at all. Even when such interventions occur, success is far from assured. Consistent, focused efforts over a period of time will probably have some of the desired results, but few presidents have the time, energy, or determination to undertake many such major efforts.

Presidents even have trouble getting the loyal and reliable support of their own political appointees. President Nixon insisted on such support and fired a number of appointees over the years because they wouldn't comply. President Carter wanted a more open decision-making atmosphere among his appointees, but this had deleterious effects for the president according to one observer (Clark, 1979a): "Decentralization of power to the Cabinet and the White House staff offices, combined with centralization of final decision-making authority to the oval office itself, has left the administration with a multitude of semi-autonomous fiefdoms, quarreling bitterly among themselves and speaking with different voices to the public."

President Reagan was loyally supported by some of his appointees on all of his policy preferences (although some of those same individuals, such as James Watt, Anne Burford, and Raymond Donovan, became politically embarrassing). But even he was opposed by some other appointees such as his first Secretary of Education, Terrell Bell.

If presidents have trouble with even their own appointees, it is even harder for them to achieve influence over those bureaucrats formally protected by civil service regulations and informally protected by alliances with client groups, other interest groups, and Congress.

However, a president really devoted to gaining some added influence can have some impact. Thus, for example, President Nixon succeeded in shaping the attitudes of the senior civil service and left them more favorable to his policies late in this administration than when he came to office (Cole and Caputo, 1979). Changes in civil service laws passed in 1978 created a Senior Executive Service more open to presidential influence. President Reagan's administration used these new powers to put bureaucrats friendly to Reaganite goals in critical positions throughout the bureaucracy.

President Nixon had an impact on the implementation of welfare policy because he made a concerted effort to do so (Randall, 1979). This impact was achieved by using two major tools at the disposal of appointees: the institution of a new monitoring and evaluation system for the program and reorganization of the Social and Rehabilitation Service of the Department of Health, Education, and Welfare, including a regionalization of it. This latter move underscores our earlier comment on the programmatic relevance of reorganization. In this case there was no strong coalition supporting liberal welfare policies to oppose the reorganization.

What difference did the moves by Nixon appointees on behalf of the president make? A careful observer of this initiative (Randall, 1979:804) summarizes:

> The overarching consequence for the welfare system of the Nixon administration was an increasingly restrictive welfare policy in the AFDC (Aid to Families and Dependent Children) program. Management tools used by that administration had the direct effect of impeding access to the welfare rolls and the indirect effect of producing a deterioration in the federal-state relationships in welfare policy.

BUREAUCRATS IN THE IMPLEMENTATION PROCESS

Bureaucrats are individuals, not machines. Government bureaucracies are simply like other organizations. Priests inhabit churches, professors inhabit universities, and bureaucrats inhabit bureaucracies. The label *bureaucrat* should be taken only as descriptive—not as a negative or positive judgment on anyone or what they do. In the remainder of this section we will outline some basic facts about what is known about bureaucrats as individuals—their personal characteristics and beliefs, types of bureaucratic behavior, the potential for individual initiative and influence, the potential for leadership, and the public's perceptions about public bureaucrats. *Bureaucrats as individuals* make concrete differences in the pace and nature of implementation (see Kaufman, 1981).

Personal Characteristics

A good deal is known about the personal characteristics of bureaucrats in the higher levels of the federal service. These echelons of the career service make a lot, although far from all, of the important implementation decisions (see Corson and Paul, 1966; Meier, 1979; and Stanley, Mann, and Doig, 1967. See also Ripley and Franklin, 1984:35–42, for a condensation of much of this knowledge). In general, higher civil servants come from a wide variety of geographical backgrounds, they are highly educated in formal terms, and they have an occupational specialty tied to their job. Many enter the civil service as their first employment after completing their education and develop their occupational specialties in the civil service. Those outsiders who enter the civil service at the higher ranks rather than working their way up through the ranks from some professional entry level are most likely to have a business background; a smaller number have a background as professional educators. But, for the most part, the higher reaches of the civil service have gained their experience as civil servants. Most are white males in their late 40s.

A large number of those entering the higher levels of the civil service from an outside career come from businesses that have had a close working relationship with the agency they enter. Likewise, when a higher civil servant leaves the civil service, he or she may well wind up working for a company that has been a client or under the regulation of the agency for which the person was employed. This means that people in the higher levels of government agencies and private companies have lots of personal ties. It also influences the decisions of the agencies over time to be more understanding of private sector needs (for evidence on this point involving Federal Communications Commission members see Gormley, 1979).

Beliefs

What kind of general politics beliefs and values do bureaucrats in the higher and middle level of the federal civil service hold? The studies that have been undertaken underscore the following generalizations (see Aberbach, Putnam, and Rockman, 1981; Aberbach and Rockman, 1976, 1977, 1978; Meier, 1979; Meier and Nigro, 1976; Rothman and Lichter, 1983; Presthus, 1974; and Wynia, 1974).

> Bureaucrats tend to adopt the ideological coloration of the agency that employs them.
>
> Bureaucrats believe strongly in the value of the free enterprise economic system.
>
> Bureaucrats believe strongly in the legitimacy of open access to bureaucratic decisions for both interest groups and interested members of Congress.
>
> Bureaucrats hold abstract beliefs about democracy and public policy slightly more liberal than the general public but not much different from the general public on specific issues.
>
> Bureaucrats most strongly wedded to abstract democratic values are likely to be in nondefense agencies, are likely to be relatively new to the bureaucracy, and are likely to have considerable formal education.
>
> Bureaucrats tend to be wary of changes in the bureaucratic and civil service system with which they are familiar (Lynn and Vaden, 1979).

It should also be noted that bureaucrats are quite circumspect about stating their beliefs while they are in office. Their situation breeds considerable cautiousness. If a higher level bureaucrat indulges himself or herself in sweeping pronouncements on policy—especially if the pronouncements are critical—it is usually on the way out of office.

General Behavior—Types of Bureaucrats

Despite the similarities in general characteristics sketched above, not all bureaucrats behave alike. They have different motives and different goals and they emphasize different values. We think that four types of bureaucrats emerge most consistently—careerists, politicians, professionals, and missionaries. (For interesting discussions of these and other types, see Downs, 1967:88; Wilensky,

1967:85–86; and Wilson, 1980a:374–82). Wilson describes the first three types succinctly: *careerists* are employees who identify their careers and rewards with the agency that employs them. They do not desire or anticipate moving to other agencies, and their most important concern is maintaining the agency's position and their own position within it. The *politicians* are employees who expect to pursue a career beyond the agency, either in elective or appointive office. Their most important concern is maintaining good ties with a variety of sources external to the agency. The *professionals* are the employees who derive greatest satisfaction from the recognition of other professionals in the same technical, substantive field on the basis of demonstrated competence and expertise. The pursuit of professional behavior appropriate to their occupation—chemistry, mineralogy, psychology—is their most important concern, and professional esteem is their most important reward.

Missionaries, as Wilensky describes them (1967:86), combine aspects of Downs' zealotry and advocacy (1967:88). Missionaries are motivated primarily by their loyalty to specific policies or to social movements that suggest certain configurations of policies as desirable. They are concerned with seeing their preferences become operational and are not primarily concerned with their own status in an agency, their personal future outside an agency, or the approval of fellow professionals.

Most agencies are usually dominated in both numbers and spirit by careerists most of the time. Missionaries are quite rare. Politicians and professionals fluctuate both in number and importance and can either singly or jointly dominate an agency's policy behavior for at least short periods of time. Careerist domination is the natural state of agencies. Missionary domination is virtually never achieved, although occasionally individual missionaries may have considerable short-run impact. The liveliest periods of agency history are likely to come when some combination of politicians and professionals are most active.

Bureaucratic Autonomy—the Power of Decision

Individual bureaucrats deliver the products and services of their agencies—both benefits and restrictions—to individual and corporate clients. They interpret legislation both informally and formally through writing rules and regulations (on the importance of the writing of regulations see Rabinovitz, Pressman, and Rein,

1976). The writing of regulations can often take years and, over the course of time, much of the presumed original intent of the legislation can be altered (for good examples in both the Carter and Reagan years see Wines, 1982).

Bureaucrats also have a vast array of powers through their application of programs and regulations to specific cases. They also adjudicate most appeals of specific decisions. Bureaucrats make the detailed decisions about resource applications.

Individual bureaucrats have lots of latitude in their activities in part because statutes are almost inevitably ambiguous or at least leave many gaps. For example, the controversy over the Meals on Wheels programs reported in Chapter 1 resulted, in part, because the law was ambiguous, and thus bureaucrats could move to cut out private agencies even though congressional intent seems to have been to include them (Ranii, 1980). In the Reagan years, bureaucrats, operating under the watchful eye of politically appointed superiors in a number of regulatory agencies such as the Environmental Protection Agency, the Occupational Safety and Health Administration, the Food and Drug Administration, the Consumer Product Safety Commission, and the Office of Surface Mining in the Department of the Interior, dramatically slowed down enforcement activities under existing statutes, thus altering the regulatory climate for a lot of businesses without new legislation being passed.

Individual bureaucrats in the middle and even relatively low in an agency's hierarchy also have lots of latitude in their activities—some by design in delegations from their formal superiors in the agency and some because subordinates do not necessarily follow directions faithfully in all cases. Sometimes the directions simply are never issued, sometimes the directions are unclear, and sometimes they are ignored or reinterpreted. Much of the time individual bureaucrats or very small units of the bureaucracy—usually located outside Washington either in the federal field establishment or in state, local, and private bureaucracies that are funded to conduct public business—have a great deal of autonomy. Any given agency, let alone the entire government, is under central control only in a loose sense. Programmatic coherence and coordination even within a single agency are usually matters of chance, not design. "Street-level" bureaucrats have what amounts to important policymaking powers (Lipsky, 1980).

We do not imply that bureaucracy has run amok and threatens the liberties of the populace. We are describing a situation that is virtually inevitable because of the political and organizational structure that has been developed over the years in the United States. There are institutional and public opinion limits on totally outrageous behavior by bureaucracies much of the time. But these limits are not foolproof, as the revelations made in the 1970s about the behavior of the Central Intelligence Agency and the Federal Bureau of Investigation indicate. This form of control is negative and is exercised only in extreme cases. Positive control of bureaucratic behavior characterized by planning, rationality, predictability, and smoothness generally does not exist. Much control within a bureaucratic unit is based on approximation and guesswork. (See Janowitz, 1978, for empirical support for this generalization and judgments about the sociological reasons for it. Wildavsky, 1979, and Lindblom, 1965, offer additional evidence plus arguments that this situation has positive aspects.) Agencies vary in the degree of centralized control over lower level bureaucrats, including those in the field (see Kaufman, 1960, for a classic study of how the field staff of one agency was controlled by the top management of the agency).

Individuals matter in bureaucracy. In 1980 one man in the Department of Energy won praise from almost everyone for making decisions in a timely fashion when the rest of the department seemed mired down and unable to process its business (Sulzberger, 1980). For many observers and clients the Department of Energy was simply the Department of Melvin Goldstein, who directed the Office of Hearings and Appeals. As one client put it: "In a pile of manure, a rose blooms brighter than in a field of flowers."

The autonomy of individual bureaucrats on important matters was depicted vividly in a story on the contest between producer interests (oil and timber) and environmentalists over the future of some public land in Wyoming (Harden, 1980):

> The Bridger-Teton (National Forest), in the parlance of the Forest Service, belongs to Reid Jackson. For a federal bureaucrat making $37,000 a year, he has enviable autonomy.... He's in charge of up to 200 employees. Without consulting his superiors, Jackson can sell up to 100 million board feet of timber, enough to build 833 houses. He can authorize major highways that would cut through the forest or

stop dead in their tracks almost any timber or mining operation inside the Bridger-Teton.

While national forest policy is made in Washington, it's Jackson who decides when and how sizable portions of the largest wilderness in the lower 48 states will be chopped down and scoured for its natural resources.

By virtue of his job, Jackson is automatically one of the most powerful men in Wyoming...Jackson's boss in Washington, assistant agriculture secretary M. Rupert Cutler, says the man in charge of the Bridger-Teton has "the best job in the Forest Service" in terms of authority to make his own decisions.

Even when Cutler has second-guessed Jackson, as he did last year in admonishing the forest supervisor for allowing timbering in an area that interfered with a study of elk behavior, the reprimand came after the fact—the timber was being cut down by the time Cutler decided it shouldn't have been.

Note that Jackson is a middle-range civil servant (grade GS–14) in the Forest Service, an agency that in 1979 had 22,685 employees. Of these, 553 held Jackson's grade of GS–14, and 264 held higher ranks. Jackson lives and works 2,000 miles away from his superiors in Washington, D.C. But he and thousands like him in hundreds of agencies wield genuine power in implementing their agencies' programs.

Even at the lowest levels of an agency's hierarchy the individual bureaucrat has latitude to exercise individual judgment and discretion. For example, the front-line interviewer in a local office of a state employment security agency screens people who come to the office looking for a job, or retraining, or unemployment insurance. The interviewer is formally responsible for knowing the eligibility criteria for the variety of programs his agency handles as well as for knowing the job requirements of the job orders placed by employers looking for workers. The front line interviewer will decide which individual applicants are eligible for which programs and who will be referred to what job openings. He or she may choose to emphasize certain programs over others. The Targeted Job Tax Credit Program, for example, was not popular in many employment security offices throughout the United States because the agency received virtually no funds to implement it and got no rewards for good performance. Thus some front-line interviewers chose to ignore the program and not issue vouchers to eligible applicants, since they got no credit for their work and their superiors weren't pushing them anyway.

Other interviewers in the same office might choose to issue vouchers to every eligible applicant out of the conviction that the voucher might help the applicant find a job and that employers ought to be rewarded with a tax credit for hiring people. Both responses involve the exercise of individual discretion, and both decisions have important impacts on the lives of individual applicants at local employment security offices—*and* on the aggregate performance of the agency in implementing the tax credit program that Congress had authorized.

Leadership

Bureaucracies and bureaucrats are not immune to the energizing effects of new persons in formal leadership positions who bring new ideas for programs and have the personalities to motivate others to agree with them. Recent examples of "strong" presidentially appointed individuals with jurisdiction over a sizable bureaucracy include two Secretaries of the Interior: Cecil Andrus (appointed by Carter) and James Watt (appointed by Reagan). They moved their bureaucracies some distance toward their respective policy goals, which, of course, were very different from each other. But persons with this combination of qualities who stay with a key post long enough to make a difference are rare. Most political appointees come and go quickly and are engaged much of the time in trying to get some leverage over the behavior of their nominal subordinates (Heclo, 1977).

The dependence of a political appointee on career civil servants and the limitations facing a new leader were made graphic in a story on a new secretary of transportation in 1979 (Sawyer, 1979b):

> One minute you are Neil Goldschmidt, mayor of Portland, Oregon, a continent away from Washington, fighting for dollars from the Feds like everyone else.
>
> Then comes a call from the White House.
>
> A federal chauffeur meets your plane, someone hands you the keys to a gold-carpeted suite on the 10th floor of the mammoth Transportation Department building in the heart of the capital and suddenly you are in charge. Mr. Insider, right?
>
> Well, sort of.
>
> Enter Edward W. Scott, Jr., the highest ranking career civil servant in the Transportation Department.... A self-described bureaucratic "lifer" who has watched department heads come and go for 18 years, Scott is one of the government's "godfathers." He reveals

bureaucratic truths: Who you can fire without ticking off the White House or a powerful member of Congress. What decisions have to be made during the first 120 days. Who should get an appointment. What reporters will ask on "Meet the Press" next Sunday.

Civil servants themselves can, of course, energize their own agencies to pursue new paths and come up with new ideas. But such behavior is atypical. A person who has grown up in an organization for 30 years and becomes bureau chief is not likely to start looking at the world differently all of a sudden and revolutionize the implementation behavior of that agency.

In short, individual leaders can and do make a difference, but the odds are against it most of the time.

The Public's Perception of Bureaucrats and Bureaucracy

The American people seem to be skeptical about bureaucracy in the abstract. For example, a Gallup Poll in 1977 revealed that two thirds of the people felt that federal employees work less hard than those employed in the private sector. Two thirds also believe that the federal government employed too many people. Political campaigns in which candidates beat up on the impersonal bureaucracy—"government on your backs and with its hands in your wallet"—are frequent.

However, one recent study about how individuals felt about their own personal contacts with government agencies and bureaucrats revealed that at the personal level they were quite positive (Katz and others, 1975). Eighty percent reported that their own experience with an agency providing services left them convinced that the agency was fair. Seventy-two percent felt that the agency had proceeded efficiently. Not surprisingly, individuals who had dealt with an agency that somehow restricted or constrained their behavior were less positive—only 51 percent felt the agency was fair, and 41 percent felt it had been efficient. But even these figures were much higher than the same individuals' opinions of "government agencies in general." Only 42 percent thought all agencies proceeded fairly, and only 29 percent thought they proceeded efficiently. The moral is that, up close, bureaucrats—especially those providing services and tangible benefits—don't seem so bad after all.

SUMMARY

Bureaucracies, also called bureaucratic units or agencies, are a normal and essential form of organization for the conduct of public and private business. Governmental bureaucracies are the most important actors in the implementation of public policy. The potential benefits stemming from bureaucratic organizations include efficient processing of business by a professional staff that treats applicants and clients without favoritism. Bureaucracies don't always perform up to their full potential, and they have associated costs. They change slowly and incrementally and produce lots of red tape even when they are relatively efficient.

Bureaucracies are inherently political in their behavior. The choices they make in allocating resources, interpreting legislation, writing rules and regulations, applying eligibility standards, and judging appeals—in short, in all of their implementation activities—inevitably confer rewards and penalties on different groups and individuals. In addition, the personal values, beliefs, and motivations of individual bureaucrats contribute in important ways to their agencies' implementation behavior. Individuals matter in bureaucracy. Especially important factors that affect implementation involve the organization and reorganization of staff and programs, the internal and external resources that can be marshalled in support of agency preferences, and the variety of bureaucratic relationships with important others—other agencies, clients, Congress, the president, and the institutional presidency.

Government bureaucracy has administered a variety of programs. Currently there are over 2.8 million civilian employees in the federal government and over 13 million more in state and local governments. Growth in bureaucracy has not just happened; it has occurred as a specific response to demands from the public (and organized parts of the public) for additional services and benefits. Bureaucracies also find allies in Congress to help them create new services and benefits. The specific programs developed can be grouped into policies that distribute subsidies, policies that regulate the conditions under which certain kinds of private activity can occur, and policies that redistribute certain benefits in an attempt to reduce inequality among classes of people. These broad categories of policies will be explored further in the next chapter.

CHAPTER 3

Federalism, Policy Types, and Implementation

In the preceding chapters we have tried to portray some of the complexities of implementation and also some of the complexities of bureaucracies. And we have tried to explain how the complexities of bureaucracy affect implementation because bureaucrats are major implementers.

The present chapter has a dual focus. In it we develop more fully two general points made earlier. The two objects of our attention here—the relation of federalism to implementation and the relation of policy type to implementation—are of major importance. *And,* critically, the first has not received a great deal of systematic attention in previous literature (for notable exceptions to that generalization see Van Horn, 1979a and 1979b, and some of the articles in Jones and Thomas, 1976). Even more critically, the second has received no systematic attention.

The first part of the present chapter, then, seeks to add to a systematic understanding of the vast impact on implementation caused by the federal system in the United States.

The second part develops a scheme for classifying policies and states a number of expectations (hypotheses would also be an acceptable word) about how implementation behavior will vary between the four major types of policy. Chapters 4 through 7 present data that allow us to explore some of those expectations.

FEDERALISM AND IMPLEMENTATION

Implementation of national programs and policies is rarely conducted wholly by the federal bureaucracy in Washington. For most programs, different levels of governmental bureaucracy are centrally involved, and the Washington-based bureaucratic units may be quite remote from actual implementation activities. The involvement of other governmental units—in federal regional field offices throughout the United States, in states and in localities, stems from the federal nature of American government. The different layers of bureaucracy engage in bargaining with each other. Even in federally funded grant-in-aid programs the federal bureaucrats only have a license to bargain with the state and local bureaucrats (Ingram, 1977).

Federalism and intergovernmental relations are vast topics and have spawned numerous books (for two useful general studies, see Wright, 1978, and Walker, 1981). The presence of a federalistic structure and the simultaneous fact that the United States is a huge country both in terms of area and population makes implementation extra challenging under any circumstances. The direction that the federal structure of intergovernmental relations has taken in practice adds extra complications as well as challenges. The use of a federal structure for many (although not all) national programs complicates both politics and formal accountability because more people and agencies are involved.

Federalism and intergovernmental relations are inherent features of the American governmental system and set the stage for the implementation of public policies. The federal system has evolved over time, and its impact on domestic policy implementation has evolved. There is every reason to expect that it will continue to change. The federal grant system is the primary apparatus for involving other units of government in policy implementation. Overall control and management of the federal system is limited—the politics of bargaining is much more prevalent than control. In the sections that follow we will elaborate on these general points about the relationship between federalism and policy implementation.

The Changing Shape of Federalism and National Policy

At heart, the meaning of U.S. federalism is simply that all policy is not national in origin or implementation. The 50 states have many important policy powers. In addition, the states have over the years created a staggering variety of local governments and authorities that also have policy powers. About 83,000 such units existed in 1982 and 85 percent of them had the power to tax.

The lines of which government has the power to do what have always been somewhat blurred, although for the first 100 years or so of the existence of an independent United States the dividing lines between state powers and concerns and national powers and concerns were fairly clear. Relations between federal and state governments were formal and distant. National and state programs were not interrelated in any particular way and funds were not comingled.

However, for roughly the second 100 years of independent national existence, since the first federal grants-in-aid to state governments for specific uses were made in 1887, the lines of who was responsible for what, who was employed by whom, who determined programmatic purposes, and who paid how much of the bill all began to blur. That blurring accelerated rapidly beginning in the 1930s. The proliferation of the grant-in-aid system—always by federal statute—has been at the heart of the development of modern federalism. The 1960s saw a particularly dramatic expansion of the grant system in terms of number of programs, amount of money involved, and the definition of grant recipients to include local governments and authorities as well as states. The 1985 federal budget estimates that by 1987 all grants for states and localities will total almost $108 billion. About 80 percent of these grants will be categorical—that is, targeted at specific purposes and programs (with the four largest areas involving health; income security; transportation; and education, training, employment, and social services).

Grants that are not categorical are given either for general purposes (called revenue sharing) or as block grants tied to a broad substantive area but with considerable flexibility left to states and localities in terms of how they spend the money.

Until the 1960s the grants from the federal government were given to accomplish purposes that were defined primarily by the states themselves. The federal government specified only a few vague national goals. In the 1960s the grant-in-aid programs changed in several major ways: the federal statutes specified more national goals, although sometimes vague and confused, that were to be achieved by the programs thus funded; the number and size of grants grew dramatically; and grants were no longer restricted to state governments but were increasingly channeled directly to a whole variety of local governmental units—cities, counties, school districts, and other special districts such as those for sewers or conservation. The direct channeling of aid that bypassed the states began in the 1950s. It grew quickly in the 1960s and 1970s.

In the very late 1960s and throughout the 1970s, a major emphasis on decentralizing federal-state-local government relations in several senses emerged: greater controls and autonomy over federally provided resources (dollars) were given to states and localities. The federal government bureaucracy was itself decentralized in large part to make it more responsive to states and localities. The first of these changes produced so-called cooperative federalism, which has had many concrete impacts on implementation and holds potential for additional impacts. The emergence of cooperative federalism and the attempt to decentralize at least some federal bureaucracies are worth considering separately here. Both phenomena will reappear in various cases in Chapters 4 through 7.

Cooperative federalism. Officials at all three levels of government began using rhetoric in the 1960s suggesting that various arrangements should be developed to make intergovernmental relationships smoother, especially on grant programs. President Lyndon Johnson took some steps. Early in his presidency Richard Nixon took up the cause and worked throughout his tenure to put flesh on it. A number of concrete results emerged from these presidential initiatives and also from initiatives coming from the state and local levels (Wright, 1978:390–93).

President Johnson in 1964 and 1965 created a number of interagency coordinating committees to simplify the administration of grants.

Beginning in 1965 the Office of Management and Budget issued a number of directives aimed at facilitating intergovernmental relations.

In 1968 Congress passed the Intergovernmental Cooperation Act which, among other things, enabled states to obtain uniform information on federal grants.

The general revenue-sharing program created in 1972 was renewed in 1976, 1980, and 1983. Until 1980 the program provided between $6 and $7 billion annually to states and a whole variety of local units of government. In 1980 states were dropped and spending was reduced to $4.6 billion annually. In 1985 President Reagan proposed killing the program altogether.

In block grants, states and localities get federal funds for a broad purpose. Then they can decide themselves how to use that money to fulfill the aim. Since the mid-1960s, there have been many proposals for block-grant programs. Only five had been created by 1981: (1) the Partnership for Health Act of 1966; (2) the Safe Streets Act of 1968, which created the Law Enforcement Assistance Administration (LEAA); (3) the Comprehensive Employment and Training Act (CETA) of 1973; (4) the community development block grant part of the Housing and Community Development Act of 1974; and (5) Title XX of the Social Security Act, added in 1974. Each of these programs has had its own problems. But on balance, they were more efficient in distributing federal aid than the endlessly growing and overlapping categorical programs. Both LEAA and CETA died under Reagan, although CETA was replaced by another employment and training block grant program.

The Reagan administration sought to increase the use of block grants but had only marginal success. Nine new block grants were created by Congress in 1981, but only a few of them had much importance. Most proposals were rebuffed by Congress. In 1982, Congress replaced the Comprehensive Employment and Training Act with the Job Training Partnership Act.

Decentralization of the federal establishment. In some ways, of course, the federal government is the federal government, and it doesn't matter where it is located. And in a country as large both in territory and population as the United States, some decentralization has always been necessary. There has been a federal field establishment as long as there has been a federal government. However, it is also true that in the last several decades there has been more conscious attention to the structure of the federal field establishment. This attention has come in part as a response to the need for improving relations with state and local governments, in part as a response to perceived problems with implementation in general. It makes sense to consider the federal field establishment—and its multiple levels—as part of the federalistic context in which domestic program implementation takes place.

The Federal Grant System

The federal grant system has been the primary instrument for involving other levels of government in the implementation of federal domestic policy and programs. The nature of the grant system has generated extensive scholarly investigation, the most thorough of which has been conducted over the last few years by the Advisory Commission on Intergovernmental Relations (ACIR), which has issued numerous volumes of reports.

There are lots of grant programs, and their aggregate cost has grown over time. Most grant programs are still categorical—which means that the funding agency in Washington defines the goals and conditions of the grant program to be operated by the recipient agency in Tuscaloosa, Moline, or Helena—rather than broad-based, general purpose in nature. Most are for specific projects not based on formula allocation of funds to recipient agencies.

There were almost 500 categorical programs by the late 1970s (Advisory Commission on Intergovernmental Relations, 1979). By 1981 there were 361 programs. By 1984 this number had shrunk to 259. Over 85 percent of all spending was concentrated in 25 programs. In 1968 categorical grants made up 98 percent of all federal aid to states and localities. Since then, general revenue-sharing and block grants have reduced that percentage. From 1976 through 1987 the percentage fluctuated between 77 and 81. The Reagan administration, despite its goals, has not been able to reduce federal centralization of categorical programs.

TABLE 3–1 Distribution of Federal Grant-In-Aid Programs by Program Area, 1960–1990

Program Area	1960	1970	1980	1985 est	1990 est
Energy, natural resources, environment	2	2	7	5	3
Agriculture	3	4	1	2	*
Transportation	43	19	14	17	16
Community and regional development	2	5	7	5	4
Education, training, employment, and social services	7	27	24	17	18
Health	3	16	17	23	29
Income security	38	24	20	25	28
General purpose and other	2	3	10	7	*

*Less than one-half of one percent.
 SOURCE: *Special Analyses, Budget of the United States Government, Fiscal Year 1986:* H-17.

The major substantive purposes of federal grants-in-aid have shifted over time, as Table 3–1 summarizes. Health has become consistently and steadily more important. Transportation has become consistently less important. Other areas have exhibited some fluctuations.

Management and Control in the Federal System

Despite attempts at management over the years, some of which are referred to in Chapters 1 and 2, not much systematic management has emerged in the federal system. There is a lack of order, routine, and predictability in the system (Leach, 1970). Thus, any given policy is likely to be processed somewhat differently from any other policy.

There is a touching but probably ill-placed faith on the part of some officials and observers alike in the ability of the federal government to manage the whole system in some rational, coordinated fashion (see, for example, Brunner, 1980, and Weimer, 1980). In fact, the federal layer can sometimes control a policy by proceeding coercively if Congress has provided coercive features in the statute, but that is not the dominant pattern.

One resource available to federal bureaucrats trying to impose controls is the actual or threatened withholding of grant funds. The disadvantage to the technique of withholding federal grant money is that the intended program purpose will certainly not be implemented in the absence of grant funds. The federal bureaucrats may try to obtain control over program performance by suing communities or agencies, but this route has the drawbacks of being time-consuming, expensive, and limited to a case-by-case approach. The Justice Department brought suit against a small town in Texas in 1980 for misusing its general revenue sharing funds by discriminating in services provided to black residents of the town. The town settled out of court and agreed in a consent decree to undertake specific improvements (*Washington Post,* December 12, 1980). The suit was successful, but the implications for federal control and management are not heartening—to monitor and catch misuses or failures to conform to program guidelines and then to alter the misbehavior in the desired direction would require a federal manpower level that far outnumbered the state and local bureaucrats, and that clearly will not occur.

Aside from the limitations of manpower, time, and resources, federal bureaucrats' power is limited by the degree of coercion contained in statutes, and most of the time the federal power is quite limited. One study of general revenue sharing and two major block-grant programs (CETA and Community Development Block Grants, Van Horn, 1979b) summarized the federal responsibilities in those programs (see Table 3–2). These responsibilities were sketchy and left the federal government with only limited tools for persuading and coercing, which they used badly much of the time. By design there was no chance of federal control.

If federal bureaucrats are cast in the role of would-be managers without the resources to manage, state bureaucrats are often cast in the role of middlemen who are pushed by the federal government in some program areas and pulled by local governmental units within their boundaries to help meet specific needs (Wright, 1978:120). And local officials are often cast in the role of entrepreneurs, hustling federal dollars wherever they can find them. As the mayor of Seattle put it (Stanfield, 1979a): "Whether you're a new-breed mayor or an old-style mayor, you continue to struggle to get new dollars and hold on to the ones you have."

The entire federal-state-local relationship in relation to dollars and grant programs takes on an air of a bazaar, with many people in many stalls and booths haggling over who gets what. This entrepreneurial or bazaar model helps explain the confusion

TABLE 3-2   Federal Responsibilities in Three Federal Programs in the 1970s

Program	Federal Responsibilities
General Revenue Sharing (1972)	No prior plan review. Collect information on fund usage, audits. Evaluation of performance.
Amendment to GRS (1976)	Adds requirement to report on participation process and nondiscrimination provisions. Adds independent financial and compliance audit each three years.
CETA (1973)	Prior plan approval by DOL. Collect information on fund usage. Monitor performance, provide technical aid. Evaluate performance yearly.
CDBG (1974)	Automatic plan approval unless vetoed. Collect information on planned and actual uses. Annual performance review and audit.

SOURCE: Adapted from C.E. Van Horn, "Evaluating the New Federalism: National Goals and Local Implementors," *Public Administration Review* 39(Jan./Feb. 1979): 19. Reprinted with permission. © 1979 by the American Society for Public Administration. All rights reserved.

that is often the hallmark of federal grant programs during implementation.

The decentralization of programs can take several different forms. Figure 3–1 lays out five different general possibilities.

Figure 3–2 portrays the agencies that are typically involved in a federal grant-in-aid program. The arrangement of agencies and actors in the diagram implies that the system functions hierarchically, but as we have stressed, such orderliness is more likely to be overwhelmed by the smell and color of the bazaar.

There is a paradox involved in the changing shape of federalism in relation to the management and control of policy implementation. On the one hand, states and localities have become increasingly dependent on the federal government's dollars. There has also been a related increase in presumed national goals, and directives and regulations intended to lead or force states and localities to pursue those goals. The paradox is that the increased money and fiscal dependency has, in effect, created more programmatic autonomy and goal independence at the state and local level despite the attempts at national regulation of state and local behavior. This situation means that the obstacles to smooth or successful implementation from the point of view of federal

FIGURE 3–1   Models of Administrative Organization for Providing Assistance to Program Beneficiaries

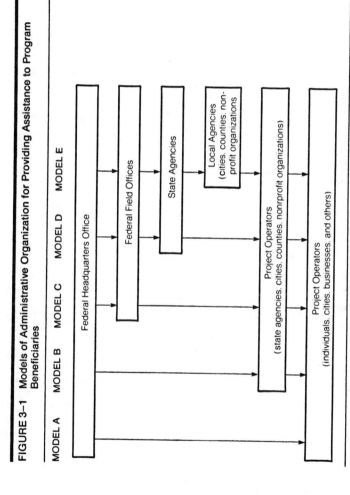

SOURCE: Adapted from U.S. General Accounting Office, 1978, *The Federal Government Should But Doesn't Know the Cost of Administering its Assistance Programs*, p. 3.

FIGURE 3-2 Illustrative Structure for Federal Aid Programs

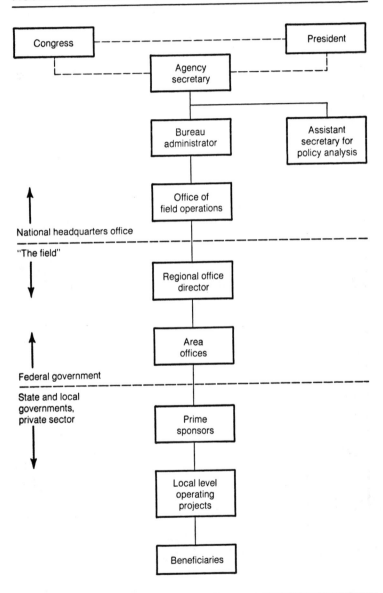

SOURCE: Reprinted from "Decentralization of Government Agencies" by R.K. Yin in *American Behavioral Scientist* 22: 533 © 1979 Sage Publications, Beverly Hills, by permission of the Publisher.

bureaucrats have increased dramatically. Accountability to the federal government by states and localities has been diminished in fact although the "feds" have tried to devise regulations to prevent that diminution.

On the more positive side, this development *may* have increased the responsiveness of programs to local needs. It has certainly increased the number of significantly influential implementers for any program. And it has made bargaining and compromise even more pervasive in many programs.

Some observers are upset by these developments. They feel that increased state and local influence diminishes the chance of achieving implementation that will lead to the achievement of national goals. Others feel that the increased influence on the parts of states and localities encourages healthy adaptations of national goals to varying local needs. Ronald Reagan's administration has kept the debate a lively one, especially with its stress on a diminished role for the federal government and increased responsibilities (with less federal money) for states.

POLICY TYPES AND IMPLEMENTATION
Policy Types
In Chapter 2 we sketched the major social purposes that governmental bureaucracies achieve—distribution of benefits, regulation of activity, and redistribution of benefits. For the remainder of this chapter we want to elaborate and expand on this classification of governmental policies and programs. Inevitably, any classifying scheme will have some imperfections. The one we use is no exception. Policies and programs may have elements of several types embedded in them. Policies also may shift from one type to another over time. But we think the classification we use has considerable utility for understanding the varying purposes of governmental policies and programs and the distinctive political relationships that surround differing types of policies. The typology has demonstrated considerable utility in relation to patterns of policy formulation and legitimation (see Ripley and Franklin, 1984), and we believe it will be similarly helpful in understanding policy implementation.

We will use the following fourfold classification of domestic policy in the remainder of this book: (1) *distributive;* (2) *competitive regulatory;* (3) *protective regulatory;* and (4) *redistributive.*

This typology derives from our own work and our use of the work of a number of other people (particularly Lowi, 1964; see also Froman, 1968; Hayes, 1978; Lowi, 1972; and Salisbury, 1968).

Two major assumptions underlie our adoption of these policy types. The first is that the perceptions held by individuals involved in the implementation of programs and policies about what is at stake in the decisions that must be made have an important impact on the nature of the politics surrounding the implementation. There is a chicken-and-egg quality to the relationship between perceptions and politics: the perceptions of what is at stake help shape the politics; the politics help sustain the perceptions. But as with most things human, change is likely. Changes in perceptions can trigger changes in political patterns, or changes in aspects of political behavior can lead to changes in the perceptions of what's at stake. And, of course, the policies and programs themselves can and do undergo change over time. These changes are also likely to alter both politics and perceptions. all of this makes for a somewhat messy, imprecise situation for the analyst to unravel, but it is faithful to the reality of politics, programs, and policies. And, in fact, we are confident that there are understandable patterns that can be explained even within the seeming confusion.

Our second assumption is that at the point of implementation the purposes of programs are clearer to implementers and to others interested in and affected by them than are the purposes of the general policies governing, usually loosely, their application. A policy may have multiple purposes that can be broken into more manageable program units for purposes of implementation. The policies are the results of compromise and often contain multiple ends that are pointed in different directions simultaneously. Those multiple ends may be pursued in the form of separate programs, each of which adopts different parts of the overall goals as its province. It is at the stage of implementation that the fuzzy and multiple goals of policies can be made specific and concrete.

Distributive policies and programs. Distributive policies and programs are aimed at promoting private activities that are thought by supporters to be desirable and beneficial to society as a whole and, at least in theory, to be activities that would not be undertaken without government intervention in the form of assistance. The assistance is provided in the form of *subsidies,* which are payments of some kind (not necessarily just straight cash) that induce individuals and groups to undertake the desired activity. Distributive programs provide tangible government benefits in the form of payments in cash, payments in kind, tax advantages, grants, low-cost loans, franchises, and licenses to the persons, groups, and corporate entities from which the government is hoping to get the desired activity. The subsidy is generally made dependent on the performance of the activity: the government, in effect, says to the potential beneficiary: "if you do X, we will give you Y benefits." The recipients of distributive subsidies may be thought of collectively as "producer" interests because the distributive policy is intended to induce certain types of productive behavior that policymakers view as desirable—behavior that may include certain farming practices, land development, investment patterns, or manufacturing certain kinds of cars. Subsidies may also be awarded to producers for *not* engaging in some activities.

Examples of distributive policies and programs include:

Land grants for railroad companies in the 19th century based on miles of track constructed.

Use of proceeds from sale of public land to homesteaders to subside development in the 19th century West.

Cash payments for purchase of agricultural crops to support prices.

Direct loans for various aspects of farm improvement, such as the purchase of equipment or soil and water conservation.

Grants to localities for airport construction, hospital construction, sewage facilities, and mass transit facilities.

Income tax deductions for interest on home mortgages and for local property taxes to encourage home ownership.

Permits to private interests to timber or mine or graze livestock on public lands such as national forests or lands held by the Bureau of Reclamation.

Grants for research to universities and private laboratories.

Provision of general revenue-sharing monies to support state and local activities of their own choosing.

Patents for inventors and copyrights for authors to encourage invention and creative writing.

During the policymaking (formulation and legitimation) stage, distributive policies are not perceived to compete with each other. Distributive policy choices are not considered in an aggregate sense—those supporting a subsidy for university research do not compete directly with those supporting a subsidy for growing or not growing wheat. Each distributive policy choice is made separately with only short-run consequences in mind. At the point of implementation, however, the element of competition may be introduced if the structure of the program does not allow unlimited benefits or if certain groups or individuals are not entitled to benefits automatically.

For example, a program that guarantees that every bushel of wheat produced will generate a direct government payment of 10 cents to the farmer up to a maximum of $20,000 per farmer does not produce head-to-head competition among wheat farmers. However, a program that allocates $5 million to the National Science Foundation for reallocation to university-based sociologists on a competitive basis does produce head-to-head competition among various sociologists and their home universities. Both programs are subsidies, but they are likely to result in different political situations during implementation because of the relative degree of competition or noncompetition. Policy formulators do not have to trade off the wheat program versus the sociological research program, except in the abstract sense of keeping total government expenditures under some ceiling level proclaimed during the congressional budget process—a level that can be altered to make room for more programs. The wheat farmers in this example do not have to compete for their subsidy, but the sociologists do.

Competitive regulatory policies and programs. Competitive regulatory policies and programs limit the provision of specific goods and services to only one or a few designated deliverers chosen from a larger number of potential or actual competitors. The regulated goods and services are thought to be important enough to the public good to require public governmental intervention for one or both of two reasons: (1) the good or service being allocated is scarce, such as the finite limit on the number of radio frequencies or television channels; (2) the public has a stake in the manner in which the good or service is provided. For example, localities needed to be guaranteed they would receive some rail freight service. These policies are competitive because more than one potential deliverer exists and in any individual decision, there can be only one winner. The other potential recipients lose. Some scarce resources simply cannot be divided. A television channel has to go to one of the parties competing for it.[1]

In recent years a number of areas formerly subject to competitive regulation have been opened to freer competition. These areas include the major forms of transportation for both people and freight and some forms of communications.

One principal implementation activity is simply choosing the winning competitors. By definition, the competitors understand that there can be only one winner in each individual contest. However, over time, those who can compete repeatedly are likely to win some competitions. Thus, until airline deregulation went into effect, an individual airline may have lost individual contests for specific routes but, over time, every individual airline won its share.

Some decisions in the competitive regulatory arena impose standards of delivery and have periodic competitions or periodic review of performance of those granted delivery privileges. These conditions and standards of service comprise the other chief implementation activity in competitive regulatory policy. For example, to have a license renewed a radio or television station must conform to certain standards of public service programming (often met in part by broadcasting taped reports from members of Congress at 6 A.M. on Sunday!).

Competitive regulatory policy is somewhat different from the other three policy types in several ways. First, it is a hybrid in that it provides, in effect, subsidies for winning competitors and also tries to promote the public interest by requiring certain kinds of behavior on the parts of the winners by regulatory measures.

---

[1] Note that competitive regulation should not be confused with the regulation of the conditions under which competition in the business world can take place. That regulation—such as is administered by the Justice Department's antitrust program or the Federal Trade Commission's administration of statutes prohibiting "unfair competition"—is intended to be protective of the public and fits into the policy category we call protective regulation.

Second, general pronouncements of policy at the national level are much less frequent than in the case of the other three types of policy. New competitive regulatory programs are only rarely legislated or amended in major ways or terminated. Most of the programs in fact emerge during the implementation process itself. Case-by-case application of general guidelines is at the heart of the implementation of competitive regulatory policy. Third, the subsidy portion of the hybrid extracts an obligation from the recipient to deliver the service. A railroad awarded a route under this model *must* operate it. A broadcaster given a television channel *must* operate it. The element of coercion in competitive regulation is stronger than in distributive policy, which does not require anyone to become a wheat farmer or to plant a certain number of acres in wheat. Distributive subsidies merely offer inducements to obtain voluntary behavior.

Examples of competitive regulatory policies include:

Authorizing and requiring specific railroads to operate specified routes.

Authorizing and requiring specific airlines to operate specified routes.

Authorizing and requiring specific trucking companies to haul specified commodities over specified routes.

Authorizing and requiring the operation of specific television channels and radio frequencies by specified operators.

Protective regulatory policies and programs. Protective regulatory policies and programs are designed to protect the public by setting the conditions under which various private activities can occur. Activities and conditions that are thought to be harmful, such as pollution of the atmosphere, unsafe working conditions, unfair competition between businesses, or unfair labor practices by employers or unions, are prohibited. Conditions that are thought to be helpful, such as fixed rates for railroad or truck shipping, truth-in-advertising, or publication of true interest rates on loans and installment buying are required.

Examples of protective regulatory policies and programs include:

Minimum-wage and maximum-hour limits for workers.

Limiting the conditions under which strip mining can be undertaken and requiring restoration of the surface after mining has occurred.

Wage and price controls.

Certification of the airworthiness of airplanes before allowing them to fly on commercial routes.

High taxation to discourage the use of scarce or dangerous commodities, such as gasoline or firearms.

Requiring the providers of credit to publish true interest rates.

Testing food additives and drugs before allowing them on the market and prohibiting harmful additives and drugs.

Setting rates for airlines, trucklines, railroads, bargelines, and pipelines.

Prohibiting certain labor and management practices defined as unfair.

At the policy formulation and legitimation stage, the objects of protective regulation—those whose behavior is regulated, such as railroads, mining companies, unions, banks, and many other corporate entities—usually perceive themselves in an adversary relationship with those proposing the creation or expansion or tightening of regulation. At the stage of implementation they may continue to view themselves in an adversarial relationship and fight the regulators, or they may attempt to capture the regulators as sympathetic friends.

Redistributive policy and programs. Redistributive policies and programs are intended to readjust the allocation of wealth, property, rights, or some other value among social classes or racial groups in society. The redistributive feature enters because a number of actors perceive that there are winners and losers—that is, that the policies and programs *transfer* the valued items to one group *at the expense of* another, distinct group. Thus the more well-off economic classes perceive progressive taxation tied to income transfer programs for the poor as redistributive, and most members of those classes, although not far from all, oppose such taxation. Similarly, some white males— again, not all—perceive programs aimed at affirmative action or equal opportunity for females and ethnic minorities as redistributing jobs and opportunities at their expense. Thus they oppose affirmative action.

In practice, government policy can and does redistribute resources in the other direction too, so that the already privileged classes and ethnic groups in society can become more privileged at the added expense of the less privileged. But these programs are not *perceived* to be redistributive in the context of debate over policy in the United States. Instead, redistribution has come to be understood explicitly as reallocation of resources in favor of the less advantaged and in the direction of greater equality. The other direction in redistribution—in favor of those already more well-endowed and in favor of continued or greater social and economic inequality—is promoted by a number of policies and programs such as regressive or proportional taxes that include most property taxes at the local level, state sales taxes, and the federal payroll tax to support the social security program. But the political disputes over such programs do not invoke the image of redistribution.

It was typical of American politics that, in early 1981, President Ronald Reagan proclaimed that the tax system should not be used for redistributive purposes. He was, at the time, proposing changes in the federal tax structure that would clearly have redistributed wealth back in the direction of the already wealthy. But he did not consider that redistribution, nor did many who joined the debate over the proposal. What he meant by redistribution, and what most people engaged in policy debate in the United States mean by redistribution, is exclusively the shifting of something of value from the more well-off to the less well-off. Thus, Reagan's proscription of redistribution in tax systems meant that he did not think a tax system should be used to shift wealth from the upper economic classes to the lower economic classes. In an objective, analytic sense, of course, virtually any tax is redistributive in some direction—but American political discourse proceeds using its own unique logic.

Even though a policy nationally proclaims or appears to proclaim redistribution in a general sense, the exact details of who gets how much at the expense of whom remain to be decided by the details of implementation. Thus the precise nature of potential redistributive impact is often, although not always, settled only during the implementation process.

Examples of redistributive policies and programs include:

The provision of food stamps for the disadvantaged.

The creation of employment and training programs that are designed primarily for the disadvantaged.

Requirements of affirmative action in hiring by federal contractors.

Requirements that governmentally provided or aided services and facilities be equally open to all without regard to race or ethnicity.

Progressive income taxation, which involves setting personal income tax rates in such a way that more affluent people pay a substantially higher percentage of their incomes in taxes than do less affluent people.

The provision of special legal services for the disadvantaged.

The provision of special health care for those who cannot afford it otherwise.

Relationships Between Policy Type and Implementation

Now is a good time to ask an all-too-often ignored question: so what? What difference does it make to the understanding of implementation that there are four types of domestic policies? We believe that implementation activities and outcomes will vary according to policy types. In part these differences are carried over into implementation from the political relationships and debates generated during the formulation and legitimation stage.

In the following pages we offer some propositions about the patterns that we hypothesize are present in implementation of different types of policy. These propositions are based in part on our reading of the literature, in part on personal involvement in empirical implementation studies, and in part on hunches. We think the expectations we present here are correct. One of the central purposes of Chapters 4 through 7 is to develop some evidence about the degree of correctness of the expectations.

The aspects of implementation that we expect to vary according to policy type are the identity of the principal participants, the nature of the relationships among principal participants, the relative difficulty of achieving what the bureaucrats would consider successful implementation, and the critical processes for achieving success.

Principal actors in implementation. The primary actors in implementation that we will discuss include the *bureaucracy* (subdivided by territorial level into the federal bureaucracy based in Washington, the regional field offices of the federal apparatus, the state governments, and local governments), *beneficiaries* (including producers, who receive direct subsidies from the government for their actions, and consumers, who benefit from the regulation of producer interests), *restricted clients* (potential beneficiaries who fail to win direct subsidies and producers whose activity is regulated), and *Congress.* Table 3–3 summarizes our expectations about how these actors will be involved in the implementation of each type of domestic policy.

Bureaucratic levels. We have made the point in Chapters 1 and 2 that the most influential actor in any implementation situation is the bureaucracy. While this is true, the territorial level of bureaucracy that is most important—whether the central federal government bureaucracy in Washington, the regional field offices of the federal bureaucracy, or various layers of state and local governments—varies according to the types of policy being implemented. In distributive policy areas the design of the program is critical to determining the relative importance of these layers of bureaucracy. No one level dominates in every distributive program all of the time; all can be active.

In competitive regulatory policy the central federal bureaucracy is consistently the most important bureaucratic actor. Typically, the federal field establishment and the state and local bureaucracies have little to do with implementing this kind of policy.

In protective regulatory policy the dominant bureaucratic layers tend to be the federal central and federal field establishments. The state and local government bureaucracies are less likely to be important.

In redistributive programs the details of program design determine the relative importance of federal field bureaucratic entities and state and local bureaucracies. Typically, the federal bureaucracy in Washington, D.C. is not directly involved in a day-to-day way with implementation.

TABLE 3–3 Principal Actors Involved in Implementation by Policy Type

Policy Type	Bureaucracy	Beneficiaries	Restricted Clients	Congress
Distributive	Central federal, federal field, state and local all active depending on details of program design	All producers if benefits are unlimited or a matter of right; some producers if benefits are limited and apportioned on competitive basis (the winners)	None if benefits are unlimited or a matter of right; some producers if benefits are limited and apportioned on competitive basis (the losers)	Sporadic oversight and intervention triggered by interruption or threatened interruption of distribution of benefits.
Competitive regulatory	Central federal most active	Some producers (the winners in competition); some consumers receiving regulated services	All producers (the losers in competition; the winners in that they have to conform to some delivery standards)	Sporadic oversight and intervention triggered when constituency interests are threatened; some focus on processes by General Accounting Office (GAO)
Protective regulatory	Central federal and federal field structures both important	Consumers of regulated activities, goods, services	Producers of regulated activities, goods, services	Sporadic oversight and intervention (anecdotal examination of impact on beneficiaries); some focus on processes by GAO
Redistributive	Federal field, state and local all active depending on details of program design; (central federal apparatus not very active)	Dependent classes and minorities	None if benefits are by entitlement; dependent classes and minorities if there are eligibility criteria or funding limits	Sporadic oversight and intervention (anecdotal examination of impact on beneficiaries); some focus on processes by GAO

Beneficiaries. Beneficiaries are active participants in the implementation of all types of policies and programs. The nature of those beneficiaries varies by policy type, however.

In distributive policy the beneficiaries are producers of some kind such as farmers, corporations, or researchers. All producers in the category of recipients targeted for subsidy are beneficiaries if the benefits provided are unlimited, if all producers can receive subsidies by virtue of their status as members of the targeted group, or if benefits are defined as a matter of right or entitlement. In these cases there is no competition for the subsidy among potential beneficiaries. If benefits are limited and must be apportioned at least in part on a selective basis, then only a portion of the producers are direct beneficiaries. They are winners in the short term. The rest are losers in the short run and are considered to be restricted clients.

In competitive regulatory policy some, but not all, producers are beneficiaries—these are the producers, such as trucklines, airlines, broadcast corporations, that are the winners in the competition for the scarce resources. Some consumers—those receiving the services presumably regulated in the consumer interest—are also beneficiaries. Citizens in Minot, North Dakota, who received a mandated number of flights to Denver or Minneapolis per day were good examples in the days of airline regulation.

In protective regulatory policy all of the consumers of the regulated activities, goods, and services are the presumed beneficiaries. All consumers who purchase medications are thought to benefit from the Food and Drug Administration's requirements for thorough testing before allowing new drugs on the market or from their decisions to withdraw drugs and food additives from the market because of health dangers discovered by research.

In redistributive policy a variety of dependent classes—the less well-off economically or racial and ethnic minorities—are the presumed beneficiaries. The programs are designed to provide them with benefits to enhance their well-being or to increase their opportunities to improve their own status in life.

Restricted clients. In a number of programs beneficiaries reap benefits because there are other individuals and groups who do not benefit but who are instead restricted, denied, or coerced. These latter individuals and groups are also clients, but they are clients in the sense of being denied a subsidy (failing to win in a competition for a scarce subsidy) or being restricted in the kinds of activities they can or cannot undertake as a quid pro quo for receiving a subsidy (thou shalt not discriminate in hiring on the basis of race or sex; thou shall set employment goals for women and minorities).

In distributive programs there are no restricted clients if benefits are unlimited for all practical purposes or if they are granted as a matter of right. Some producers are restricted if benefits are limited and therefore must be apportioned on some sort of competitive basis. Those who lose, at least in relative terms, in such a competition can be thought of as restricted clients.

In competitive regulatory policy all producers in the target population of producers are restricted in some sense. The losers in the competition for the right to undertake certain activities—for example, the broadcast companies that do not get to broadcast over Channel 10 in El Paso—are restricted by that loss. The winners in competitive policy are also restricted clients in the sense of having to conform to some standards in delivering their services: Thou shalt provide no smoking seats for your passengers on any route you fly with federal approval; thou shalt dedicate six hours a week of your air time to providing public service programs if you get an assigned radio frequency.

In protective regulatory situations the producers of the regulated activities, goods, and services are the restricted clients. Mining companies must conform to federal standards in rehabilitating land after strip mining. Automobile companies must meet federal standards for gasoline mileage.

In redistributive programs there are no restricted clients if benefits are extended by entitlement to all individuals in certain categories. The dependent economic or ethnic classes are restricted, however, if there are eligibility criteria that require some action or proof on their part, or if resources for programs are insufficient to serve all members of the entitled group. In the latter situation, recipients who get served by the programs may do so on a first come, first served basis until the funds are used up; the remaining members are the restricted clients.

Congress. Interested individuals and subcommittees in Congress get involved in implementation only occasionally. While oversight and intervention are sporadic both can be triggered in any of the four policy areas.

In distributive policy intervention can be triggered by an actual or a threatened interruption of the distribution of benefits if the constituents or interest groups facing the cut-off make their problems known in the right places in Congress forcefully enough.

In competitive regulatory policy the trigger comes primarily when constituents or national interest groups feel their interests are threatened and report the threat vociferously to interested parties in Congress. The General Accounting Office (GAO)— formally an arm of Congress—also engages in some studies of processes used in this arena.

In protective regulatory policy the trigger is related to forceful complaints of either too much or too little zeal in enforcement. Consumers complain of too little zeal and can trigger members of Congress ideologically in sympathy with them. Producers can complain of too much or misplaced or unfair zeal and can activate members of Congress in agreement with them ideologically. Again, GAO undertakes some special inquiries in this area.

In redistributive policy some subcommittees or committees of Congress may intrude in implementation by seeking information on how programs are performing. They may engage in examination of impact on beneficiaries, usually limited to anecdotal evidence. Occasionally, an interest group's claim that benefits are being denied is forceful enough to elicit some congressional interest. GAO also mounts some studies of bureaucratic processes in redistributive programs.

Expected relationships among principal actors. As described above, the identity of the principal actors varies systematically from policy area to policy area. In both distributive and redistributive programs the identity of bureaucratic levels involved is subject to variations in program design. A principal concern of all layers of bureaucracy in implementing all types of programs is a desire to maintain orderly routines for delivering benefits, services, and subsidies to recipients, and thus to minimize complaints and conflict about the processes and outcomes. Much of the time, particularly for the federal bureaucracy, these concerns are paramount. If a program is functioning smoothly in terms

TABLE 3-4 Relationships and Success in Implementation by Policy Type

Policy Type	Nature of Relationships between Actors	Relative Difficulty of Successful Implementation*	Processes Critical to Successful Implementation*
Distributive	Federal bureaucracy (central and regional) mainly concerned with smoothness of process and absence of complaints representing beneficiaries Central federal bureaucracy is close to national groups representing beneficiaries Federal field, state, and local bureaucracies close to local groups representing beneficiaries General level of conflict: low	Low	System management and operating routines to deliver the goods
Competitive regulatory	Federal bureaucracy mainly concerned with smoothness of process and absence of complaints Central federal bureaucracy maintains formal distance from competing interests; may work closely informally General level of conflict: low, with short, higher bursts	Moderate	Operating routines to make decisions and review performance
Protective regulatory	Federal bureaucracy mainly concerned with smoothness of process and absence of complaints Central federal bureaucracy in either adversary relationship with restricted clients and friendly relationship with beneficiaries or vice versa General level of conflict: moderate, some sustained higher bursts	Moderate	Involvement of federal implementers to enforce restrictions
Redistributive	Federal bureaucracy (central and regional) mainly concerned with smoothness of process and absence of complaints; may promote some evaluative efforts on both process and impact Central federal bureaucracy has distant, impersonal relationship with beneficiaries and restricted clients State and local bureaucracies have close relationships with beneficiaries—sometimes friendly, sometimes hostile General level of conflict: moderate to high	High	Bargaining relationships between bureaucrats and beneficiaries

*Be sure to see the text, pp. 86–88, for a discussion of the meaning of successful.

of processes and if there are no complaints about those processes, then the program is usually judged to be a success by the implementers. Table 3–4 summarizes our expectations about the nature of relationships among implementers.

In distributive policy the federal bureaucracy, both in Washington and in the regions, is mainly concerned with smoothness of operational processes for delivering benefits to recipients. The central federal bureaucracy proceeds in a close relationship with national interest groups representing the beneficiaries. State and local bureaucracies also operate in close harmony with local interest groups representing beneficiaries and some individual beneficiaries. The general level of conflict between bureaucrats, beneficiaries, and even restricted clients is low.

In competitive regulatory policy the federal bureaucracy is again mainly concerned with smooth processes. The central federal bureaucracy maintains formal distance from competing interests but may well work very closely with them informally. The general level of conflict in this policy arena is low with only short bursts of higher conflict surrounding critical decisions.

In protective regulatory policy the federal bureaucracy is primarily concerned with smooth processes once again. The national office can either be in an adversary or friendly relationship with beneficiaries or with restricted clients, depending in part on the ideology of the national office and patterns of congressional and national interest group support and pressure. The general level of conflict is moderate, with sustained bursts of higher conflict particularly when new regulations are first enforced.

In redistributive policy the federal bureaucracy maintains its high level of interest in smooth processes. It may also promote some reasonably good evaluative efforts to assess both process performance and program impact on beneficiaries. The central federal government offices maintain a distant, impersonal relationship with beneficiaries and restricted clients (with the possible exception of some important national interest groups). State and local bureaucracies have close relations with both beneficiaries and restricted clients. Sometimes these are amicable, sometimes they are hostile, depending on the values promoted by the state and local bureaucracies. The general level of conflict in implementing redistributive programs is moderate to high.

Relative difficulty of successful implementation and associated factors. "Successful" implementation can mean many different things to many different people. When policy actors, especially bureaucrats, speak of *success* they may really have some form of *efficiency* in mind. We shall use their word *success* but mean nothing more than they do by the word. We will return to the concept of success in the final chapter of this volume and, at that point, will give it some meaning of our own.

One measure of success involves assessing how well goals—both procedural and substantive—were met by a program. That is surely a valid definition of success. A major problem arises in many concrete cases, however, because there are no stated goals or at least none of sufficient clarity to provide standards against which performance can be measured. Another measure of successful implementation is simply to accept as successful activity that seems to be in some generally productive direction even if that direction has not been specified ahead of time. This is sloppier but it is, in fact, often used either explicitly or implicitly. Another loose standard, also frequently used, is the time required to produce some forward movement. The assumption is made that the shorter the time elapsed before such movement, the higher the degree of success. As indicated above, the smoothness with which operating processes function and the absence of complaints or conflict about those procedures are regarded as indications of successful implementation by many bureaucrats, especially at the federal level.

We want to return to a consideration of the definition of *success* in implementation in our last chapter. In the last two columns of Table 3–4 we use the adjective *successful* only in the rough sense that most bureaucrats tend to use it: general productivity by their own standards, no great time lags in apparent forward movement, and relative lack of controversy. We do not imply that these are satisfactory or complete criteria. The last two columns in Table 3–4, in effect, summarize our propositions about how to achieve success by the standards of most bureaucrats and the processes critical to achieve success by those standards.

Throughout this book until the last chapter we shall use *success* and *successful* in the loose sense used by bureaucrats and summarized above. Our main aim, however, is not to make pronouncements about success (or efficiency, for that matter) in the examples we develop in Chapters 4 through 7. The principal aim is to offer evidence that is relevant to the exploration of the propositions offered in this chapter.

No implementation is easy. But, for a variety of reasons, redistribution is the most difficult and distribution is the least difficult. The two regulatory policy arenas fall somewhere between relative difficulty and relative ease. The reasons for this judgment include:

1. More varied and diffuse bureaucracies involved in the more difficult areas (see Berman, 1978).
2. Less powerful beneficiaries in the more difficult areas.
3. Relatively powerful restricted clients in the two regulatory areas.
4. Greater difficulty in establishing the critical processes in the areas in which successful implementation is least likely.
5. Greater controversy over the program purposes in the more difficult areas.

No single factor or set of factors, absent or present, can guarantee successful implementation, no matter how success is defined. Scholars and bureaucrats studying implementation have not yet developed and probably never will be able to develop a formula to guarantee successful implementation. But that will not and should not deter students of implementation from continued attention to the topic of what makes implementation work or fail.

In the empirical chapters yet to come, we will be attuned to factors both present and absent that affect implementation either positively or negatively, and we will look for any systematic differences in the influence of those factors across types of policy. One such feature that we can speculate about at this point is the nature of critical operating processes that characterize implementation relationships and that are essential to the success of implementation as perceived by most bureaucrats (what follows was stimulated by Elmore, 1978). The last column of Table 3–4 summarizes our propositions.

Critical to implementation in the distributive area is the establishment of relevant and sufficient operating routines and management of those procedures to insure that the delivery of the benefits, services, and subsidies to recipients occurs without problems, delays, or errors. If the goods are not delivered efficiently, implementation in the distributive area cannot succeed.

In competitive regulatory policy the establishment of operating routines is again critical for making fair decisions about which competitor receives the limited good and for regulating and reviewing the activity of beneficiaries.

In protective regulatory programs the personal involvement of the bureaucrats in the central and regional field offices of the federal government is critical to insure that regulations issued to restricted clients are enforced so that consumers can benefit.

In redistributive policies and programs a critical process that is necessary, but not sufficient, for implementation is the establishment of a bargaining relationship between bureaucrats and beneficiaries in which the beneficiaries are treated as equals and their claims are heard regularly, taken seriously, and inspected on the basis of their merit, even if they are not granted.

OTHER INFLUENCES ON IMPLEMENTATION

To claim that policy type determines everything that varies in implementation patterns would be naive. We wish it were so, but Chapter 1 indicated there are lots of other important influences. In the empirical material that follows in Chapters 4 through 7 we will describe other factors that help explain systematically why some implementation processes look different from others. At least three seem worth looking for as we assess some cases of implementation.

First, the clarity of the goals for a program and the degree of consensus among the implementers on those goals are important. The greater the consensus and the greater the clarity the more likely that the implementers will work effectively (see Van Meter and Van Horn, 1975:461–62). Greater lack of clarity and greater lack of consensus are both likely to result in major implementation problems.

Second, the degree of change from past practices required by a program seems important (Van Meter and Van Horn, 1975:461–62). The greater the degree of change, the harder it is to implement the program. The more minor or marginal the change, the easier it is to implement.

Third, as implied by our discussion of types of beneficiaries and restricted clients, those people and groups that are the targets of implementation are also important. If some important segments of them have a high degree of consensus in opposing implementation, it is unlikely that implementation will take place. If some important segments are united in favoring rapid implementation along the lines favored by the bureaucrats, then the path of implementation is made easier (see Ball, 1976).

SUMMARY

All layers of governmental bureaucracy—the federal central offices, the federal field offices, states, and localities—are involved in domestic program implementation as a result of federalism. The prevalence of intergovernmental relations is an essential part of implementation. Often the central structure in Washington is remote, operationally as well as physically, from the implementation of national programs.

Federal grants constitute the primary apparatus for involving other layers of government in the administration of national programs. Through the introduction of special purpose block grants and general revenue sharing, an era of cooperative federalism has emerged; most grants to states and localities, however, are still of a narrow, categorical nature.

Overall control and management of the federal system is constrained by its size, complexity, and proliferation of individual programs. No one is in charge. The ability of the federal government to control the behavior of states and localities receiving federal grants is inherently limited. Those layers of bureaucratic actors not based in Washington have and use latitude in implementing programs.

The types of domestic policies and programs that are implemented are divided into four categories based on their intended purposes and impacts. Characteristic political relationships surround their formulation and legitimation. Distributive policies and programs are those that are intended to produce certain types of behavior voluntarily on the part of affected groups by offering incentives (subsidies). Competitive regulatory policies and programs award a limited resource to one of several competing recipients and regulate the activity of the beneficiary. Protective regulatory policies and programs are ones that limit and regulate the activity of all producers in specific areas for the benefit of the public good. Redistributive policies and programs alter the allocation of goods in society in favor of less-advantaged and less-privileged groups of people.

We expect that certain aspects of implementation will be the same within programs clustered by type of policy. Thus, implementation will vary systematically across policy types. Areas in which we expect such differing patterns include the identity of primary participants in implementation (levels of bureaucracy, beneficiaries, restricted clients, and Congress—with bureaucracy being the most influential actor in implementation regardless of policy type), the nature of the relationships among primary actors, the relative difficulty of achieving successful implementation, and the critical processes for achieving what bureaucrats often refer to as success. The patterns we expect are summarized in Tables 3–3 and 3–4 and will be explored in the cases presented in Chapters 4 through 7.

CHAPTER 4

The Implementation of Distributive Programs

In this chapter and its three successors we want to augment what has been so far a general discussion of bureaucracy and implementation by dissecting some actual examples of implementation. *Example* is a more accurate word than *case* because case studies imply a finite, bounded, and tidy set of events with a beginning and an end, whereas implementation is a long-term, messy process around which it is hard to draw definitive boundaries in terms of either time or events. Case studies are much easier to do when describing formulation and legitimation of a policy because the passage of major legislation is traditionally accepted as the end of a story that makes sense in itself. There are no such automatic flags to signal the end of implementation. Thus we do not tell complete stories of policy implementation, nor are we interested in doing so. Rather we want to lay out enough facts so that we can analyze what they tell us about implementation not just for that instance but for that general type of policy. We will also be sensitive to other general points that seem to be illustrated by the examples, even if they have nothing to do with the fourfold classification of policies and programs.

DISTRIBUTIVE PROGRAMS: INTRODUCTORY CONSIDERATIONS

There is a myth that the patterns of actors, politics, and decisions tied to distributive policies and programs are quite easy to understand and predict because all activity and decisions are dominated by unchanging subgovernments—triangular alliances of persons from Congress, a relevant bureaucracy, and affected interest groups—and that these subgovernments always get everything they want. At the stage of formulation and legitimation there is some truth to the myth. On some issues what appears to be an unchanging subgovernment does in fact dominate decision making and get the lion's share of its preferences virtually unchallenged. However, in an earlier volume we took a harder look at the dominance of subgovernments in distributive policy formulation and legitimation (Ripley and Franklin, 1984: chapter 4) and concluded that the myth of subgovernments' unchallenged prowess was flawed. The pattern was considerably more complicated. There were differing conditions under which subgovernments played different roles. The notion of subgovernments (or "iron triangles") is a useful one in empirically based discussions of distributive policy formulation and legitimation, but it should not be used as a shorthand to imply uniformity and it should not be regarded as an immutable condition. Subgovernments exist and succeed more often than not in the formulation and legitimation of distributive policy, but the idea should not be reduced to a simple-minded formula that implies no change and automatic outcomes and success.

If the notion of subgovernment dominance is complicated at the stages of formulation and legitimation but still remains a useful concept, at the stage of implementation it becomes even more complicated and perhaps not terribly useful. *If* subgovernments are prevalent in the implementation of distributive policy, they have to be mainly local in character, since implementation occurs primarily at the local level. The subgovernments active in decision making at the national level during policy formulation and legitimation will not be faithfully replicated at the local level. Nor will they automatically dominate local decisions during implementation. Local subgovernments may indeed have some ties to the national level policy formulation subgovernment. Local members of the dominant national bureaucracy in federal field offices or local member affiliates of the dominant national interest groups might well be involved in local implementation decisions. Key members of Congress or their staff might also get involved sporadically in specific local decisions. Inevitably, however, new actors—purely local in character—will in many instances get involved in implementation of distributive programs. Mayors, city council members, county commissioners, local social service agencies, local interest groups, and private citizens can all appear as important decision makers. The membership of subgovernments in the implementation phase—assuming subgovernments exist and dominate at least some of the time—is less predictable and less stable, especially when all of the localities are considered in the aggregate, than when compared to the composition of subgovernments in the policymaking stage.

One key factor pushes toward the emergence of dominant local subgovernments: the implementation of distributive programs is often tied tightly to questions of policy reformulation and relegitimation—that is, to policymaking. This is true to some extent of the implementation of all policies and programs, regardless of type, but seems to be most true in the distributive arena. Policymakers constantly make adjustments to policies in implementation as they unfold, primarily to keep the tangible benefits that are being distributed to clients flowing smoothly. Since individuals in the dominant national subgovernments (in the numerous cases in which such subgovernments form around specific distributive policies) feel, correctly, that they have a great deal to gain politically by managing distributive policies, they take a constant interest in implementation. They typically perceive their efforts at coalition-building during policymaking to be tied to the tangible benefits they can produce. Members of Congress yearn for votes from constituents, support—both votes and campaign funds—from interest groups, and continuing favorable decisions from federal bureaucracies charged with making implementation decisions. Bureaucrats think of their budgets and the scope of program authority as defined by key members of Congress, by the support of their constituents, and particularly by interest groups claiming to speak for the beneficiaries. The interest groups are most concerned with guaranteeing an uninterrupted flow of existing benefits to themselves and their constituents, increasing the resulting support of the constituents, therefore, keeping the existing interest group representatives in their jobs at ever more handsome salaries, and obtaining an even fatter package including new benefits.

In some areas the implementation process itself is set up to require continued intervention and involvement of the policy formulation subgovernment. The classic example is the process, mandated in law, for approving individual Army Corps of Engineers projects. In this process each implementation decision is also a policy decision in that it involves Congress in what formally is a policy role but informally is an implementation role. In other substantive areas such decisions would be left to a bureaucracy or bureaucracies (see Drew, 1970; Maass, 1950).

Each individual project originates at the local level, when representatives of concerns that can see profit in a corps' project (industrialists, real estate developers, barge companies) get together with the corps' district engineer and draw up a proposal for a dam, canal, reservoir, or other project. They then proceed to enlist the aid of their senators and representative(s) to sponsor legislation to authorize a study by the corps of the feasibility of the proposed project. Many proposals never advance beyond this stage. Those that do are referred to the House and Senate Public Works committees. These committees make decisions about which projects should receive feasibility studies by the corps and also about which of the projects that have received the corps' approval will be authorized for funding and construction. The Appropriations committees provide the funds for the feasibility studies and for the construction of authorized projects. Once a proposal has received authorization for a feasibility study, the corps' engineers in the district conduct the study, which may entail many years and volumes of technical reports. The engineers report their recommendations for or against a proposal based on determinations of whether the economic benefits to be derived from the project would be equal to or greater than the costs of the project. At congressional insistence, the criteria used to evaluate the economic benefits are extremely flexible. Every two years, in an authorization bill, the Public Works committees identify the projects authorized for feasibility studies and those authorized for construction.

Even in cases in which the decision process does not formally involve the policy formulation subgovernment in implementation decisions, the same kind of interaction may well arise on a fairly frequent basis. Fiorina (1977:48–49) argues that members of Congress create federal programs and expand bureaucracies responsible for them in part for their own political gain. His argument seems especially appropriate for distributive policy:

> In sum, everyday decisions by a large and growing federal bureaucracy bestow significant tangible benefits and impose significant tangible costs. Congressmen can affect these decisions. Ergo, the more decisions the bureaucracy has the opportunity to make, the more opportunities there are for the congressmen to build up credits.
> ...Congressmen...earn electoral credits by establishing various federal programs.... The legislation is drafted in very general terms, so some agency, existing or newly established, must translate a vague policy mandate into a functioning program, a process that necessitates the promulgation of numerous rules and regulations and, incidentally, the trampling of numerous toes. At the next stage, aggrieved and/or hopeful constituents petition their congressman to intervene in the complex (or at least obscure) decision processes of the bureaucracy. The cycle closes when the congressman lends a sympathetic ear, piously denounces the evils of bureaucracy, intervenes in the latter's decisions, and rides a grateful electorate to ever more impressive electoral showings....
> The bureaucracy serves as a convenient lightning rod for public frustration and a convenient whipping boy for congressmen. But so long as the bureaucracy accommodates congressmen, the latter will oblige with ever larger budgets and grants of authority.

Another key factor, however, works against the emergence of local implementation subgovernments modeled on Washington-based formulation subgovernments. Policies viewed from the national level and in the aggregate as being distributive may be perceived to be quite competitive and even redistributive at the local level when they are implemented. An agricultural subsidy enacted at the national level, for example, which bestows benefits on all farmers who qualify and whose size is limited only in a faint and indirect sense by theoretical competition with other programs, is viewed from the national level as an embodiment of classic distributive policy. But when that same agricultural program gets down to the point of implementation, with fixed benefits to distribute and with local actors such as county agents and farmer committees involved, it may appear to be much more a contest of tenant farmers versus landowning farmers or sheep ranchers versus cattle ranchers or large landowners versus small landowners. Perceived—and therefore quite genuine and fiercely fought—competition quickly destroys a quiet, efficient subgovernment that keeps everybody happy. We will discuss specific instances of these mixed distributive/redistributive policies in both this chapter and in Chapter 7.

Some would argue that the new congressional budget process adopted in the mid-1970s changed perceptions of distribution at the national level. In principle, this process requires budget restraint through the necessity of adjusting actual spending to a pre-agreed total figure. However, a process that promises a balanced budget in May and then prophesies a $50 billion deficit in July, as it did in 1980, or that seems to have no effect on annual deficits ballooning to a quarter of a trillion dollars in the late-1980s, is hard to take seriously as a limit on distributive program costs (or any other costs, for that matter).

In the remainder of this chapter we want to look at examples of routine (that is, relatively quiet and conflict-free) implementation of distributive programs and also at complications that can and do arise to make implementation of such programs nonroutine. As we gathered raw material on examples for this section, it was far easier to find instances of complications than of "routine" situations. This is a hint that implementation, even in the seemingly least complicated areas of distributive policy, abounds with complications. This underscores a general point: *implementation is never easy in an absolute sense* even though, in a relative sense, some programs are easier to implement than others.

ROUTINE IMPLEMENTATION
Conditions Allowing Routine Implementation
There are two principal conditions that allow (but do not guarantee) routine implementation—that is, implementation in which decisions can be made in a timely fashion, carried out without major snarls and delays, and provoke either no conflict or only a minimum of conflict among different individuals and organizations involved in the implementation. The first condition is that there must be established (routine) processes for making implementation decisions and carrying them into effect that continue to be used. The second condition is that there must be general

agreement on a stable distribution of influence over implementation decisions that predictably and consistently (routinely) gives the most influence to the same small and readily identifiable set of actors over time without serious challenge or conflict.

Few programs meet both of these conditions in a straightforward and stringent fashion. But several examples show how the conditions work to allow a sizable measure of easy or routine implementation.

General Revenue Sharing

The State and Local Assistance Act of 1972 was enacted for the purpose of distributing some federal revenues to states and localities with a minimum of federal strings. Popularly known as general revenue sharing, it allocated money by formula to all local units of government in the nation for them to use on their own local first priorities (see Van Horn, 1979a and 1979b for good summaries of experience with the program in the 1970s). In its first five years it provided about $30 billion for some 38,000 subnational political jurisdictions.

Implementation of general revenue sharing at the federal level during the 1970s was generally routine. The formula contained in the statute was applied to generate the amounts of money to send to the state of New York, Oscaloosa, Iowa, Snohomish County, Washington, and their 38,000 cousins. The Office of Revenue Sharing in the Treasury Department wrote and mailed checks on a periodic basis.

The law was written in such a way that normal budget procedures in place at any given subnational level simply continued to apply to the disposition of this new money. The processes and political treaties that had been arrived at in a city and were contained both in the city charter and in informal agreements about the roles, responsibilities, and relative influence of the mayor, city manager, budget office, city council, and local interest groups all remained mostly unchanged by the federal statute. In the 1972 act there was no specific requirement for citizen participation in planning, only a requirement that planned and actual uses of the money be published. Some priority expenditure categories were listed but they were really only statements of federal preference and were not binding. The federal government had no prior review powers over the plan for expenditure at any subnational level. The basic federal role was one of collecting information on usage, auditing it, and evaluating performance. Evaluation involved analysis with no sanctions or rewards attached except to the extent it might have any impact on subsequent congressional action.

The 1976 amendments removed priority expenditure categories but required public hearings, named groups that should participate in decision making, and required planned uses to be publicized both before and after hearings. A requirement was added that there had to be reports on the participation process and on implementation of nondiscrimination provisions to the federal government. Auditing was also increased. But the number of strings were still quite minimal when compared with categorical grants. The sovereignty of the local processes remained basically unimpaired.

In short, by design Congress created a dispersion of money that allowed specific implementation decisions to be made in accord with 38,000 different sets of existing budgetary processes and local political environments, and there was no additional conflict created over who had the right to make decisions. The supremacy of the local officials was reinforced. Naturally, in some localities and states budgetmaking was already somewhat politicized and involved more than just the ranks of officials. But the statute added no meaningful new potential for conflict or challenges to the decision-making authority.

This is a case, then, in which the program met both of the conditions allowing relatively trouble-free and routine implementation. Established subnational routines were simply left alone without interference to work as they ordinarily would with this new infusion of money.

Aid to Maritime Industries

A classic area of distribution involves programs for merchant shipping and the maritime industries of the United States (see Lawrence, 1966, and Jantscher, 1975). There are numerous specific programs of maritime subsidy. The principal ones are:

An operating subsidy that exists, in theory, to offset the higher operating costs of American merchant shipping lines compared to foreign lines.

A construction subsidy that goes to shipyards so that they can reduce their prices and make their products more competitive with foreign-built ships.

Tax subsidies that, in effect, function as interest-free loans to ship-owners to buy ships and equipment from U.S. manufacturers.

"Cabotage" laws that require that ocean commerce between U.S. ports be carried in ships built and registered in the United States. Money is not disbursed from the Treasury Department for this subsidy, but these provisions add to the cost of shipping, paid, in effect, by the consumers of the goods carried in the ships affected (Jantscher, 1975).

Requirements that certain percentages (from 50 to 100) of certain kinds of cargo going overseas be carried in ships registered in the United States.

This handsome package of subsidies is relatively impervious to change, and most of it has been in existence for a number of decades (the operating subsidy since 1936, for example). Their implementation is relatively free of controversy and automatic. The same interests—shipowners, shipbuilders, maritime unions, relevant bureaucrats, and relevant members of the House and Senate—that dominate the creation and continuation of the subsidy laws also work together easily and naturally to make sure the benefits are distributed. The distribution of a tax subsidy, of course, requires only the proper numerical manipulation on tax forms. The implementation is set in the context of no coherent overall maritime policy. Rather, each particular subsidy has its own supportive group at the policy level. Thus each separate package of goodies is implemented separately and seemingly without difficulty. The interests being subsidized are in a strong position to guarantee the continuation both of favorable policy decisions and of what we have called routine implementation that they find satisfying.

The only hints of controversy from within the subsidized interests (virtually everyone in the maritime trade) is when companies feel that some other subset of one or more companies is getting a bit more than it should. Thus, a decade or more of huge loans to Seatrain Lines, Inc. (almost $400 million in loans and loan guarantees from 1969 through 1980, according to *The Wall Street Journal* of February 10, 1981) brought some protests from competing firms—but, significantly, no slackening in the brisk pace of subsidy for Seatrain. In an odd situation in the early 1980s the owners of modern oil tankers—who had been handsomely subsidized to build the ships—resented the fact that a statute from 1920 prevented them from getting into the highly profitable business of carrying oil from new Alaska fields but instead reserved that trade for older tankers, whose 20-year subsidy contracts had expired (Wines, 1983a). Occasionally, subsidies collide in this most pampered of U.S. industries.

Programs for Veterans

The Veterans Administration (VA) is the third largest agency of the federal government in terms of budget—smaller only than the Department of Defense and the Department of Health and Human Services. In terms of employees it is smaller only than the Defense Department and the U.S. Postal Service. It relies on federal bureaucrats for implementation of its many programs. In all program areas a classic subgovernment seems to dominate implementation as well as formulation of the programs themselves. One observer has dubbed the close relationships dominating both policymaking and policy implementation as the "khaki triangle"—the VA itself, the veterans affairs committees in Congress, and the groups representing veterans, such as the American Legion, the Veterans of Foreign Wars, the Disabled American Veterans, and the AMVETS (Keisling, 1982).

Implementation is handled in a way to preserve a huge system that can only grow. For example, administrators of VA hospitals have incentives to keep their hospitals full—even if that means giving more care than a medical situation really warrants, longer hospitalization than necessary, and elaborate care to veterans technically eligible but not required to receive care (those who are not needy and whose problems are not service-connected).

The VA actually encourages hospital administrators to admit unneedy patients. Since the VA budgets for each hospital on the basis of the previous year's occupancy rate, a typical administrator quickly realizes the advantages of keeping his hospital full. A conscientious bureaucrat who attempted to save the federal government's money would suffer a sizable budget cut. He'd be forced to close beds, lay off employees, and suffer the inevitable wrath of the surrounding community—not to mention the district's congressman (Keisling, 1982:26).

The same incentive structure is reproduced in other major areas of VA benefits.

COMPLICATIONS

We previously identified two critical conditions—allowing but not guaranteeing relatively easy, fast, routine implementation— the continued use of existing processes for making and carrying out implementation decisions and a stable pattern of influence in which a relatively small set of actors is consistently the most important and is deferred to by others. However, routine implementation can become nonroutine if disruptions are introduced. In the following examples we address six kinds of complications that can upset or prevent routine implementation:

The addition of new responsibilities to the agenda of established actors with established processes.

The intrusion of national elected officials'(president or members of Congress) priorities.

The addition of new decision makers.

The intrusion of competing laws responding to (and helping create) changing conditions.

The necessity of making decisions withdrawing or reducing benefits.

The intermingling of distributive and redistributive concerns.

The Addition of New Responsibilities

Implementation of existing programs through specified institutional channels that are proceeding smoothly and routinely can be either upset or found to be inapplicable if new responsibilities are added to the implementing agencies. Two examples illustrate the point: the addition of the medicaid program to the agenda of a large number of state and federal agencies already handling a number of health-related programs with established routines; and the addition of the supplemental security income program to the workload of the federal Social Security Administration. It should be noted that these examples also illustrate how programs that are purely redistributive in intent at the policy level (and are perceived as such during formulation and legitimation) become, in effect, perceived as both distributive and redistributive during implementation. It is also fair to say that these two cases illustrate problems inherent in giving programs designed to be redistributive to agencies that are used to functioning in the distributive arena. Their operating routines are designed for and have been used on distributive programs. They turn out to be ill-adapted to programs that are redistributive in intent.

Medicaid. The medicaid program is a federal-state matching grant program enacted in 1965 to provide reimbursements to medical personnel who extend health care services to eligible patients (see Mead, 1977 for more information on the medicaid program). The program grew steadily from $3.5 billion in its first full year of implementation, 1968, when it served 11.5 million people to over $14 billion in fiscal year 1976, when over 23 million people were served.

The implementation of the program involves the federal and state governments and private individuals and organizations. The federal government provides matching grant funds to state governments, which then reimburse medical personnel who provide health services to the eligible recipients. The federal contribution varies from state to state, depending on per capita income, but it averages about 55 percent of the total costs. The program is aimed at the neediest recipients. Welfare recipients must be included as eligible recipients, but the states are given some discretion in choosing other recipients. The states are primarily responsible for administering the program, even though most of the money is federal. Many states contract the reimbursement part of administration to a fiscal agent, often an insurance company.

The goal of the program is to provide adequate medical care for the target population at reasonable cost. In fact, implementation problems have reduced the quality of medical care and greatly increased costs.

Some of the problems result from aspects of program design. Others result from changing economic conditions. In the short run, the persons who implement the program do not have control over these factors. However, there are also problems that are much more attributable to failures on the part of the implementers.

Those in charge of the program at all governmental levels did not have adequate or appropriate information on which to base decisions. There were also problems in communicating information between levels. The quality of the information generated at the lowest working levels was poor. The problems of relying on this inadequate information were compounded as the information was aggregated for higher levels of administration.

Another critical problem arose from overreliance on established administrative routines that were not appropriate for the complex monitoring required by medicaid. But officials at both the federal and state levels refused to change procedures. Instead they insisted on retaining inappropriate procedures that gave them no management control over their program.

The rigidities introduced at both the federal and state levels by the existence of civil service systems, augmented by civil service unions, impaired the ability of the managers to manage the system and often left them with underqualified people in key positions. The managers were powerless to move these weak links.

In some instances, interest groups representing the service providers, particularly the medical profession, worked successfully to reduce regulations and cost controls. This resulted in some increased costs.

Insufficient coordination with other organizations with overlapping and competing jurisdiction and responsibilities also created problems. At the federal level, medicaid should have been coordinated with medicare and maternal and child health, but actual coordination was weak. State agencies that logically should have been coordinated with one another in implementing medicaid often pursued independent courses, in part because of the differing policies of the different federal agencies providing them with funds.

The medicaid program provided some valuable benefits for some needy people. But the program was much less efficient at providing those benefits quickly and with adequate controls over costs than the designers had envisioned. Government neither succeeded nor failed with medicaid. It performed at a mediocre level, largely because of problems in implementation. And many of the problems arose both because routines established for other programs did not work well for medicaid, and the institutions involved seemed unable or unwilling to invent appropriate new routines.

Supplemental security income. The Social Security Board of the federal government was created in 1935 following the passage of the Social Security Act and replaced by the present agency, the Social Security Administration (SSA) in 1946. It quickly established routines that allowed it to do its major job of implementation well and efficiently: the delivery of benefit checks to the correct people on time (see Johnson, 1977a, 1977b, 1977c for more information on the Social Security Administration).

Over time the SSA has grown enormously in three ways: new programs have been added to its responsibilities, the number of beneficiaries its programs serve has increased, and the dollar amount of benefits it distributes has multiplied. The original program and still by far the largest of those administered by the SSA is called the Old-Age, Survivors, and Disability Insurance (OASDI) Program, created by the original act in 1935. This provides retirement pensions to covered workers, disability benefits for them, and retirement benefits for survivors.

The great success of the SSA in delivering checks for the correct amount to the correct people on time for many years under the OASDI program led Congress and administrators in the Department of Health, Education, and Welfare to propose adding new responsibilities. The routines were in place, the SSA was widely acknowledged to be supreme in its field and expert at it, and problems of implementation looked as if they would always be small and manageable. And so new programs were added—medicare in 1965, black lung disease benefits in 1969 (black lung is a disease of coal miners), supplemental security income in 1974, and Aid to Families and Dependent Children in 1977. These programs collectively distributed hundreds of millions of checks for billions of dollars in benefits to millions of recipients. The numbers are staggering. To administer these mammoth programs, and to undertake a variety of other duties not described here, not the least of which is maintaining records on the close to 400 million or so Americans who have received social security cards since 1936, the Social Security Administration has 10 regional offices, six program service centers, and over 1,300 local offices.

The great crisis in implementation came with the addition of the supplemental security income (SSI) program in 1974 and lasted for years. The SSI was a new kind of benefit program, with a huge number (four million) of a new kind of client that social security personnel had never dealt with before. And there were new implementers in state and local governments who had the latitude to augment basic eligibility requirements set by Congress. The old established routines for delivery were not applicable to the new program, and creating new procedures was far more time-consuming and difficult than anticipated. The SSI program was intended to provide welfare recipients with an extra income, but state and local governments' records on their welfare recipients were not complete or accurate, so the SSA had to obtain new documentation on an individual basis. When it came under fire for being slow to deliver checks to needy people, the agency shifted priorities and wrote checks without thoroughly checking eligibility, only to come under criticism for issuing benefits to people who weren't qualified. After three years of trying to meet the demands of the new program, implementation was still problem-ridden (Johnson, 1977a):

> Almost everything went wrong. Many of the state and local welfare rolls turned out to be hopelessly in error; case after case had to be reconstructed from scratch. Dealing with the new claimants themselves often came as a shock. In all of its experience, Social Security had dealt only with those who had paid their money into the system through payroll taxes. Those, in other words, who had earned their benefits. Now, picking up the welfare load, they were dealing with the core of the urban poor....
>
> Social Security strained and began paying its welfare checks, but the first time it failed. "All of a sudden we wake up and find all hell's broken loose," the agency executive recalls. "The press, the Congress, the advocacy groups of the poor are raising hell because we didn't get those checks delivered on time to those people."
>
> "And here's an agency that if it never did anything else right it had a 40-year record of delivering checks and delivering them on time—by the hundreds of millions."
>
> ...Social Security people began working around the clock, 30,000 of them, to try to bring order out of the program. A decision was made to get those checks out—fast.
>
> ...After intensive efforts for more than a year, and great strains and pressures on personnel, Social Security thought it was winning its battle. Then came the greatest shock of all. It became painfully clear that a great deal more money was being given to people than

they were entitled to. And a great deal of money was going to people who weren't eligible in the first place. There were massive over- and underpayments.

The Intrusion of National Elected Officials' Priorities

The distributive arena is particularly porous to intrusions from members of the House and Senate and even presidents when they see political advantages to be gained for themselves. These intrusions can and do create sizable complications in what otherwise might develop into routine implementation. Several examples suggest the disruptive or complicating impact of such intrusions. Note, however, that such intrusions are not unusual in the distributive arena; therefore, these are common complications.

Water projects. At the beginning of the chapter we indicated that Congress has created a large role for itself in approving the implementation of Army Corps of Engineers projects. Such congressional involvement in water projects extends across the board, regardless of whether the principal federal implementation agency is the Corps of Engineers, the Bureau of Reclamation in the Department of the Interior, the Soil Conservation Service in the Department of Agriculture, the Tennessee Valley Authority, or some other agency that also gets involved from time to time. Congress has typically been aggressive in adding money and instructions for making new starts on water projects. Presidents have been much more conservative (for three years, from 1976 through 1978, Presidents Ford and Carter proposed no new starts, although Congress mandated 54 anyway). The preceding table summarizes the record of starts recommended and mandated for water projects from 1971 through 1980 (Mosher, L., 1980:1189).

A classic case of the creation and sustenance of a massive project because of the political weight of a single senior senator—with support from other members of Congress from his region—is that of a barge canal known as the Tennessee-Tombigbee Waterway. This is a 300-mile river-widening project linking the Tennessee River in far northeastern Mississippi with the Gulf of Mexico at Mobile, Alabama, via the Tombigbee River in southwestern Alabama. Senator John Stennis, chairman of the Senate Appropriations Committee, maneuvered constantly and effectively to

	Proposed by President	Added by Congress	Total
1971	25	47	72
1972	16	22	38
1973	15	23	38
1974	4	16	20
1975	7	27	34
1976	0	21	21
1977	0	33	33
1978	0	0	0
1979	26	42	68
1980	16	0	16

keep Congress behind the project. Congress has continuously appropriated more money so that implementation could proceed. This corps project, which opened in 1985, went forward, in part, on the basis of analyses of projected benefits that a number of critics—but not enough to win in Congress—found dubious and misleading.

In general, the Reagan administration had a consistent preference for less domestic spending. However, it is instructive that the Reagan administration did not attack the Tenn-Tom project. And, at a broader level, in early 1984 the Reagan administration rejected a cost-saving fixed formula for splitting the cost of water projects between local beneficiaries and the federal government. Rather, the president opted to keep his Western supporters happy.

Military employment, water and sewer grants, and Model Cities grants. Bureaucrats are not helpless victims of intrusions from Congress in implementation routines. They can and do act to limit such intervention. One study (Arnold, 1979) of federal bureaucrats administering three distributive programs (military employment, water and sewer grants, and Model Cities grants) concluded that in programs in which agencies are given discretion over the geographic location of facilities or resources, bureaucrats will make those allocative decisions in such a way as to build coalitions in Congress to support policy decisions that they favor. Depending on the exact nature of the program and the statutory limits within which they are operating, they may seek to expand a coalition by increasing geographical coverage and/or increasing the size of benefits. They are also likely to target particular individuals in Congress to give their states and districts favorable treatment. These individuals hold key committee and subcommittee positions vital to the good health of the agency in general. Such coalitions can be valuable resources for warding off unwelcome attempts to intrude in implementation decisions.

Military employment (see Arnold, 1979:chapter 6) is, of course, not a single program but reflects a whole series of decisions about location of facilities, transfers of facilities, and closing of facilities. After careful analysis Arnold calculated that bureaucrats in the Pentagon (Department of Defense) adjusted their locational and closing decisions roughly 10 percent of the time to take account of the need to maintain their supportive coalition in Congress.

The Water and Sewer Facilities Grants program administered by the Department of Housing and Urban Development was a separate program from its creation in 1965 to its inclusion in the Community Development Block Grant program in 1974 (see Arnold, 1979:chapter 7). It was very popular with members of Congress and the local officials whose sewage and water facilities could be upgraded by winning grant awards at no visible, direct cost to local taxpayers. Demand for the grants in the form of applications far outran the supply of money, and so the bureaucrats had to make some choices about which applications got funded and which ones did not. Only about 20 percent of the applications were successful. Arnold estimates that roughly one fifth to one quarter of all specific decisions were made by bureaucrats on the basis of primarily political, coalition-building criteria rather than on strictly technical criteria such as need, feasibility, and cost.

The Model Cities program (see Arnold, 1979:chapter 8; and Ripley, 1972:chapter 5) stemmed from a presidential task force on urban problems in 1965 whose recommendations were put into statutory form in 1966. This program was also folded in to the Housing and Community Development Act of 1974. In the course of legislating the program the criteria for eligibility were relaxed to make more cities eligible for funds. Congressional pressure and bureaucratic initiative and response resulted in a higher number of awards (150) than was first envisioned as appropriate for a targeted demonstration program. The program began with some redistributive goals but quickly became primarily distributive in implementation. The awards for 150 cities allowed the program to affect more than half of all congressional districts (226 of the 435). Arnold did not make a precise estimate of the number of decisions made centrally on political rather than technical grounds. His overall conclusion was that "political considerations were important, but they were not determinative" in terms of any individual grant. But the expansion of numbers to build a larger coalition in the first place meant that virtually every decision had a general political basis behind it.

The Addition of New Decision Makers

Another condition that upsets the chances for establishing and maintaining routines for smooth implementation of distributive programs is the introduction of new decision makers to the implementation network. Over time these new decision makers can, of course, become part of the routines, but at the time of their initial addition, they undoubtedly cause some dislocation of routines.

The tradition of democratic participation in the implementation of agricultural programs through a variety of committees is an old one, going back to the 1930s. Many of the program committees have become part of the routine. However, the details of participation and choice of committee members are altered from time to time by Congress. Such changes create, in effect, new participants and disrupt well-established decision routines in existing programs (see Talbot and Hadwiger, 1968:291–95). Price-support programs, soil conservation programs, programs of the Farmers Home Administration, federal extension programs, and land banks and cooperatives affiliated with the Rural Electrification Administration all have various committee arrangements—some of which are changed from time to time by statute—that help make implementation decisions.

The Community Development and Block Grant program (CDBG) offers another example of a new decision maker (or at least a decision influencer) getting involved. The program had developed as a major channel of money provided to a large number of local jurisdictions as a matter of right and on the basis of a formula. By early 1985 the number of " entitlement jurisdictions" had expanded from an initial 594 to 735 and accounted for close to $3.5 billion in spending annually (Peirce and Guskind, 1985).

During the period of expansion and routinization of the program the General Accounting Office (GAO) got involved because of a critical report about a number of procedures that, in its view, led to diminished program execution. In the subsequent program year (the fourth) the Department of Housing and Urban Development (HUD) responded. Dommel and Associates (1982:257, 259) summarize how the criticism of an outside agency—GAO—helped cause the principal federal agency—HUD—to put pressure on localities and to increase its own oversight role permanently:

> Partly as a result of the GAO criticism, HUD began to give more attention to program execution and increased pressure on communities to spend their grants more quickly. In 1979 HUD adopted a "use or lose" policy, warning communities that if they were not able to make sufficient progress in implementing their CDBG programs, HUD would begin to reduce their grants. Forty-five communities were given official warnings about the possible loss of funds, but by mid-1980 only Houston, Texas, had actually lost funds under the policy....
>
> [A] general effect of the use or lose policy was that HUD was drawn into closer oversight of execution of all aspects of the program and closer scrutiny of local management, organization, and procedures. From the perspective of local officials the evolution toward increased HUD oversight of program execution suggested a return to the level and detail of federal involvement that had characterized the categorical programs.

The Intrusion of Competing or Altered Laws

Implementation of one program is often complicated by laws governing another program that has some ties to or impact on the first program. Even a major distributive program of mammoth size such as the creation of the interstate highway system, originally planned to be 42,500 miles in length, is not impervious to competing laws that both respond to and help create new attitudes and conditions.

When the law was passed in 1956 virtually everyone was in favor of it, and the interests that sought to benefit most—auto makers, concrete makers, construction companies and unions, oil companies, tire manufacturers—were in the lead in pressing for massive efforts to complete the system quickly without a whole lot of regard to cost, 90 percent of which is paid by the federal government. Localities and their officials eagerly competed to be included on interstate routes and to get priority funding so their segments would be completed quickly.

However, reality in other forms and eventually in other laws began to intrude. The environmental movement in the late 1960s and early 1970s helped create laws that required environmental impact statements before new segments of road could be undertaken. The statements were time-consuming, and construction could not proceed until they were completed. Even then sometimes nothing more happened either because the impact statement revealed unacceptable impacts or because local pressures began to move against completion, especially in urban areas.

A classic case of such a development occurred in suburban Dayton, Ohio, in the 1970s (Bernstein, 1980). A suburban offshoot of a major interstate highway passing just north of Dayton was begun in the 1960s and almost 10 miles of it were completed by 1973—running from the interstate to a cornfield. Then the Federal Highway Administration required an environmental impact statement before releasing the rest of the funds for the rest of the road. The statement was due in 1974 but was not produced until 1979. Meanwhile, local decision makers and interest groups had begun to reassess their earlier unanimous support for this particular highway and began to drop off the bandwagon in a very public way. The Dayton City Commission announced its opposition unless compensation was provided to the city to make up for the expected loss of jobs and population to the suburban area in which the highway would be located. The Black Political Assembly of Dayton also came out against it because of expected further decline of the inner-city black neighborhoods attributable to suburbanization spurred by this particular highway project.

Bureaucrats in the U.S. Department of Transportation charged with implementation responsibilities rejected the impact statement as insufficient and wanted to know more about the impact on the whole urban area. A regional planning commission responded to that federal request with a report that showed that the city would indeed suffer economically from the completion of the remaining 16 miles of the bypass and suggested the kinds of support the benefited suburban areas could offer to the city to get its support. But the suburbs—like suburbs most places—were not very interested in helping their declining central city.

Finally, in late 1979 the Department of Transportation announced that it would approve only enough funds to get the highway spur out of the cornfield and to the next major existing highway crossing (3 miles); federal funding for the remaining 13 miles was dead. The $80 million that had been committed for the project were to remain available for Dayton to use for alternative transportation purposes—if it could raise required matching money.

The trade of an approved interstate project that has become objectionable over time for other transportation projects because of changing laws such as those on environment or changing perceptions of what is desirable for local economic development has been repeated elsewhere (*New York Times*, December 3, 1978). As of late 1978 about $5 billion of such trades had been approved by the federal government. The federal government also facilitated this shift in implementation strategy by increasing federal shares for alternative projects. For example, the previous formula for noninterstate highway projects was 70 percent federal and 30 percent local, and the previous formula for mass transit projects was 80 percent federal and 20 percent local; both of these were changed to 85 percent federal—much closer to the 90 percent federal share for interstates.

In short, new laws and new attitudes and concerns have intruded and changed the conditions for implementation of this popular and expensive (about $100 billion were spent) program. Completion of all of the original interstate highway system will not occur because the Reagan administration announced its intention in its first year in office to drop some of the remaining segments not yet built.

Decisions Withdrawing or Reducing Benefits

Inevitably some implementation decisions involve the reduction or termination of benefits even in popular distributive programs. Such decisions not only provoke congressional and local opposition, but in fact, the federal bureaucrats charged with implementing such decisions may sabotage them as best they can. For example, one director of the Office of Economic Opportunity ordered by President Nixon to participate in its dismantling opposed those moves effectively enough to lose his job for insubordination.

In 1979 the secretary of the army wrote the deputy secretary of defense that if the Pentagon (Department of Defense) wanted to close the training center at Fort Dix, New Jersey, they would have to do so without the cooperation of the Department of the Army. Such an open and flat refusal by one bureaucrat to obey a superior bureaucrat is rare. Opposition and footdragging is usually done more quietly. In this case the opposition worked: Fort Dix was given a reprieve in late 1979 until sometime after the 1980 election. This allowed the secretary of the army, the New Jersey congressional delegation, and the base employees that did not want to lose the 3,300 jobs at the base to win, at least temporarily (Sullivan, 1979a, 1979b).

The Intermingling of Distributive and Redistributive Concerns

We have already indicated that what may appear distributive nationally may appear redistributive locally and vice versa. This fact often complicates implementation decisions, as the previous examples of medicaid and SSI have already demonstrated. This intermingling means that national expectations about implementation and shaping of implementation processes may become warped because national shapers think of the program in profoundly different ways than do people at the local level making concrete implementation decisions. Cases of this phenomenon will be discussed in Chapter 7. Such large programs as the Economic Development Administration's basic grant programs, major parts of the Comprehensive Employment and Training Act, and the Job Training Partnership Act and the Community Development Block Grant program all fall into this category where dissonant expectations and decisions at the federal and local levels are based at least in part on differing perceptions of what's at stake.

SUMMARY AND CONCLUSIONS

We began this chapter with a general expectation that perhaps implementation of programs could be counted on to go relatively smoothly in most cases. However, we conclude the chapter with the altered view that complications are a way of life in all implementation, including distributive programs.

Some of the expectations we articulated in Chapter 3 and summarized in Tables 3–3 and 3–4 are borne out by the examples of implementation in this chapter. However, some of those expectations need to be revised a bit:

1. Congressional participation in implementation decisions in this arena may be more frequent than we first expected. It is still sporadic and triggered in part by the interruption or threat of interruption of benefits. But it is also triggered by the desire for more benefits. Congress can also help create processes that will give it at least a right of refusal to act in implementation situations, or a built-in role for itself in implementation as it has in Corps of Engineers' projects.
2. Federal bureaucrats are primarily concerned with maintaining nonconflictual relationships in the implementation of distributive programs. They try to make decisions that will protect and expand congressional coalitions vital to their agencies' health, survival, and prosperity.
3. Our expectation that operating routines and the nondisturbance of those routines would be particularly important to successful implementation in this area was buttressed by the cases at which we looked—both those where routines were relatively undisturbed (such as aid to the maritime industries) and those where they were more disturbed, such as the supplemental security income and the Social Security Administration.
4. We still stick with our comment in Chapter 3 that distributive programs are relatively the least difficult to implement successfully, but the word relative needs to be underscored. There are lots of potential and actual problems in successfully implementing even distributive programs, but we continue to suspect that these problems are less threatening than those in relation to the other three kinds of policies.

CHAPTER 5

The Implementation of Competitive Regulatory Policy

What we call competitive regulatory policy involves, centrally, *competition* by prospective deliverers for the right to deliver some good or service and *choice* of the winning competitor by a government agency. Conditions are then usually placed on the winning competitors to require them to deliver the good or service in accord with some standard. Implementation involves both the choice process and the development and enforcement of the subsequent conditions. Those conditions are presumably in the public interest and are partially protective too. Thus there is some blurring between the two major types of regulation— competitive and protective—but the element of competition between potential deliverers is, we think, distinctive enough to generate a different pattern of politics than that which exists for protective regulation. We outlined those projected differences in Chapter 3. In the present chapter and the next one we will investigate the two types of regulation separately to see if our projections are correct or if they need major amendment.

Discussion of policy in this arena sometimes focuses on the question of whether entry into a given sphere of activity should be regulated at all. Some contend governmental regulation of entry is useful; others contend that the public is better served by allowing market forces to regulate entry. The debate over the validity of competitive regulation has been heated in recent years and, in fact, the federal government has withdrawn from a central role in many areas of activity.

Note that the competition is most often for the right to deliver a good or service to the public—as with various modes of transportation or broadcasting. The right to proceed requires a government decision. Sometimes, however, the competition by potential deliverers is for the right to deliver directly to the government itself. Such is the case for various kinds of governmental procurement activities, with defense procurement being by far the most important. Here too, the government must choose between competing deliverers and, in the course of doing so, it will specify the conditions the winning deliverer must meet during the course of delivery.

COMPETITIVE REGULATION: INTRODUCTORY CONSIDERATIONS

Recall that general policy pronouncements about competitive regulatory activities are relatively rare. The creation of a federal agency designed to operate in this area (coupled with the specification of the scope of its functions) is the principal occasion for such pronouncements. Major amendments affecting the nature of the agency or the scope of regulatory activities provide a second major occasion for these pronouncements. And, in recent years, a third occasion has come at the end of debate and compromise over the question of drastic reduction or elimination of agencies and functions.

Examples of the first kind of policy statement—with the competitive regulatory aspects and the protective regulatory aspects mixed—include the creation of the Interstate Commerce Commission in 1887 to regulate railroads in a partially competitive mode, the creation of the Federal Communications Commission in 1934 to do the same for radio broadcasting, and the creation of the Civil Aeronautics Board in 1938 to operate in the realm of competitive regulation for commercial airlines.

Examples of the second kind of occasion include the inclusion of television under the purview of the FCC and major amendments to the Interstate Commerce Act effected by the Hepburn Act of 1906 and the Mann-Elkins Act of 1910.

Examples of pronouncements of the third kind include the debates in the late 1970s that led to major deregulation in relation to airlines (the Airline Deregulation Act of 1978), trucking (the Motor Carrier Act of 1980), and railroads (the Staggers Rail Act of 1980).

There are also some specific competitive regulatory areas in which no landmark statute creates an agency and its regulatory enterprise, but policy ground rules are built up through a series of specific statutory decisions and implementation actions. The best example of this type of competitive regulatory policy implementation is in the field of defense procurement.

Because of the relative paucity of statutes, a great deal of policy is promulgated on a case-by-case basis by bureaucrats. The bureaucrats do not, of course, act in a vacuum. Rather, they often define policy through implementation decisions in negotiation with affected producers and consumers. And in many cases, Congress, in the form of individual members of the House and Senate (as contrasted to the collective intervention reflected by statutes), intervenes. congressional intervention is triggered when constituency interests are either threatened or presented, potentially, with what appear to be golden opportunities.

Because bureaucratic dominance in this policy area is so great operating routines are particularly critical to the implementation of competitive regulatory policy.

As indicated in Chapter 3, competitive regulation is a policy hybrid. In many ways it looks like pork-barrel distribution. Over time, persistent supplicants all tend to win some decisions from the distributing agency. Subcontracting by primary beneficiaries (awardees) helps spread out the benefits to other supplicants who may have lost in their bid for a prime award or contract but who pick up some piece of the action by making supplication to the primary awardee or contractor. The intervention by individual members of Congress to facilitate supplications by constituents also looks like the classic distributive case.

But there is at least a short-run scarcity of resources that provides a clear competitive element to this policy area. There is only one television channel at a time in a given geographical area that can be awarded by the FCC to a single competitor. The other competitors either lose altogether and forever or they wait for another channel to open. If they are nationally based they can compete for a license in another geographical area. The air force typically only needs one new fighter plane model at a time and feels there should only be one prime contractor to deliver the whole assembled product, from wings to foxtails on the antenna. Thus Boeing wins and Convair loses, at least for the moment, after a process in which each company has spent many millions of dollars and thousands of hours of employee time in developing and urging its case to the decision makers.

In the long run the competition and the notion of winning and losing may be mostly mythical. Convair loses today but wins six months from now on some equally lucrative project. Happy Talk Associates loses channel 3 in Kalamazoo this year but will pick up channel 9 in Altoona next year. But the competition is real in the short run, and the actors involved—bureaucrats, companies, interfering members of the House and Senate—all behave as if the competition is genuine and winning and losing is everything. In such cases, it should be noted, winning is much more important than how the game is played. The gameplaying clearly involves some illegal activities some of the time. There are folks in prison or with prison records who can attest to that. And it involves other activities that may at least be seriously questionable on ethical grounds even if no one goes to the slammer as a result.

There are also some protective features for what goes on in the competitive regulatory arena. The winner of a competition will sometimes have to agree to pay for the gains of winning by simultaneously agreeing to adhere to standards of service in providing whatever was involved, whether it be TV programming or a new tank. The enforcement of those standards of service becomes part of the implementation of the protective dimension of competitive regulatory awards and, in many cases, seems to be taken somewhat lightly by both awardee and awarding (and, subsequently, enforcing) agency personnel.

The drive for deregulation—both in the competitive sphere and in the protective sphere—is based on some assumptions about motivations, identities, and behavior of sets of actors. In the competitive regulatory sphere—when deregulation is proposed—

the central elements in the vision of what deregulation (or self-regulation or market regulation—the terms are often used loosely and interchangeably in political discourse about the phenomenon) will look like will include the following:

> There will be no government bureaucrats involved any more. Rather the bureaucratic actors (although the term is rarely used to apply to anyone outside of government) will be those in private sector organizations responding primarily to market forces.

> The beneficiaries of such policy will be both producers and consumers—producers because they will be allowed to produce their goods and services rationally (market forces are assumed to represent rationality) and consumers because they will reap the benefits of genuine market competition (lower prices, better service, and more choice).

> Clients of this kind of policy will be restricted only by the forces of the market.

> Congress and its members, once they enact the deregulating statute and eliminate both former regulations and the agencies charged with specifying and enforcing them, will not be involved.

There are a number of questions that the opponents of deregulation can and do raise in any given debate. A critical question raised by many students of politics is whether members of Congress can be content to stay out of the action once deregulation has been created. It will be very difficult—indeed, impossible—for members of Congress to behave that way in some areas. Surely they will not permanently exit areas, such as defense procurement, in which major resources and tangible benefits are distributed. And, after airline deregulation, some members of the House and Senate continued to support subsidies to airlines to serve communities so small that market forces would leave them without scheduled air service.

What follows will first deal with the "normal" pattern of competitive regulation. Normality involves interactions of government agencies, supplicants, and intervenors. Second, we will look at deregulation (which, presumably, includes self-regulation and market regulation features that replace governmental regulation).

THE NORMAL PATTERN: GOVERNMENT AGENCY, SUPPLICANTS, AND INTERVENORS

What does the implementation of competitive regulatory policy look like in practice? To add some specific reality to our general portrait we want to pay some attention to examples in four different policy areas. As you read the examples recall the hybrid nature of competitive regulatory policy. There are important aspects of distribution in all of the examples (tangible benefits in the form of either direct money making or the award of money-making opportunities are at stake) and aspects of protective regulation in some (some benefits have compliance price tags attached).

Airlines and the Civil Aeronautics Board, 1938–1974

Between its creation in 1938 and 1974 the CAB behaved in the classic manner. That is, its policies consistently favored those it was regulating in terms of entry into the airline passenger market and in terms of pricing to guarantee financial stability and, indeed, profitability (see Behrman, 1980). The statute, in effect, gave some direction to the CAB in this direction (although there were also other, contradictory options built into the statutory language). And the CAB, with its airline supporters (the regulated interests) and with sporadic interventions by Congress, shaped its policy decisions to support stability and profitability for over a third of a century.

The Civil Aeronautics Act of 1938 created the CAB and gave it powers that made it the czar over which airlines could serve what cities and what prices they could charge for tickets. The airlines themselves were heavily involved in writing the statute and got virtually everything they wanted included in it.

The policy statement in the act, as is often the case, laid out contradictory aims:

> Supporting a good economic condition in the air transport industry.

Promoting "adequate, economical, and efficient service."

Promoting "competition to the extent necessary to assure the sound development of an air-transportation system."

Similarly, in the sections of the act dealing with entry into service the language gave very ambiguous directions that could be interpreted in a variety of ways. The applicants had to be " fit, willing, and able." Stressing these criteria would, presumably, increase the number of carriers on some routes. The transportation had to be "required by the public convenience and necessity." One legitimate interpretation of this phrase would be to assume that existing carriers could, by expanding the number of flights, serve the public convenience and necessity. Therefore new carriers should be kept out of important routes, and established carriers should not be granted new routes.

In practice the CAB opted for tight restrictions in the interest of airline profitability and protection against competition in its implementation decisions for the first 36 years of its existence. Its post-1974 stance will be examined in the discussion of deregulation. In general, policy decisions used a standard set of decision rules:

New carriers should, in general, be discouraged.

New carriers that were granted routes should be in some special category such as unscheduled. In general, new carriers should not compete with existing airlines.

Where politically possible, unprofitable service should be dropped so as to minimize the necessary federal subsidy (a formula built into the statute) and thus please federal budget cutters. This simultaneously allowed the airlines to focus on their profitable routes.

Where the reaction from political officials (especially members of Congress) to dropped service were sufficiently clangorous, then keeping good relations with Congress was worth the extra cost in subsidy.

The scheduled airlines with the most to gain also had the most regular, direct, and easy access to the CAB. They organized an association and worked out their joint self-protection collectively. Both publicly and privately they urged their united positions before the CAB and before interested committees and members of Congress. They helped particularly loyal members of Congress with campaign contributions.

Implementation was relatively easy for these 36 years. The decision rules governed most cases, the privileged competitors remained privileged, and the newcomers remained genuine competitors in name only, existing on the economic fringes of the industry if they survived at all.

Defense Procurement

Defense procurement is quite different from the case of airlines, which presents a classic instance of a mix of competitive regulatory and protective regulatory purposes being served by the same regulating agency. Defense procurement can be competitive in the short run. A pitched battle for the prime cruise missile contract, for example, is very real to the competing companies and their personnel. But the elements of protective regulation—except for choosing the winners—are relatively small. The winning contractors are supposed to deliver the item for which they contract, on time, and at the specified price. However, in practice, all of these deliverables can vary. The item for which the contract is written may come out looking quite different by the time it is finished. Time deadlines are routinely extended. And, so-called cost overruns are routinely allowed, so that in many cases the initial contract represents only a part of the actual cost of the finished product to the government and, therefore, to the taxpayer.

The element of competition may not be as great in the defense procurement area as it first appears. In a study of the 1960s and 1970s Gansler (1980:75–76) found that over 90 percent of all defense procurement dollars were provided on a "negotiated" basis, not on a strictly competitive basis. And about two thirds of those negotiated dollars (or 60 percent of the total) were negotiated with only a single contractor (a "sole source"). Under these conditions, Gansler concludes that "the supplier can effectively name his price."

It is also worth noting that defense competition is somewhat limited because, for any given defense system (for example, nuclear submarines, fighter aircraft, helicopters) there is often a high degree of concentration. That is, only a few of the largest firms in each area are in a position to compete (see Gansler, 1980:42–44, 164–166).

Three aspects of defense procurement are particularly interesting. (1) In the long run defense procurement decisions subsidize a very wide range of contractors. (2) Even in the short run no single contractor is likely to suffer deprivation very long. (3) Despite the implied guarantees of survival and, probably, prosperity for most defense firms, the companies mount intensive lobbying in connection with individual contracts. No individual company is content to rely on the nature of implementation process itself to produce its "fair share" of contract dollars. Each company is eager for a larger share and the guaranteed profits that come with such shares.

We will take a brief look at each of these three general points in the following pages.

The long run: Dispersed awards. Defense procurement involves awesome sums of money and flocks of companies seeking that money. Over time implementation decisions of the defense department bureaucracy subsidize a very large number of companies that compete with each other in the short run but that are all dependent on the government bureaucrats in the long run.

The "iron triangle" model is alleged by some analysts to apply to the entire decision process in the defense procurement area. Gordon Adams (1982:11) in an empirically rich study concludes that "A powerful flow of people and money moves between the defense contractors, the Executive branch (DOD and NASA), and Congress, creating an 'iron triangle' on defense policy and procurement that excludes outsiders and alternative perspectives." However, there is good evidence that, in terms of final procurement decisions and outcomes the congressional point of the triangle is weaker than the other two (see Hughes, 1980).

A large number of companies are involved in defense contracts. The largest companies do a huge volume of business but no few companies are dominant. In 1984, for example, total defense contracts involved about $132 billion. The 10 largest contractors received just over one third of the business. The largest single company—McDonnell Douglas in 1984—received less than 6 percent of all contracts, although the amount involved was $7.7 billion (*New York Times*, May 12, 1985).

Between 1970 and 1979 the eight largest companies (Boeing, General Dynamics, Grumman, Lockheed, McDonnell Douglas, Northrop, Rockwell International, and United Technologies) received "over $100 billion in DOD contracts, 25 percent of all DOD awards. Nearly $25 billion of this was for research and development—37 percent of the DOD total for R&D. They also received over $11.4 billion in NASA contracts, 36 percent of the NASA total" (Adams, 1982:7–8).

The above figures represent only prime contracts. These large companies conducted a great deal of their business through subcontracts with a whole host of companies.

In short, defense procurement represents big business for a sizable number of U.S. corporations, both large and small. It became even bigger during the accelerated defense buildup during the Reagan administration.

The short run. Each short-run, one-time decision tends to be viewed by the competitors as life-or-death competition. That psychology produces the heavy lobbying typical of implementation in the defense procurement area that we will discuss in the next section. Congresspersons often get involved in individual implementation choices after Congress authorizes a new piece of equipment and the Department of Defense sets the specifications and announces the competition. They reinforce the views of their constituents (companies) and allies that life or death hangs on the outcome. There is some evidence, however, that the bureaucrats and probably the most savvy defense lobbyists do not view each choice that way. They see the slightly longer run, balancing process in which company A wins a contract this month and therefore city A benefits, but company B in city B, which lost the first contract, gets a major plum six months later.

A specific case very much like the above model involved the award of the prime cruise missile contract by the Department of Defense in March, 1980. Great media attention was paid to the final competition between General Dynamics Convair Division (headquartered in San Diego) and Boeing (headquartered in the

Seattle area). Over $5 billion were at stake, and the welfare of the companies and their two principal towns were assumed to be critically involved. Prosperity was predicted for the winner and at least modestly hard times were predicted for the loser. Boeing was selected as the recipient. San Diego went into mourning.

The most instructive part of the story, however, comes hard on the heels of the laying of the funeral wreath for Convair's hopes for the cruise missile contract. A few days later the bureaucrats in the Pentagon let it be known that Convair would almost surely get the contract for a medium-range, air-to-surface missile for both the Navy and Air Force that was predicted to mean even *more* business than the $5.2 billion that went to Boeing in the original cruise missile competition. The dynamics of defense procurement implementation—as a longer view would have predicted—had rescued Convair and San Diego. Such rescues go on all the time. The real point is that they are not rescues at all but simply part of the routine implementation of defense procurement in which each decision is cast in the trappings of competition, but miraculously enough, the winning competitors tend to rotate over time. Thus, DOD preserves the stable of contractors it finds essential to national security.

Lobbying. Defense companies employ lots of professional lobbyists to make their cases in regard to any individual competition. A number of these lobbyists are retired military officers or members of Congress or civilian DOD officials and already have good ties into what President Eisenhower called the military-industrial complex.

The focus of lobbying at the stages of formulation and legitimation is to join forces with a number of defense-oriented organizations (including many DOD officials) to push the president and Congress for more defense money in general and for more money for specific weapons systems for which the lobbyist's company could be a bidder. Thus, for example, a lobbyist for Boeing would push for more defense money in general and especially for more money for aircraft.

The focus of lobbying at the implementation level—when the situation is defined as competitive in terms of what company gets what share of the contracts—is still diffuse. Pentagon bureaucrats are the direct decision makers and therefore the focus of much attention. Other DOD officials at field locations are also approached as they help make decisions. Members of Congress continue to be lobbied because it is assumed that they have channels of influence into the bureaucracy that will let them help sway the decision. Congress itself continues to be a target of lobbying since appropriations are needed for specific projects, and appropriations represent a critical implementation decision. Likewise, on the question of budget management, the release of funds as well as the inclusion of certain proposals in budgets sent to Congress, the Office of Management and Budget becomes a target of lobbying.

When approaching members of Congress to get them to lobby the bureaucracy too, the major line used by defense-company lobbyists has to do with constituent benefits. The bait used to get members' attention involves projections of dollars, jobs, and other benefits going to different states and localities depending on the award of a contract.

A typical lobbying struggle took place in 1979 (Wilson, 1979) over who would be the primary builder of Navy and Air Force Fighter engines for the foreseeable future—General Electric or Pratt and Whitney. Some $6 to $8 billion were estimated to be at stake. Both companies had large lobbying staffs—the one at Pratt and Whitney was headed by Clark MacGregor, a former Minnesota congressman and the chairman of President Nixon's re-election committee in 1972. Robert Giaimo, a congressman from Connecticut and member of the Appropriations Defense Subcommittee was quite visible in the Pratt and Whitney coalition, no doubt because that company is a major employer in Giaimo's state of Connecticut. Joseph Addabbo, a New York Democrat and chairman of the Appropriations Defense Subcommittee, was counted as a major gun in the General Electric arsenal.

Lobbying is not confined to the United States. When foreign countries who buy U.S. products make major weapons decisions, lobbyists from U.S. companies will surely be present. The various foreign bribery scandals such as the Lockheed bribes that have sent a number of Japanese politicians into limbo, if not prison, suggest an intensive effort. More legitimate lobbying abroad along the model of constituent politics is also apparent. For example, in 1980 when Canada was deciding on a new mainstay fighter plane for its air force, McDonnell Douglas and General Dynamics sent lots of lobbyists north of the U.S. border to influence the decision. The former's F–18A and the latter's F–16 were the two finalists in the competition, which was finally decided in late 1980 in favor of the F–18A. The lobbyists met with members of Canada's national parliament and also with politicians at the provincial level to outline for them the economic benefits that would accrue to their constituents because of subcontracts that would go to Canadian firms. General Dynamics used the argument with Quebec politicians that they should push for the F–16 because Pratt and Whitney, which would supply the engines, has a plant near Montreal and would get some of the work. The president of Pratt and Whitney upped the ante by pledging to build a new plant in Quebec costing $30 million if the F–16 were selected. He said construction could start immediately. McDonnell Douglas also sweetened the pot, promising among other things to build a $70 million plant in Quebec to produce some of the engine parts.

U.S. arms manufacturers have also tried to lock up sales abroad by helping market other products from countries that are prospective arms purchasers to third countries. Thus, in recent years, for example, Northrop has helped sell Turkish wine to third countries in return for aircraft sales to Turkey. It also helped produce a Liberian buyer of Canadian paper cups as part of selling airplanes to Canada, and it helped Swiss companies peddle elevators and drills to places such as Egypt and Spain for yet more aircraft sales (*Washington Post*, July 6, 1982).

The Federal Communications Commission and License Renewal

One of the most critical decisions—at least in theory—in the field of federal competitive regulation of broadcasting is the decision on whether to renew the licenses to broadcast given to the owners of television and radio stations. Licenses expire every three years. Channels and frequencies are, by definition, scarce, although they are not absolutely fixed and can be increased in a variety of ways that will be noted in our later discussion of the FCC and deregulation. The number of potential recipients competing for awards far outnumbers the number of channels and frequencies which are usually very lucrative for the owners. Thus contests for the initial award of a channel or frequency are spirited, and there are sometimes contested cases of license renewal.

There is substantial evidence, however, that the FCC has over the years developed a style of implementation that tends to treat renewals as virtually automatic. The statute gives the FCC room to make serious reviews on a number of grounds of performance by license holders at the time of application for license renewal, thus opening the way for successful challenges. The formal process for handling TV license renewals is outlined in Figure 5–1. The process for radio license renewal is similar. In fact, however, the FCC has generally sought to stabilize its relationship with supplicants that already hold licenses by granting them renewals without much fuss. (For a classic study of the low-profile FCC approach to renewal controversy and relations with their clients and regulated interests in general see Drew, 1967.)

Challenges are not frequent, no doubt in large part because potential challengers are well aware of the FCC's preference for renewal. The unattractiveness of the cost of a challenge coupled with the high probability of losing deter most from mounting the effort. Between 1961 and 1978, for example, only 17 challenges— either from groups simply opposing renewal or from competitors—were made in relation to TV license renewal. Seven of the cases were still pending in early 1979 (see Holsendolph, 1979). Of the 10 that had been decided in almost two decades, 8 were decided in favor of the current license holder who had filed for renewal. And even the two awards that went against the incumbent were made on nonsubstantive grounds: one station's owner was discovered to have been behaving fraudulently and the second one simply had not filed the application in a completed and timely fashion. Thus, no challenge was supported on the basis of substantive merits during these 18 years.

The FCC's performance in the field of radio licensing was even more clearcut. Between 1961 and 1978, challenges to incumbent licenses were made 31 times, and in every case the license of the incumbent was renewed. Incumbents had little to worry about in dealing with the FCC at the stage of life-and-death.

In commenting on this performance a three-judge federal Court of Appeals opinion in early 1979 asserted that station owners had quite reasonably developed "a renewal expectancy." Implementation, then, turns out to be easy: incumbents win and

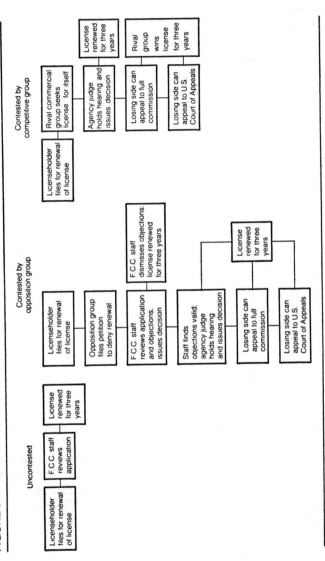

FIGURE 5–1 How the FCC Renews Television Licenses

Uncontested

Licenseholder files for renewal of license → F.C.C. staff reviews application → License renewed for three years

Contested by opposition group

Licenseholder files for renewal of license → Opposition group files petition to deny renewal → F.C.C. staff reviews application and objections; issues decision

FCC staff dismisses objections; license renewed for three years

Staff finds objections valid; agency judge holds hearing and issues decision → License renewed for three years

Losing side can appeal to full commission

Losing side can appeal to U.S. Court of Appeals

Contested by competitive group

Licenseholder files for renewal of license → Rival commercial group seeks license for itself → Agency judge holds hearing and issues decision

License renewed for three years

Rival group wins license for three years

Losing side can appeal to full commission

Losing side can appeal to U.S. Court of Appeals

SOURCE: *New York Times*, Feb 7, 1979. © 1979 by the New York Times Company. Reprinted by Permission.

challengers are denied. The FCC, having made what might have been a tough decision in the first award of a license, if there was competition for that first award, apparently has no stomach for making subsequent tough decisions. The decision rule in favor of incumbents makes life easier for implementers and incumbent beneficiaries.

The Interstate Commerce Commission and Licenses for Moving Companies

Another pattern of stability and of close relationships between an agency awarding a license for which there can theoretically be competition involves the Interstate Commerce Commission and the nationwide moving van companies (see Holsendolph, 1980). There were, as of early 1980, only 19 companies licensed to be nationwide movers. The value of each license was estimated at $15 million because of their scarcity. These 19 companies had attained nationwide status in one of two ways. Some had been grandfathered in as nationwide movers when the Motor Carrier Act of 1935 that defined the ICC's powers in this area was passed. Those already engaged in nationwide moving via truck were guaranteed the right to continue. The additions to that initial core came about not through new nationwide moving license awards but through individual movers patiently and incrementally adding one or a few states at a time to an existing license. The ICC licenses a number of movers for only a few states. Implementation decisions for nationwide moving licenses followed three clear rules that made implementation easy for the ICC: (1) existing nationwide movers were protected and their territory could never be challenged; (2) larger movers could gradually add states and had some hopes of achieving nationwide status; (3) applications by smaller movers or new movers to become nationwide companies were automatically rejected.

The stability and coziness of the implementation decision pattern was disrupted by an unusual exception. In the early 1960s a regional mover in St. Louis (optimistically named Allstates Transworld Van Lines, Inc.) applied for a nationwide moving license. This company was already experienced and had the special qualifications of not only being a minority-owned and -operated enterprise but of focusing on moving to and from inner cities. It fought with the ICC for a national license for almost two decades. The existing 19 carriers all opposed the award. As the contest developed, Allstates found it necessary to enlist the support of a number of politicians from around the country to bring pressure on the ICC to grant the license. In addition, other federal agencies were motivated, for a variety of reasons, to join Allstates' case and request favorable action from the ICC. These included the Justice Department (which, no doubt, was impressed that all 19 existing carriers were white-owned), the Transportation Department, the General Services Administration, and the Department of Defense. The last two departments were satisfied customers of Allstates.

Allstates eventually prevailed, and in early 1980 the ICC awarded the license, making Allstates the 20th company with a nationwide moving license. But the extraordinary circumstances and the extraordinary campaign required to win it (and the fact that no one at the ICC could remember another similar award ever having been made) make this particular area of competitive regulation look very much like a tightly controlled subgovernment situation.

DEREGULATION, MARKET REGULATION, AND SELF-REGULATION

We have been considering implementation examples in which a federal agency is, at least theoretically, an active participant. In contrast, what is popularly called deregulation has at its core the removal—either gradually or all at once—of an active role for the federal agency. In theory, either self-regulation by the parties formerly regulated by government agencies or, more likely, the regulatory forces of a competitive market (market regulation) are supposed to serve the public interest even better than the regulations imposed and implemented by government agencies. Table 5–1 summarizes the major statutes reducing regulation since 1976. Actions not requiring statutory changes have also enhanced the deregulation effort in some areas.

In many ways, the deregulation movement is too new to test the performance claims of either its proponents or opponents. And such a test is, in any event, beyond the scope of this volume. What we want to look at is the patterns of implementation in deregulation compared to those in regulation. In a sense, of course, the most interesting question is whether Congress can really withstand the urge to reinsert itself (and, therefore, a

TABLE 5-1   Deregulation Statutes, 1976–1982

Act	Year	Key Elements
Railroad Revitalization and Regulatory Reform Act	1976	Allowed railroads limited rate setting autonomy; was the first piece of deregulation legislation in the recent wave
Airline Deregulation Act	1978	Instructed the Civil Aeronautics Board to place maximum reliance on competition in its regulation of passenger service; provided that the board's authority over domestic fares and mergers would end Jan. 1, 1983 and that the CAB would be abolished January 1, 1985
Staggers Rail Act	1980	Limited the Interstate Commerce Commission's jurisdiction over rates to those markets where railroads exercised market dominance; introduced price competition
Motor Carrier Act	1980	Allowed truckers to form subsidiaries and expand into additional regional markets; ended necessity of demonstrating public need; placed fewer restrictions on certain industry hauling practices; eased entry and introduced price competition
Depository Institutions Deregulation and Monetary Control Act	1980	Allowed mutual savings banks to make commercial, corporate and business loans equal to 5 percent of their assets; allowed payment of interest on demand deposits; removed interest rate ceilings
Bus Deregulatory Reform Act	1982	Allowed companies to obtain operating authority without applying to the ICC in many circumstances
Thrift Institutions Restructuring Act	1982	Authorized savings and loans to make commercial loans equal to 10 percent of their assets; allowed investments in nonresidential personal property and small business investment companies

SOURCE: New York Times, February 10, 1985.

federal presence) into situations in which constituents are pressing claims or in which members of Congress can appear to be parceling out major money-making opportunities. In the first instance, a senator from North Dakota faced with clamor from the leading citizens of Minot, Bismarck, Grand Forks, and Fargo for the restoration of decimated commercial air service is probably hardpressed to continue to favor total deregulation. Or in the second instance, any member of Congress who realizes the credit and potential future campaign contributions he or she can get from intervening in the granting or renewing of a trucking license is likely to think twice before becoming an all-out supporter of no role for the ICC in trucking regulation.

In the pages that follow we want to look briefly at three areas where deregulation is beginning to occur. It should be kept in mind, however, that it is too early to discern all of the patterns surrounding implementation in these cases.

One final introductory point is useful to make: deregulation is no more neutral in intent and implementation then regulation. Both are policies and both have goals, both implicit and explicit. In the case of deregulation policy makers make assumptions about how the market forces will work. In the case of regulation policy makers make assumptions about how government intervention will work. In both cases the assumptions include assessments of what tangible and intangible benefits are at stake and who stands to win or lose.

Of the three areas addressed only one—airlines—has been deregulated (at least in part) long enough to see very much. Thus the airline example will get most of our attention.

The Vanishing of the CAB and Much Airline Regulation

In the few years between 1974 and the passage of the Airline Deregulation Act late in 1978, the CAB (opposed by many of the airlines) took the lead in pushing for deregulation and, indeed, for the abolition of the CAB itself. For a variety of reasons that make an interesting story in themselves (see Behrman, 1980) the economic arguments in favor of deregulation were espoused by the CAB and then by Congress in short order. However, our concern here is not that intriguing piece of policy formulation but rather the aftermath. What has deregulation meant so far?

Deregulation immediately and dramatically relaxed service (entry) and price restrictions and ended them altogether within a few years. The CAB itself went out of business on December 31, 1984, literally with a Marine bugler playing "Evening Colors" as the flag was lowered. Both the economic and political adjustments to deregulation produced some fluctuations in the early post-1978 years and neither the industry nor the government stance toward it is immutably fixed for the future. Deregulation all by itself did not cause all of the fluctuations. Other economic factors, for example, have had important effects that are hard to sort out from each other and from the effect of deregulation. These include the general health of the economy (which has a major impact on the travel habits of individuals), the price of aviation fuel, and the state of the relations between individual airlines and the many unions with which they deal (pilots, flight attendants, mechanics, baggage handlers).

Six general results (although somewhat unstable over time) seem to characterize the situation in mid-1985 (as this is written). First, the fare and service structure is enormously varied. Heavily traveled routes typically have competitive fares that are quite low, although the price of tickets on different flights and for different periods of the week and different length trips can vary enormously. New York–Los Angeles is a typical route with these characteristics. Fares on more lightly traveled routes between medium-sized places—Columbus, Ohio, and Charleston, South Carolina, might serve as an example—are much higher on a per mile basis and there are fewer options for cutting those fares. In a real sense, travelers on the more expensive routes subsidize travelers on cheap routes. Ask any travel agent about the complexity of searching for the best fares between any two end points and you will quickly become aware of the great variety of options and, sometimes, the desirability of taking a more round-about and longer route rather than the most direct and shortest route. It is even sometimes cheaper to buy a ticket to a destination beyond where you want to go, get on a flight that stops where you want to go, and get off there. (At one point, for example, it was cheaper to buy a ticket from Washington to San Francisco and get off at St. Louis on a one-stop plane rather than buying a ticket from Washington to St. Louis!) Clearly, deregulation has resulted in aggressive fare and service competition.

Whether any individual consumer benefits or not depends on where he or she lives and where he or she wants to go.

Second, the financial health of the airlines—once reliably protected by CAB coddling—has been highly unstable. Deregulation has been one cause of fluctuations, although certainly not the only cause. In the period from 1978, when deregulation began, through 1984, 120 airlines—including commuter and charter firms—went bankrupt. Even if only scheduled, noncommuter airlines are counted, the number that went bankrupt in this period was 28. In some years even the largest and seemingly best-managed airlines lost money. By 1984 industry revenues were high (a record $44 billion), but net profit was low ($800 million—1.8 percent on revenues). Some airlines still lost massive amounts of money and some of the weakest were teetering on the edge of extinction.

Third, small cities were losing much of their "certificated" air carrier service—carriers often thought of as the "real" airlines. But some of that service was being replaced by commuter carriers using very small airplanes. A residual subsidy program—the Essential Air Service Program—was still in place in 1984 (at a small annual cost of $35 million) to prevent elimination of all scheduled air service to some localities. But Congress may or may not renew the program when it expires in 1988.

Fourth, airplanes are more crowded because airlines must increase their *load factor* to become or remain profitable.

Fifth, airports handle more flights that are more concentrated at the most popular times (*peak periods*). The number of flights increase when more people travel but also because more smaller airliners are in use to increase load factors. Peak periods have become even more popular as airlines fight for passengers who want to travel then. All of this activity has resulted in a pattern of increased delays in landings and takeoffs at the busiest airports. (The mass firing of illegally striking air traffic controllers in August 1981 and the slow rebuilding of the controller work force also contributed to the problem.)

Sixth, even though the CAB is gone a residue of regulatory activities remains and has been moved to the Department of Transportation. These include allocation of takeoff and landing slots at major airports (although the government sometimes asks the airlines to come up with their own cooperative solutions), international negotiations, antitrust matters involving computer reservations systems owned by a few airlines, and some consumer regulations involving such matters as smoking and nonsmoking sections, compensation for lost baggage, and being "bumped" when a flight is oversold.

In the midst of all these changes, who has been involved doing what in terms of implementation decisions? Thus far the government agencies have resisted any temptation to leap back in to the fray. The CAB unswervingly stayed on its course of promoting the orderly implementation of deregulation and the orderly closing of its doors. Members of Congress have bemoaned the loss of service to various favored towns in their states and districts, but beyond the level of individualized grousing, their efforts have thus far been channeled toward supporting more use of a subsidy program for commuter air carriers rather than into any effort to rescind broad-scale deregulation.

What the course of the CAB and the relative restraint of members of Congress means so far is that, indeed, airline executives are making the implementation decisions. Before deregulation the dominant sentiment among these individuals was opposition to it, although there were notable exceptions. The dominant sentiment among these individuals has become positive.

The ICC and Deregulation of Trucking

In July of 1980 President Carter signed the Motor Carrier Act of 1980, which deregulated trucking. The act made entering new routes extremely easy. It left pricing decisions up to the truck lines. It also left considerable discretion with the Interstate Commerce Commission (ICC) on how far and how fast to allow deregulation in trucking to go.

As of mid-1985 the economic and political reactions to deregulation of trucking had some clear similarities to the reactions to airline deregulation but it also had some striking differences, particularly in terms of the political situation.

Some of the economic consequences first observed were quite similar to those in the airline industry. Fare and service competition abounded. New truckers—including thousands of independents—sprang up. There were also thousands of bankruptcies.

But the political situation was much more unsettled than in the case of air transport. Two principal features created uncertainty about the future. First, unlike the CAB, the ICC was bitterly divided internally over how far and how fast to go with deregulation of trucking (this division also occurred simultaneously—perhaps even more strongly—with regard to deregulation of railroads). Second, also unlike the air transport case, many shippers and many truckers wanted some sizable portion of reregulation. They found unregulated trucking too threatening to economic stability and predictability. (This demand for reregulation was also paralleled in the case of rail transport, especially by some powerful shippers and shipper organizations.)

From early 1983 until late 1984 the ICC had only four of its seven allotted seats filled. The chairperson wanted to deregulate very slowly while the other three members wanted to go much more rapidly. Meetings and decisions were both few and bitter. And, to complicate matters, no one seemed to be clearly in charge of the professional staff. Because the chairperson had more influence over staff than the other members of the ICC, the staff tended to enforce existing regulations rather than seeking ways of reducing them. The ICC was, in short, in a mess. Simultaneously, a concentrated and well-financed campaign for reregulation put pressure both on the ICC and especially on Congress.

By the end of 1984 the three vacant seats on the ICC had been filled but there was still no reliable majority. And, to complicate matters even more, the ICC was scheduled to shrink to five members by January, 1986, which created an extra dimension of instability. Some members were sympathetic to going slowly in promoting deregulation by using the ample latitude given the ICC by statute. Others wanted to go full tilt. Some had sympathies with some of the reregulation efforts and were supported in those sympathies by some members of Congress.

In short, the implementation of deregulation of trucking not only resulted in short-term economic confusion and uncertainty (which is, to some extent, to be expected) but it also resulted in an as yet unresolved political confusion and instability.

The FCC and Gradual Deregulation of Broadcasting

The broadcasting privilege, by its nature, is a scarce resource. Some regulation of entry into it seems inevitable, almost surely by a government agency. However, there are many points on the regulatory spectrum controlling entry into broadcasting, ranging from those at one end promoting easy entry in many different forms of broadcasting to those at the other end promoting the dominance of standard forms of broadcasting by established networks of conventional radio and television stations.

In the last few years the FCC has moved of its own accord (no doubt nudged by some economic interests that stand to gain) to increase the options available to consumers. It has also moved to reduce its regulatory activity. At the same time, congressional supporters of deregulation in broadcasting have also begun to push various statutory changes, particularly those that reduce or end FCC powers in reviewing program content and renewing licenses. But powerful forces also oppose many deregulation proposals and there are often clashes between FCC members and members of Congress about the best way to deregulate (Schwartz, 1980; Wines, 1983b).

The FCC has reduced many of the restrictions on cable television so that cable operations could carry a broader range of programs. It has allowed more than one subscription television station to be established in a community. It has proposed changes in its rules that would allow up to 139 new VHF channels (channels 2 to 13) throughout the country. These are much more lucrative than the UHF stations (channels 14 to 83). The FCC has proposed changes that would increase the number of AM radio frequencies available by reducing spacing between them. It also made changes in both satellite transmission and satellite reception rules to allow direct broadcast from satellites to individuals, rather than having such transmissions under the control of intermediaries, such as networks.

Predictably, officials of the three large networks are upset with these moves by the FCC because their favored position is being somewhat endangered. The chairman of the board of one of the networks, for example, said in the autumn of 1980 that the FCC decisions would lead to the promotion of "pay television and other systems by arbitrarily discriminating against free television." He asked that government "get off our backs," surely an ironic comment about an agency promoting what it views as "*de*regulation." Perhaps the moral of the story is that depending on how regulation or deregulation is defined it is going to favor some interests and be viewed unfavorably by other interests. Neutrality is not achieveable no matter what government does *or* does *not* do.

SUMMARY AND CONCLUSIONS

1. Normal competitive regulatory implementation is routine, relatively free of controversy, and highly protective of established interests. All four cases we examined—defense procurement, the ICC and moving licenses, the FCC and the renewal of conventional radio and television licenses, and CAB's treatment of airline entry and pricing before 1975—reflect this situation.

The interests well served—those in Congress, in the regulated businesses, and in the regulating agency—all agree that this arrangement for implementation is fair, legitimate, and sensible. Those with competing interests may protest but they have little audience because they have little standing.

The above situation—which we have dubbed normal—looks a lot like the situation with regard to the normal implementation of distributive policy.

Complications can arise that shatter this normal situation, however. These complications can include the following:

The intervention of powerful outsiders with different values. Senator Edward Kennedy's support of airline deregulation fits this category, as does the intervention of the Department of Defense, Department of Transportation, General Services Administration, and Department of Justice on behalf of the applicant for the 20th national movers license.

Changes in key personnel that involve people with different commitments and goals. For example, President Ford and President Carter appointed two successive CAB chairmen dedicated to deregulation who helped turn the climate of opinion in relation to deregulation dramatically in just a few years.

Changes in technological conditions. Some of the new broadcasting developments in the 1960s and 1970s (such as satellites) made new options available for adaptation to home use.

Division of opinion among the regulated. Some airlines, for example, helped push for deregulation. The lack of a unified airline front helped allow the climate to change.

These upsetting factors are similar to some of those identified in regard to distributive policy implementation at the conclusion of Chapter 4.

2. The balance between forces favoring regulation and deregulation became quite volatile in a number of areas in the 1970s, and this volatility continued and spread to more areas in the 1980s. The forces unleashed by deregulation may create conditions that later generate calls for reregulation. For example, if airlines curb costly competition by either explicit or implicit price-fixing agreements, consumer groups are likely to work hard with sympathetic members of Congress to forbid such practices and to return to some form of regulation, although not necessarily the previously discarded form. We are not suggesting there is an automatic cycle of free market to regulation to deregulation to reregulation, but it is certainly worth noting that the economic and political forces underlying the debate over various options will not wither away. Political and economic climates have changed in the past; there is every reason to expect they will do so in the future.

3. When the actors in the implementation of competitive regulation are assessed, some surprises emerge. The two largest surprises are that regulatory agencies are not uniformly in favor of continuing regulation in unchanged form or even at all. The CAB did a complete about-face, and the FCC is making movements of its own volition in some areas of its responsibility. The ICC, however, underwent a period of bitter internal division.

In a similar vein, all regulated interests do not hanker to be free. Regulation often may involve more protection than hassle. Thus the majority of airline executives before 1975 predicted dire results if their particular form of regulation-protection was removed. Similarly, many broadcast network executives are quite unhappy about FCC movement away from their favored form (the existing one) of regulation-protection.

However, agencies and regulated interests do not take wholly predictable positions because ideas about regulation (economists' theories, among others) are important in the political debate and because the underlying structure of economic interests can be perceived differently by different regulated interests.

4. In Table 3–4 (Chapter 3) we summarized expectations about the nature of relationships between actors, the processes critical to successful implementation, and the relative difficulty of successful implementation of competitive regulatory policies. Our examples in this chapter seem to confirm the general accuracy of those expectations:

The federal bureaucracy is mainly concerned with nonconflictual processes and the absence of complaints. The central federal agency (the major bureaucratic actor) keeps a formal distance from the regulated interests but often may work closely with them informally. Conflict is generally low, but there may be short-term higher bursts.

Operating routines are critical to successful implementation.

There is some moderate difficulty in achieving successful implementation (defined as peaceful and quiet protection of existing interests) both because there are some outbursts of disagreement between agency and regulated interests and because dissenters may challenge the basic assumptions and procedures of the whole enterprise.

5. To these generalizations, we would add some comments about deregulation although we do so with considerable tentativeness.

The federal bureaucracy is involved in leaving some fields or at least in minimizing its role. The private interests being deregulated are beginning to grope for new alliances and arrangements that will allow them to cope with changed conditions. In their groping they may seek to form alliances within the private sector, with members of Congress who might help them overcome problems through new legislation or intervention in specific implementation decisions, or with other federal agencies and programs that have some potential for helping them solve problems caused by deregulation.

Bargaining relationships in the formation of new alliances are more important to successful implementation of deregulation than operating routines.

The degree of difficulty of successful implementation of deregulation is not clear to us. The rigid theorists (usually economists) favoring deregulation claim it is simple. Unlike some of them, our faith in Adam Smith and the magic powers of the market as a cure for human ills is not strong. Earlier reliance on such powers led to identifiable problems that may well have been imperfectly addressed but were viewed as intolerable without some governmental response.

6. The congressional role in the implementation of competitive regulatory policy can be very important on a case-by-case basis. Congressional abstinence from meddling will probably also contribute to a fair test for various instances of deregulation—although expecting Congress to stay out of such politically rich decisions may be like expecting the town lush to give up the bottle voluntarily for more than a few days following a temperance rally.

CHAPTER 6

The Implementation of Protective Regulatory Policy

PROTECTIVE REGULATION: INTRODUCTORY CONSIDERATIONS

Protective regulatory policy can both prevent certain types of private activity and require private activities in explicit terms. The job of the implementer is to enforce those requirements and prohibitions. The enforcement dimension means that the policy by nature usually is perceived to be much more threatening than competitive regulatory policy, and it is perceived to be much more coercive than many other policies, including virtually all of those of a distributive or competitive regulatory nature.

Protective regulatory implementation is a hands-on activity. The implementers (federal officials in the central offices and in the field) typically must interact directly with the regulated interests either to require mandated activity or to prevent prohibited activity. Thus, if the regulation is to be successfully implemented, the implementers must, almost by necessity, act aggressively toward the regulated. This means that many of the interactions during the implementation of protective regulatory policy will be characterized by *hostility*, which is specific rather than abstract. The interactions are also cast in *adversarial* terms because the restricted clients do not get rewards, rather they receive directions, punishments, or constraints upon their actions.

This policy area is activist in that implementers must take positive steps to implement. In both distributive policy and in some aspects of competitive regulation the affected interests take the lead in promoting implementation because they have something to gain. In the protective regulatory arena the affected interests (the regulated) prefer *non*implementation and will certainly not take the lead in stimulating implementation.

There are a large number of actors almost constantly involved in many protective regulatory implementation activities. Government agencies, and factions within agencies with different visions of good implementation, are involved constantly. The interests and individuals being regulated (producers) are involved. The consumers of the goods and services that are regulated are involved. Since there is lots of hands-on contact between government and private interests, Congress—both as subcommittees and as individuals—is involved sporadically, but sometimes heavily. Courts also become involved with a fair degree of frequency. The agency situation is complicated not only by the possible presence of factions in the Washington office but also by geographical decentralization that occurs because a lot of implementation activities take place in field offices. Factional divisions from the central office over the proper way to proceed can carry over into the field offices. To complicate the bureaucratic picture even more, there are policies in which state and local enforcement agencies also become involved.

Occasionally a regulated interest will welcome the regulation, but more usually such interests will resent and resist it. The principal modes of resistance include:

Keeping a low profile and hoping that the agencies will proceed slowly or not at all.

Cultivating good relations with an agency or at least with a significant faction in it. Critics claim that when this happens the agency has been captured by the regulated interests. A more neutral way of putting it is that self-defense is promoted by attempting to minimize conflict and to reach accords that "everyone can live with."

Triggering long, costly fights with the agency by rallying congressional allies, interest group allies, dissident agency allies, and through legal means such as filing lawsuits that involve a new set of actors in the judiciary and that also eat up lots of time and energy for everyone, including the implementers.

Another form of resistance that is increasingly used is attacking the need for regulation at all and working for deregulation. Those in favor of deregulation have attacked a number of protective regulatory activities as being counterproductive, expensive, and unnecessary. Major statutes have been passed deregulating the pricing limits (a protective feature) as well as opening up market entry and exit (a competitive feature) in a variety of fields, including airlines, trucking, and railroads. Additional deregulation has involved domestic oil and gas pricing, oil pipelines, and barge lines. Statutory dilution of regulations aimed at guaranteeing pure food and drugs, safe workplaces, environmental quality, fair business competition, fair labor relations, and various aspects of consumer protection has not occurred. However, in a number of these areas the Reagan administration has clearly been unaggressive in enforcing existing regulations and has interpreted their meaning in less restrictive ways.

There is also a large element of instability in the protective regulatory field. Actors, being numerous, come and go as their interests are involved or not. They also change substantive positions. The coalitions that form usually do not extend beyond single regulated industries or sectors. This means that over time there is a kaleidoscopic aspect to the implementation of protective regulatory policy. Similar kinds of shifting, temporary alliances and the resulting instability also occurs during the stages of policy formulation and legitimation for protective regulatory policy (see Ripley and Franklin, 1984).

Central features of the implementation of protective regulation are summarized below (for a rich treatment of these and other complexities see Meier, 1985):

1. Protective regulatory policy implementation is marked by hostility and by the opposition of the regulated interest to many of the activities of the implementing agency.

2. Protective regulatory policy both prevents and requires activities. It can also create an element of competition in certain circumstances. Despite a normal situation in which regulating agencies and regulated interests are hostile to each other, there are occasions in which potentially regulated interests welcome such regulation, usually to obtain some sort of competitive advantage. Some assert that the relationship between a regulated producer and the regulating agency is inevitably one of the former capturing the latter. This sometimes happens as, for example, with both oil regulation and nuclear regulation in the last few decades (Chubb, 1983). But the phenomenon is certainly neither inevitable nor uniform (Quirk, 1981).

3. Deregulation beyond lessening control over pricing decisions is harder to create in meaningful terms in this policy area. But debate over other means and other reductions is occurring and is likely to increase.

4. The number of actors involved from both the public and private sectors in regulatory activities in many specific subject matter areas is very large at any given time. This makes central control over implementation very hard to achieve.

5. The complexity of the substantive fields being regulated, the individualized nature of specific enforcement decisions, and the large number of actors also create an unstable situation in terms of shifting alliances and shifting positions of actors on certain implementation questions. Different patterns will be likely to characterize different subject matter areas; and in some cases the pattern in a single field may be very unstable and change rapidly over time. Various forms of hostility are likely to prevail, but various forms of cooperation can also emerge.

6. Congressional intervention can often by stimulated in this area and is sometimes critical in specific implementation decisions.

7. Courts are especially active in the protective regulatory arena because a large number of lawsuits occur. The constraints on the behavior of both regulators and the regulated coming from judicial action are substantial.

In the immediately following section, these summary statements will be illustrated with a variety of very brief examples. The section after that illustrates the dynamics of the implementation process by discussing some specific instances in greater detail.

THE SHAPE OF PROTECTIVE REGULATORY IMPLEMENTATION: SOME BRIEF EXAMPLES

Prevailing Hostility

Hostility, in most instances, comes about because those on the receiving end of the implementation perceive their financial interests to be adversely affected. Hostility is heightened if the regulated interests perceive the regulations to be trivial, unimportant, silly, or unclear. The hostility is additionally heightened if the process of deciding on what regulations do and do not apply takes a long time, and normal private activity cannot go forward during the period of decision. Yet another increment of hostility is added if the regulations appear to change in midstream, if the implementing bureaucrats appear to be inconsistent, or if the bureaucrats simply have changed their minds.

A good example of an adverse impact on financial interests of regulated groups for reasons that surely were perceived to be trivial was the intervention of the Army Corps of Engineers to hold up real estate development in a section of San Diego because of its concern for preserving the mesa mint, a tiny plant on an endangered species list (Carson, 1980). Owners of thousands of acres in San Diego who were ready to develop them both for residences and for industrial purposes in mid-1979 were delayed for many months, and given the price of land in San Diego in 1979 and 1980, these owners were obviously forgoing attractive financial opportunities because the Corps of Engineers was charged by law with protecting endangered species. This was, incidentally, surely an odd role for the corps to find itself in, given its reputation over many decades for engaging in construction at all costs on public lands.

Another example of adverse affects on financial interests of a regulated company—so adverse that the company vowed its very existence was endangered—must have been particularly infuriating to the regulated company because privately, officials of the regulatory agency involved, the Department of Energy (DOE), admitted that the company was correct in its allegation (Kramer, 1979). A small oil company in Kansas invested $300,000 of its own capital to produce gasohol with encouragement of DOE.

Then, however, DOE regulations, in effect, prevented the company from obtaining the gasoline to mix with the alcohol to make the final product. Obviously a company that has borrowed capital must sell products in order to pay the interest on the debt and to stay in business. DOE encouragement was countered by simultaneous regulations that made this impossible. A DOE official said privately that the company's description of the situation and the blame of DOE regulations were accurate. The problem was compounded by a huge backlog of appeals mired in DOE bureaucracy.

Changes of regulations are particularly galling to regulated groups when they have already invested resources to comply with the first set and when yet more resources would be necessary in order to comply with a second set or when a greater financial burden is imposed. In 1980, for example, the Department of Commerce's National Marine Fisheries Service (NMFS) proposed changes in the regulations applying to tuna fishing designed to protect porpoises (Harris, 1980). Porpoise herds typically swim over tuna schools, making it difficult to net the tuna without also tangling porpoises in the nets. Various detailed regulations including fines for violations were issued by NMFS. Compliance by tuna fishers resulted in a reduction of killed porpoises from 200,000 in 1973 to under 17,000 by 1979—less than half of the U.S. quota in an international agreement on porpoise protection.

Tuna boat owners invested a considerable amount of money in methods of fishing that still used the porpoises as spotters but reduced the number accidentally caught and killed to acceptable levels. However, NMFS proposed new ways of estimating porpoise population and an acceptable depletion of that population that would, even in the view of NMFS, cut the U.S. tuna catch by about 40 percent. A reduction of this magnitude would mean a total loss of about $71 million for the U.S. tuna fishers. The American Tuna Boat Association said that even this grim forecast understated the economic damage that would be done. It predicted a catch reduced by more than half, which would drive a number of tuna boats out of business. It would also make tuna more expensive since the smaller number caught would have to be supplemented with more expensive imported tuna to meet demand.

Hostility about regulatory implementation can also be stimulated by nonfinancial effects. For example, the Department of Health, Education, and Welfare introduced regulations to protect human subjects of government-sponsored research projects. The regulations have brought increasingly anguished cries from researchers based in universities who claim that the regulations provide precious little legitimate protection but that, in many instances, simply delay or actually prohibit certain kinds of research, particularly in the social sciences (for a good statement by a distinguished political scientist see Pool, 1979).

Hostility toward regulations can, in some cases, become strong enough to force their abandonment or at least their relaxation. And in extreme cases, hostility generated and managed by powerful interests can result in the demise of an entire regulatory enterprise and set of bureaucrats that have no important political supporters and allies. One such agency that disappeared was the Renegotiation Board, with a staff of about 200 at the time of its termination (Singer, 1979a). It had been created in 1951 to help recover funds from defense contractors by applying laws regulating their profits. Congress in the mid-1970s got involved in a debate over how to strengthen the board. In fact what happened was that the opposition of the defense contractors—an enormously wealthy group with widespread political ties—and their allies in Congress prevailed and simply killed the board.

During the Reagan administration agencies responsible for protective measures generally became much more friendly to industry and producer points of view. Hostility between agencies and industries was clearly lower in the 1980s than in the 1970s. However, even this pattern was not uniform. For example, the National Highway Traffic Safety Administration received praise from consumer groups and criticism from the automobile industry (*The Wall Street Journal*, April 19, 1985).

Competition and Subsidy in Protective Regulation

Protective regulation is occasionally implemented in such a way that it produces a subsidy. In this case the regulated may well ask for regulation or at least will not oppose it. In other cases protective regulation can be implemented in such a way and at such a time as to give a competitive edge to one set of interests at the expense of a competing set of interests. In these cases the favored regulated interests are likely to press for regulation in the form favorable to them. Several specific examples illustrate these points.

In late 1979 when the Rock Island Railroad was on strike, before it had ceased to exist altogether, the Interstate Commerce Commission ordered a dozen normally competing railroads in the states served by the Rock Island to operate its trains, using its equipment, in order to prevent part of the grain harvest from spoiling (Shifrin, 1979). The Rock Island normally carried about 10 percent to 15 percent of that harvest. This order was not resisted by the other railroads, no doubt because they were guaranteed that they would be repaid for costs *plus* a 6 percent profit.

When the Federal Aviation Administration (FAA) issues rules controlling use of airspace around airports, it is, in effect, making some competitive judgments about commercial aviation interests, especially the scheduled passenger airlines, private aviation, and owners of business planes and other private aircrafts. Since both sets of interests know that the FAA will not go out of existence and that there will not be and should not be unregulated air traffic, they both lobby the agency for regulations favoring the dominance of their own form of air traffic.

In 1979 the Ashland Oil Company used existing federal regulations implemented by the Department of Energy to force rival oil companies to supply it crude oil so that it could refine it and make sizable sums of money (Berry, 1979). It sold its own wells to increase its cash position and keep the stockholders happy with increased dividends, and it stopped research for new oil. By these moves Ashland shucked fixed costs for the upkeep of wells and exploration costs and risks. DOE regulations made it mandatory for other oil companies to supply it with crude oil to keep up its production and market share. Needless to say, Ashland did not object to these profit-producing regulations, whereas its competitors—the other oil companies—were less than thrilled with the regulations that forced them to subsidize a competitor.

Beginning in 1964 a number of international consortia of corporations that included U.S. corporations began explorations in the middle of the Pacific Ocean to determine whether manganese and other metals were present in sufficient quantities to make mining the floor of the ocean profitable (Pincus, 1980). This is an enormously costly form of exploration; actual mining operations would be even more costly. It is believed that exploration itself has probably cost hundreds of millions of dollars and actually beginning production would be so costly that a consortium beginning it should have about $1 billion to invest. When Congress began to consider a law regulating U.S. company participation in such activities so as to preserve the sea floor environment, even though the sea floor is the property of no single country, the companies involved in the exploration joined in supporting the law so that they could prevent new competing companies and consortia involving U.S. corporations from entering exploration.

Deregulation

Deregulation of protective governmental activity is also a priority of those favoring deregulation in general. As Ronald Reagan's transition task forces worked between the election in November 1980 and his inauguration in January 1981 they proposed a number of postponements, reductions, and abandonments of various protective regulatory activities. Once in office the Reagan administration set out both to change the laws establishing federal protective regulatory powers and to change enforcement patterns by making them more producer-friendly. In general, the administration met with failure in their statutory efforts. However, in a large number of areas—extraction of timber and minerals from public lands and air and water pollution come to mind first—the administration achieved many of its goals either through bureaucratic action or, more usually, through nonaction.

The Difficulty of Control

Central administrative control over government regulators and their activity is difficult to achieve for several reasons. At the agency or department level, control is hard to achieve in part because a number of these agencies are relatively young and such agencies are particularly prone to confusion and low levels of performance. At the presidential level the inherent weaknesses of that office for controlling policy implementation in any field are also at work. At both the agency level and at the government-wide level the seemingly inherent complexity of much protective regulation also makes control particularly difficult.

In the late 1970s two agencies that came into being for purposes either wholly or partly regulatory were particularly inept in establishing routines that allowed for timely, predictable, consistent implementation.

The first of these was the Department of Energy. Created in 1977, DOE was an aggregation of some 50 federal offices concerned with various aspects of energy (Mossberg, 1980). Even after departmentalization most of these units kept going in their own direction with little central control. Two major and overlapping regulatory divisions were created by statute in the department. The secretary and his office were unable to gain any kind of effective control over the parts of the agency and, therefore, over policies. To compound problems, about 80 percent of the Department's annual budget of about $10 billion in the late 1970s was not administered by department officials at all but instead was contracted to a variety of governmental and private agencies. Even some proponents of the creation of the new department, just a few years later, were willing to consider scrapping the whole enterprise.

The second agency in a mess was the Consumer Product Safety Commission, established by statute in late 1972 (Curry, 1977; Thomas, 1978). In its attempts to regulate products it was unable to reach decisions that pleased anyone, and in many cases, it seemed unable to reach decisions at all. Some of its problems were compounded because Congress required the commission to contract with outside groups to draft mandatory safety standards. This gave the regulated interests some considerable influence in the process but also delayed results and either invited more disagreement over implementation standards in the end or simply prevented such standards from emerging in any comprehensible form.

Control of regulatory efforts involving several agencies is even harder to establish than control within a single agency. In 1977, for example, President Carter told 75 different federal agencies to develop regulations that would implement the presidential policy of discouraging industrial and commercial development in geographical areas subject to repeated flooding (Duhl, 1979). More than two years later only 15 of the agencies had created such regulations. Thirty seven of the 75 agencies were judged to be most directly affected. Only 12 had published regulations in the 25 months following the president's Executive Order. Thirteen more had begun action aimed at producing regulations, although final action could still take a long time. And the other 12 of the 37 agencies had done nothing at all! One administration official working to get bureaucratic compliance summed up the situation succinctly: "The government is so goddamn unwieldy. It takes forever to get anything done."

Regulated interests also prefer situations in which only one agency has clear authority. In 1982, for example, the Reagan administration sought to remove regulatory authority over transportation of hazardous materials from the federal Department of Transportation and return that authority to the states. The administration sought this change both as a way of cutting the Department of Transportation budget and because, in general, it favored giving more power to the states in a variety of fields. However, those who carry hazardous materials (trucking companies, railroads) and the manufacturers of containers in which they are carried united to lobby for retention of the regulatory power at the federal level. They weren't enthusiastic about the federal regulations or agency, but they preferred dealing with one agency instead of 50.

Differing Patterns of Interaction and Influence

There is no single pattern of relationships linking a regulatory agency with its outside clients and interested parties. Patterns vary between agencies at any given time, and the same agency may well relate to outside forces in different ways at different points in time.

A summary of a number of specific detailed examinations of major regulatory agencies (Wilson, 1980a:chapter 10) concluded that only one of six federal agencies primarily in the protective regulatory business that were examined related consistently to its clientele in a way that suggested it was engaged in the classic subgovernment relationship. This was the Federal Maritime Commission.

In two cases—the Antitrust Division of the Department of Justice and the Federal Trade Commission—no stable pattern of influence over agency behavior seems to be present.

In the remaining three cases—the Food and Drug Administration since the 1950s, the Occupational Health and Safety Administration, and the Environmental Protection Agency—the relationships were stable in the sense that the actors were the same: the agency, the relevant congressional actors, and both a pro-industry group from outside and an anti-industry group from the outside. But, because of the contest implied by the access of the latter two groups, policy emerging through implementation decisions could hardly be characterized as stable or as routinely serving everyone's or anyone's interests. One outcome in such situations may be that policies take a very long time to emerge. In the Food and Drug Administration, for example, as of early 1985 the agency had postponed a decision to ban six artificial colors that caused cancer in laboratory animals for the 26th time in the 25 years since the proposal to create such a ban was first made in 1960.

An agency may be divided in its approaches and loyalties at any given time. Sometimes such divisions pit one part of an agency against others. For example, the enforcement unit in the Securities and Exchange Commission (SEC) became increasingly isolated in its proconsumer stance as the rest of the SEC tried to limit regulation in the late 1970s (Miller, 1979b). Or, to take a very homely example, when that part of the U.S. Department of Agriculture (USDA) responsible for inspecting chicken carcasses allowed a speedup of the dressing line in poultry plants to 70 chickens a minute, the USDA inspectors themselves were opposed—not because they particularly wanted to nail the producers but because they felt it impossible to catch many flaws (bruises, diseases, contamination) at such speeds (Sawyer, 1979a). Agency managers were trying to be responsive to industry requests that would make their business more profitable; line inspectors viewed the matter quite differently.

Congressional Intervention

Congressional interventions on a reasonably frequent basis seem almost inevitable in the protective regulatory arena. By definition, government is coming in contact with constituents, either individuals or groups, and restricting allowable activity. Restricted interests are not shy about appealing to members of Congress, and members, ever alert for political ramifications, are unlikely to ignore the appeals. Thus members often appear, sometimes unexpectedly, as participants in the implementation decision process.

THE DYNAMICS OF PROTECTIVE REGULATORY IMPLEMENTATION: FOUR CASES

The Office of Surface Mining and Strip Mining

The implementation of strip-mining legislation is a good example of how controversial and jerky implementation in the protective regulatory area can be. In its very short life, the Office of Surface Mining in the Department of the Interior has undergone major alterations in direction and emphasis of implementing activities. The courts have played a central role in shaping the content of the agency's actions. The shifts have occurred because there is a multiplicity of actors trying to define the nature of federal enforcement in a decentralized implementation setting, while at the same time the national government has responsibility for setting goals and standards of performance and ensuring that states comply with them.

Getting started: what did the law say? The Surface Mining Control and Reclamation Act was the first federal law to require that strip-mined land be restored to its original premined contours through mandatory reclamation by strip-mine operators. The law aimed to prevent unnecessary degradation of land and water resources through mudslides, erosion, and water pollution, which are the traditional aftermath of strip mining. Prior to the 1977 law, state efforts at regulation and reclamation had been ineffective or nonexistent. State legislatures were frequently in thrall to powerful state mining lobbies, and not interested in restricting them.

Under the new law, states were required to develop programs for controlling strip mining and reclamation in accord with stringent and detailed federal standards specified by the Office of Surface Mining (OSM), the federal agency charged with implementation responsibility. The new law and subsequent regulations written by OSM were very detailed, and described every step of the process from applying for permits to planting vegetation on recontoured hillsides. Following OSM approval of the state program, direct implementation responsibility would be turned over to the states, and OSM would retain an oversight and monitoring role. To spur timely state participation, OSM would allocate grants for reclamation to states with approved programs;

funds would come from a new trust fund financed by fines and appropriations.

The evolution of the 1977 statute was both contentious and drawn out; the bill was twice vetoed by President Ford, and the legislative debate dragged on for six years. The controversy continued when implementation of the law began: coal companies and state officials fought environmentalists, citizen groups, and zealous federal inspectors. Representative John Seiberling (D-Ohio), one of the sponsors of the bill, noted in mid-1982 that OSM was destined to become a battlefield: "There was a tremendous amount of bitterness on both sides (after the bill was signed)....It's a good thing we have several hundred years supply of coal. Nobody can wreck it all at once." (Quoted in the *Washington Post*, June 6, 1982).

The new program was undoubtedly harsh medicine for the newly regulated interests to swallow. As journalist Dale Russakoff observed, the new law "did to the coal states what the Civil Rights Act in its early years did to the South. It declared that the states had failed to protect their citizens, in this case from the ravages of strip mining. And it yanked away local control, in this case over the coal fields, until state laws were brought up to federal standards." (*Washington Post*, June 7, 1982).

The setting for implementation. Several contextual features were important in affecting the implementation of the strip-mining act. First, an enormous amount of hostility was generated during formulation and this carried over into implementation. The final bill was a diluted form of the original proposals, but the compromises did not placate opponents of regulation.

Second, perceptions were changing about public opinion concerning the relative balance of priorities among a clean environment, energy needs, and employment needs as the national economy slumped.

Third, the Reagan administration unabashedly stressed state control, a diminished federal role, deregulation, and unshackling the productivity of the private sector. Nowhere was this philosophical point of view embraced with greater ardor than in the Department of the Interior under Secretary James Watt. This represented a major change from Carter administration policies.

(After Watt resigned in 1983, emphasis changed again to a more moderate position reactivating a federal role.)

Fourth, all across the department, emphases shifted to accommodate Secretary Watt's priorities and concept of stewardship. The traditional proconservation stance of the department was replaced by favorable attitudes toward development and resource extraction.

Fifth, any new agency administering a new law is bound to find itself struggling to get organized. The Office of Surface Mining, in addition to dealing with the ordinary complications of trying to set up a new agency and administering a controversial new law, also found itself embroiled in controversy practically from its first day in business.

Finally, a wide array of actors were involved in implementing the law at various levels of government, complicating the already technically complex program area. At the federal level, the major actors were bureaucrats and political appointees in the Department of the Interior (including the office of the secretary, the solicitor general's office, and OSM), judges in the federal court system, lawyers in the Department of Justice, and various congressional committees that engaged in oversight. State and local level actors included state bureaucrats and governors' staffs, coal companies, utilities dependent on coal, and a diverse collection of environmental and citizen groups. All of the state and local groups made frequent use of the courts to argue their points of view.

Implementation activities: 1977 through 1980. OSM's activity in its early years was marked by conflict and delay. Created in August of 1977, the agency received no operating funds for seven months. Hiring managers and inspectors was set back and opening field offices was postponed. Nonetheless, by September 1978 over 100 inspectors were on board and over 800 inspections of mines had been completed.

The major focus of OSM's implementation activity was on translating the language of the statute into specific rules and regulations. From the outset, the regulations were highly controversial, sparking continual skirmishes in and out of courts from 1977 through 1984. At every turn the rules were attacked by opponents and defended by proponents. Coal companies were fighting to save the money that reclamation would cost. Governors and state officials in the two dozen coal states were fighting for the intangible issue of states' rights and to save jobs that were perceived to be threatened by increased cost of operations. Environmentalists challenged what they perceived to be weak enforcement.

Court cases dragged on and on. Cases filed by companies opposed to the interim regulations that governed the agency during the initial transition period were decided in favor of the government, but cases challenging the constitutionality of the law were decided at the district court level in favor of the challengers. It took until June 1981 for the Supreme Court to rule on the constitutionality of the law. The decision was unanimously in favor of the law. In the context of uncertainty created by shifting court opinions, coal companies could not make rational economic decisions about investment and operations.

In March 1979 the agency published the final version of the rules for the states to use to prepare their own programs. Because the rules were two months late, and followed a long period of public hearings and some dispute with the Council of Economic Advisers over the economic impacts of the rules, states were given until August to submit their plans. State programs were to be operational in June 1980.

OSM was tough in reviewing and approving the program plans developed by states, and the rate of plan approval was slow. By November 1980, only three states had won unconditional approval, and another one had been conditionally accepted (*Washington Post*, Nov. 24 1980). The target date for state implementation was pushed back to early 1981.

OSM staff worked energetically in the field during the initial years to inspect mines and issue Notices of Violations (NOVs) and Cessation Orders (COs). Aggregate statistics on inspections, NOVs, and COs showed a big increase between 1979 and 1980 as the agency was gathering steam and a big drop between 1980 and 1981 as the Watt team took over. Table 6–1 summarizes these specific enforcement actions.

Implementation activities: 1981 through 1984. At a staff briefing during his first month in office, Secretary Watt promised he would be making changes in the policies and operations of

TABLE 6-1 DSM Enforcement Actions, 1979–1981 (Totals for United States)

	1979	1980	1981
Inspections	20,306	34,987	27,070
Notices of violations	4,461	6,924	2,368
Cessation orders	815	1,627	594

SOURCE: Adapted from data presented in Menzel (1983:416).

OSM. He encouraged staff who were not comfortable with his new stance to "seek other opportunities" (*The Wall Street Journal,* January 30, 1981).

Watt delivered on his promise. Although he was never publicly disloyal to the Surface Mining Control and Reclamation Act (SMCRA) directly—and, in fact, verbally supported it—his commitment to enforcement was doubtful from the start, since at the time of his appointment as secretary he was party to a lawsuit challenging the law, as were the men he named as director and deputy director of OSM.

Watt set the tone for all of OSM. Recruiting individuals who shared the administration's views on deregulation and decentralization was an important first step. A reorganization plan for transforming OSM from the lead implementer to an overseer of state implementation was quickly drafted. Even supporters of SMCRA did not doubt that such a transformation was envisioned in the original legislation. But both the timing and the extent of the reorganization could be questioned, and were, during a hearing before Congressman Morris Udall's subcommittee on Energy and Environment of the House Interior and Insular Affairs Committee. Udall (D-Ariz.) had been the primary sponsor of SMCRA. Although skeptical of Watt, Udall's committee was persuaded that the reorganization was a necessary part of federal implementation, that the federal role was due to shift to a watchdog role as states took over direct implementation, and that the transition was already under way as planning for a reorganization had already begun during the Carter administration (see Menzel, 1983:413).

Staff cutbacks followed as units (especially for inspection) were reduced and regional offices were dismantled. The authorized staff level dropped from over 1,000 to 650. Holdover staff perceived to be overly zealous enforcers were transferred to other jobs. By mid-1982 only one of the 50 Carter managers had held on; staff morale and expertise, especially in the highly technical and legal areas, plummeted (*Washington Post*, June 6, 1982).

The flurry of revisionist activity continued as OSM enthusiastically adopted the president's Executive Order of February 19, 1981, stating that burdensome and counterproductive government regulations should be rewritten or eliminated. The vast tome of SMCRA regulations, developed with such difficulty over the preceding three years, was extensively rewritten, changing the rules for strip-mining enforcement in midstream and significantly relaxing stringent regulations. States' regulations were permitted as long as they were judged to be "as effective as" the federal rules, no longer "as stringent as" the federal rules. OSM shifted from specifying requirements for how a state was to get to a particular goal (e.g., by detailing how a sedimentation pond should be built) to a results-oriented test (does the pond hold the runoff?). As in the development of the original regulations, these rewritten rules were immediately subjected to a spate of lawsuits, most of which were filed by horrified environmentalists.

The final mark of change in implementation under Watt was the reduction of effort in enforcement. Table 6–1 showed how the issuance of violation notices and cessation orders dropped off in 1981. Other activities also declined as OSM trimmed its sails. Notification of penalty assessments (the communication to the violator that a fine was to be paid) dropped to a trickle. Actual collection of penalties owed to the Treasury, estimated at about $150 million, ground to a virtual standstill.

Resolving a 1981 suit brought by environmental groups, Federal District Court Judge Barrington Parker ordered the Department of the Interior to assess and collect civil penalties against violators. Testimony in the case disclosed an accumulated backlog of 1,700 cessation orders that were unenforced, unserved, and uncollected.

The pace of agency compliance with the court order was excruciatingly slow, as few staff were assigned to the special task force created to deal with the court order. During hearings before the House Government Operations Committee in June 1984, Congressman Robert E. Wise (D-W.Va.) expressed his frustration to agency officials: "...you have been working on this for a year and a half. A hundred and fifty cases means less than 10 a month. We are probably going to be into the year 2000 before we get this thing finished." Immediately after the congressional inquiry OSM added 20 part-time staff and the pace of case review increased dramatically.

Spurred by complaints about the lack of enforcement and the controversy surrounding regulations, the House Government Operations Committee began an investigation of OSM activities in assessing and collecting fines for strip-mining violations. The 49-page report (*House Report 98-1146,* October 5, 1984) from the eight-month investigation is packed with examples of confusion, mismanagement, incompetence, and occasional deception. The committee concluded that OSM had "failed miserably" to carry out its responsibilities for collecting penalties and implementation of other enforcement provisions of the law:

> The process for the assessment and collection of civil penalties is, at best, lengthy. It is made even more cumbersome by inordinate administrative delays. The systems developed by OSM to assist in its collection efforts are ineffective and inefficient. These problems, coupled with the lack of priority attention within OSM, have resulted in the growth of a debt from unpaid civil penalties which is large, stale, and in many cases uncollectible.
>
> The Office of Surface Mining has made virtually no use of other enforcement authorities contained in the Act. When it has, it has frequently waited too long to pursue such remedies, thereby losing the opportunity to get operators to correct violations while they are still in business.
>
> The Committee further concludes that many of the problems are the result of the Department's failure to plan properly for carrying out its responsibilities under the Act. This is due either to the lack of a full understanding, or a conscious disregard, of the requirements of the statute.

Two court cases were concluded in October of 1984, that, together with the severe reprimand from the oversight committee, may signal a new start for implementation at OSM. The first case resolved a suit brought by a coalition of seven environmental groups against OSM for relaxing the regulations. The judge ordered that scores of regulatory decisions made during the Watt era must be reversed as they were too weak and not consistent with the intent of Congress (*New York Times,* October 7, 1984).

In a second major settlement, resolved out of court after five years of litigation, the new Secretary of the Interior, William Clark, admitted that OSM had failed to enforce the law. Openly departing from Watts' policies, Secretary Clark promised to pay more attention to enforcement and agreed that the plaintiffs (Save Our Mountains and the Council of Southern Mountains) should have an unprecedented role as external watchdogs with access to future implementation activities in OSM (*New York Times*, October 14, 1984). The new head of OSM, *John D. Ward,* a former Colorado coal executive, reinforced his boss's attitudes: "There are some things in it [the law] that are pretty onerous. But for the most part, these are things that had to be done anyway. We decided that there must be other things in life than lawsuits." (Quoted in *the New York Times*, October 14, 1984).

Maybe Mr. Ward's optimism will prevail and some measure of calm will descend on OSM for the first time. That is possible, but unlikely, given its tumultuous history. In fact, Ward resigned in April, 1985, and was replaced by *Jed Christiansen,* the fourth OSM Director in 13 months. In late May, 1985, Representative Udall said "the problems are getting worse, not better.... The entire strip-mine program...is in trouble" (*Washington Post,* May 28, 1985). Neither the coal industry nor environmental groups will relinquish the judicial forum as a means for arguing with the government. It is also possible, but also unlikely, that the turmoil within OSM will subside as new staff are hired and enforcement is redefined again in the regulations. This saga will continue to unfold. Because the stakes are so large—millions of dollars for reclamation versus despoiled landscapes—neither side will support quiet, routine implementation.

The Federal Maritime Commission and Shipping Regulation

After the passage of the *Sherman Antitrust Act* in 1890 shipping companies had routinely continued practices that violated that law by meeting to fix prices. Congress by 1916 accepted this practice but concluded it needed to be regulated to prevent abuses. To do so in the field of maritime shipping, Congress in 1916 passed an act that created the *Shipping Board* and gave it the charge of regulating U.S. cargo shippers engaged in foreign trade from U.S. ports or between U.S. ports in the 48 states and American possessions overseas, such as Alaska, Hawaii, Guam, and Puerto Rico. After numerous name changes over the years the Federal Maritime Commission (so named in 1961) inherited this charge. (See Mansfield, 1980, from which the following discussion is drawn.)

The principal tools given to the FMC to regulate the cost of shipping—with the intent of protecting shippers from unfair discrimination and overly high prices—are the power to approve or disapprove price-fixing agreements made between groups of shipping companies and the power to reject rate tariffs (schedules) that are judged to be discriminatory against different classes of shippers.

In the following discussion we will focus on two questions about the performance of the FMC in the 1960s and 1970s: how did the FMC implement its protective regulatory mandate, and why did it behave the way it did?

FMC implementation activities. Every carrier and every conference of carriers is required to file a statement of rates (a tariff) with the FMC. The statute was amended in 1961 to give the FMC the power to disapprove any rate that it "finds to be so unreasonably low or high as to be detrimental to the commerce of the United States."

What does the FMC do with this power? Virtually nothing. The agency rejects only about 1 percent of the total pages of statements of tariffs filed. Almost all of those rejections are for short periods of time and occur because of matters of procedure or form (width of margins, for example!), not because of substance.

Nor does the FMC do anything about rates informally. If shippers appeal to the commission for relief from rates charged by carriers that they consider to be unfairly high, the commission, in effect, tells them to negotiate directly with the shipping company and that the FMC really cannot do anything.

In the area of rates, then, the FMC generates lots of paperwork for itself and from the carriers, but the paperwork is meaningless and is examined for form, not for content. The content of the tariffs is not examined and, in fact, in some cases appears not to meet the statutory requirements for specificity. Tariffs are filed in such a way that they ratify the discounts given to large shippers by carriers and higher rates for smaller shippers.

So much for tariffs: the FMC is feckless and simply ratifies the power of the carriers and shipping companies to do about what they want to do. The second area of presumed FMC power is over conference agreements. Again the statutory language gives broad discretion and simultaneously provides no standards for implementation. The FMC must disapprove any agreements reached by such conferences if they are "unjustly discriminatory or unfair as between carriers, shippers, exporters, importers, or ports, or between exporters from the United States and their foreign competitors," if they work "to the detriment of the commerce of the United States," or if they are "contrary to the public interest." When agreements are filed for FMC review they must include a statement of justification. However, FMC staff members have no idea about what standards they should use in evaluating such statements. Thus once again, no substantive scrutiny is offered. A paperwork requirement is enforced, thus keeping the carriers happy and protecting some 300 staff jobs in the FMC.

The political context. Substantively, then, the FMC has virtually no impact. The carriers rule the world of rates and agreements. Shippers that are large can negotiate favorable treatment for themselves directly with the carriers. Shippers that are small are out of luck. What is the political setting for this protective regulatory agency and activity? What forces—both present and absent—seem to have created this situation? At least six factors play a part.

First, the personnel of the commission—especially the commissioners themselves—are none too swift. Interviewees, in talking about commission members, used words such as *semistupid* (that was praise!), *ignoramus, crook, human dregs*, and *not playing with a full deck*. The moribund nature of the commission has, no doubt, helped attract such sterling public servants over the years.

Second, the statutes are so vaguely worded that there is no mandate to do anything specific. Given weak personnel the agency is unlikely to use the vagueness to expand its activities. Rather it will use the vagueness to justify inactivity beyond paper shuffling.

Third, the large carriers and shipping companies are dominant. Since the FMC has defined its role as reactive, and since no one is pushing it to be active, it reacts most often to the large carriers. One measure of the pressures on the FMC from its clients, both beneficiaries and restricted clients, is that about 30 law firms represent the carriers but only one represents shippers.

Fourth, shippers do not approach the commission very often for relief. The large shippers have enough economic power to get what they want—discriminatorily favorable rates—directly from the carriers. The small shippers do not protest either, both because they cannot afford Washington representation and because they are in competition with each other and any success that one of them had at the FMC would be automatically granted to their competitors too. Also, a number of shippers immediately give their goods to a freight forwarder, who gets his fee as a flat percentage of the ocean freight rate. That forwarder obviously has no incentive to appeal for lower rates.

Fifth, Congress—despite occasional hearings revealing the swamp described above—really has no interest in the FMC. The small shippers are not interests important to the relevant committees. Congressional committees are instead responsive to the large carriers and carrier associations, the large shippers, and the maritime unions, whose members benefit from carriers making lots of money that can then be translated into increased wages at bargaining time.

Sixth, the central part of the executive branch—the president, his appointees, and the Office of Management and Budget—does not care much about the FMC either. The OMB regularly prevents any legislative proposals from the FMC from going forward.

The FMC does not represent a case in which a clientele (the large carriers) have captured the regulatory agency (the FMC) in any direct sense. Rather, both economic and political forces are lined up so that an inept agency can simply be ignored as it shuffles its papers and measures the margins, while carriers and shippers conduct business on their own terms without regulatory intrusion.

The Federal Trade Commission and Antitrust Activity

Congress created the Federal Trade Commission (FTC) in 1914 and gave it broad powers and responsibilities in both the antitrust and trade regulation areas. These have been summarized succinctly by Katzmann (1980b:154–55).

Among its many antitrust responsibilities, derived principally from the Federal Trade Commission Act and the Clayton Act, the FTC is charged with preventing unfair methods of competition and unfair or deceptive acts or practices in or affecting commerce, and with forestalling mergers or acquisitions that might substantially lessen competition or tend to create a monopoly. Moreover, the commission is to prevent unscrupulous buyers from using their economic power to exact discriminatory prices from suppliers to the disadvantage of less powerful buyers and is to prohibit suppliers from securing an unfair advantage over their competitors by discriminating among buyers. To these various ends, the FTC conducts investigations of alleged violations of the antitrust acts, monitors the implementation of antitrust decrees, investigates the organization, business, conduct, practices, and management of corporations engaged in commerce (except where statutorily exempted), and makes reports and recommendations to Congress.

The FTC has broad powers to fashion appropriate relief if the laws have been violated. The commission may issue a cease-and-desist order prohibiting the continuation of acts judged illegal. It may seek to restore competitive conditions by mandating relief that attacks structural imperfections in the market. For example, the agency can order respondents to dispose of illegally acquired companies or make trademarks, patents, trade secrets, or expertise available to competitors at reasonable royalties—or even without royalties.

Unlike the moribund FMC, the FTC has often been an active regulatory agency. As such, it has also usually been controversial and at the center of pulling and hauling by various interests with different preferred outcomes. In that respect it is like OSM. In the period between 1970 and 1985 it went through several distinct phases. From 1970 until about 1976 it reacted mainly to pressures from within the agency. After 1976 some externally aggressive actions brought intensified negative pressure—particularly on Congress—from a number of different segments of business. Even some moderation of aggressiveness during the Reagan administration did not reduce the controversy over the FTC (although more claims began to be heard that the FTC was not vigilant enough in policing businesses). Authorization legislation for the agency expired in 1982 (although the agency was kept alive by continuing resolutions) and, as of mid-1985, Congress had proved incapable or unwilling to pass new reauthorization legislation. The agency began to focus on individual violations rather than entire industries. This outraged consumer groups but may mollify congressional critics (*The Wall Street Journal*, July 3, 1985).

The sections that follow focus, first, on the period from 1970 through 1976 and, second, on the period after 1977.

1970–1976: FTC balancing in case selection. The most important part of the FTC's implementation activities comes at the point of selecting the cases it chooses to pursue (see Katzmann, 1980a:chapters 9 and 10; and Katzmann, 1980b). These choices both specify the companies or groups of companies to be investigated and, at the same time, determine whether the FTC will pursue a large-scale, structural case against an entire industry, or at least the largest companies in it, or an individual case of alleged illegal conduct on the part of a single firm, perhaps a small one.

The two major bureaus in the FTC—the Bureau of Competition, which is dominated by lawyers, and the Bureau of Economics, which is dominated by economists, each have their favorite kind of case. The former bureau likes cases of misconduct because they are relatively easy and result in trial experience, a major value for the lawyers in the agency, most of whom expect to move on to other jobs and are at the FTC to gain certain kinds of experience, including trial experience.

The economists in the Bureau of Economics, on the other hand, favor the structural cases in which they think the benefits to large classes of consumers will be greater. These individuals are often looking for a career in government, perhaps in the FTC itself, and so they want an active agency and do not mind if some cases take many years to resolve because of their size, legal complexity, and the resourcefulness of the powerful companies and combinations of companies being investigated. The FTC's activities in relation to cereal manufacturers and food cooperatives are examples of structural cases.

Between 1970 and 1976 the FTC pursued both kinds of cases with some balance. In 1970–76 the economists and lawyers in the FTC competed for the attention and favor of the five commissioners, especially the chairperson, who has considerable influence on the general direction the agency takes. In those years the commissioners endorsed a balanced range of activity, with some structural efforts and a large number of specific misconduct investigations. After 1977—when a new chairman was appointed for the commission—more of the highly visible structural cases were undertaken.

This relatively low-profile strategy on the part of the FTC in 1970-76 helped produce a relatively benign and nonthreatening political climate for its labors. When it began to change directions in 1977 its political visibility and its problems dramatically increased.

In the first part of the 1970s, however, potentially hostile overseers of agency behavior remained quiescent. The central part of the executive branch (the president, White House Office, and Office of Management and Budget) did not involve itself very heavily in the selection process for commissioners, except perhaps for the chair. The FTC budget goes through the Office of Management and Budget, but OMB did not use the occasion to seek any influence over agency behavior with regard to selection of cases or anything else of any importance.

Congress also behaved quite passively toward the FTC during this period. Nominations for commissionerships were routinely approved. The appropriations committees did not use their powers to influence the caseload in the first part of the decade, although this influence became very visible and critical in the second part. Nor did individuals or committees in Congress seem to be heavily involved in a routine way in either stopping proposed investigations or generating them.

Interest groups—both so-called public interest and consumer groups on the one hand and business groups on the other—did not have much impact on case selection. The processes of the commission denied them much direct access, and they did not spend a lot of resources trying to gain access to the commission through Congress, a favorite and often effective way of getting to aloof agencies.

In short, the FTC during this period was not captured by industry, but it was not perceived to be threatening enough to businesses to motivate them to build anti-FTC coalitions. The competing needs of the economists and lawyers on the FTC staff were the main determinants of caseload and selection of individual cases. The result was a politically and economically balanced program of activity, which neither satisfied any one set of interests nor appeared to any powerful interests to constitute an intolerable threat.

The FTC after 1977. The relatively quiet period of the early 1970s came to an abrupt halt after the appointment of a new and aggressive chairman in 1977. The new management began a more ambitious program of both regulation-writing and structural investigations. This activity generated increased hostility from the business community, which then made effective appeals to Congress attacking both individual case selections and the general powers of the FTC. Congress, in turn, by 1980 put some brakes on the FTC and gave clear signals that it did not want such vigor in pursuit of freer competition (for good reviews of some aspects of these years see Gellhorn, 1980, and Singer, 1979b).

The culmination of the congressional attack on the FTC came in the spring of 1980 (see Sarasohn, 1980a, 1980b, 1980c, and 1980d). For four years the agency had been without authorization and, therefore, without regular appropriations from Congress. Business lobbyists increased their anti-FTC activities to push against specific FTC actions (such as an antitrust suit against the citrus cooperative, Sunkist, and proposed rules for the funeral industry), to push for tight and frequent congressional checks on FTC activities; and—in some cases—simply to push for the demise of the agency.

The controversy came to a head as conferees labored on an authorization bill in early 1980. President Carter personally met with the conferees to try to mute the most restrictive provisions of the bill and to indicate what he would and would not veto. In the turmoil over authorization and temporary funding the FTC was forced to close its doors for three days (May 1 and June 2–3), a symbolic slap by Congress. The president's intervention worked in the sense that the most stringent limits were softened and a resolution was finally reached.

But, as a result of the new legislation, future implementation activities faced a different political context. A much larger formal role for Congress was added and, by inference, the regulated interests with access to Congress also had obtained a larger role. The most important of the numerous new limits facing the FTC was the insertion of a two-house legislative veto of agency regulations that excluded a role for the president. Any final rule proposed by the FTC would become effective in 90 days unless both houses adopted a resolution disapproving it. This was the first insertion of legislative veto provisions for an independent regulatory agency without the requirement that the president approve the veto too. In its first use of the new power, the House voted 286 to 133 in May 1982, to disapprove a proposed FTC rule requiring used-car dealers to disclose information about defects in the vehicles they were selling. Even the coming of the Reagan administration and

Reagan appointees to the FTC did little to enhance the status of the agency with Congress or a whole variety of interest groups.

The Environmental Protection Agency: Clean Air and Water Implementation

In 1970 Congress approved President Nixon's creation of the Environmental Protection Agency as a result of perceptions of growing threats to the environment. The new agency inherited 15 programs that had previously been scattered in five different locations in the federal executive branch. The history of the EPA in the 1970s as it sought to implement its various programs is one in which the agency was constantly under pressure from a number of different sides. The two most active coalitions were the pro-industry side, which is leery about controls, and the pro-environmentalist side, which is leery about industry capturing the agency. These outside pressures resulted in some statutory changes and some changes in the attitudes within the agency. But these changes did not result in a clearcut victory for any of the forces contending for the soul of the EPA. It remained an agency under close scrutiny and heavy pressure that almost surely will always be in that position given the costly and controversial nature of its mandates. But it also remained an agency willing to innovate when given the latitude to do so by Congress and the president.

To keep our task manageable, we will focus only on EPA activities in the area of air and water pollution, even though it is engaged in many additional fields. We will also focus on two phases in the EPA's brief history: 1970–76, when it was engaged in applying legislative goals and timetables, and from 1976–77 to the end of the Carter administration, a period when it began to incorporate some economic incentives in its implementation and enforcement activities. (The story of the EPA in the 1970s told here in brief form is based on Marcus, 1980; Clark, 1979b, and Navarro, 1980). The early Reagan years certainly put the EPA in the spotlight as a center of political controversy, but although the stories from that period are interesting, general lessons for implementation are scarce.

The 1970–1976 experience. In the Clean Air Act of 1970 and the Federal Water Pollution Control Act of 1972, Congress established standards for clean air and water and directed the EPA to order polluters to clean up their acts so that pollution standards could be met by fixed calendar deadlines. The deadlines were short, and the instructions were quite explicit.

The EPA set out to achieve what Congress told them it must achieve. However, it was clear that despite the presence of the "thou shalt create clean air and water in five years" mandate in the statutes and despite the EPA's sincere activity, results were slow to emerge and did not fit expectations. At least five major roadblocks appeared in the real world of implementation: economic feasibility, technical feasibility, administrative feasibility, political feasibility, and legal intervention.

1. *Economic feasibility*. Strict pollution control is very expensive. For example, EPA is estimated to have generated costs of over $15 billion in 1978. When the costs of water and air pollution legislation, especially the latter, were calculated assuming the law was literally applied on the timetable specified in the 1970 and 1972 acts, three different administrations (Nixon, Ford, and Carter) all sought to put some restraints on the EPA in terms of requiring the agency to assess economic feasibility in their implementation decisions. The result of these interventions was, of course, that literal implementation of the statutory language was diluted and/or delayed.

2. *Technological feasibility*. Simply saying that pollution should be controlled does not generate the technology to do so in some practicable and timely manner. Inevitably, delays in technological advances and some technology that was dubiously effective put crimps in EPA timetables, and delayed and diluted timetables.

3. *Administrative feasibility*. The statute writers in 1970 and 1972 did not realize how complicated the information-gathering and evaluation tasks would be in connection with EPA activities. Guidelines and standards had to be based on information and yet most of that information did not exist except in widely disaggregated and geographically scattered form.

4. *Political feasibility*. Several dimensions of political problems intruded on EPA implementation activities. First, some activities stirred ire and opposition from local politicians and their congressional allies. This opposition was stimulated by negative local public reactions to some EPA proposals. For example, the EPA's plan for air pollution control in Los Angeles required gasoline rationing in order to restrict car usage and resultant pollution. Needless to say, the Angelenos were horrified by the

prospect of restricted auto usage and threw a number of fits and prevented any action along these lines. The EPA's plan for New York City included proposals for higher bridge tolls to reduce the number of cars entering the city and a prohibition on taxis' cruising the streets looking for fares. City officials were unwilling to take the necessary steps to undertake either action.

In short, even a federal agency as centralized as EPA needs cooperation from local officials because those officials must become implementers if actions are to be undertaken in some areas, and EPA needs at least some public neutrality rather than public outrage.

A second dimension of political feasibility involved the constant pressures and activities emanating from two major clusters of interest groups—those from industry seeking delay and reduction of regulation and those from environmental groups seeking application of deadlines and aggressive agency activity. During the writing of the 1970 and 1972 statutes the environmentalists' interests were more strongly endorsed than those of the regulated industries. However, during implementation in the 1970–76 period the balance began to shift, and by the time of the 1977 amendments to the Clean Air Act, industries got a considerable portion of what they wanted.

In the lobbying during the implementation process before 1977 industry was particularly eager to get various deadlines and specific goals dropped or amended in a more lenient fashion.

Regional politics also got involved in the struggle among groups. An unholy alliance of industrial interests located in the East, coal producing interests in the East, and environmentalists joined to oppose what they perceived to be the advantage given to the relatively cleaner western states by the 1970 legislation and the interpretation of it during implementation. Thus they pushed EPA and Congress toward a series of measures that would equalize, in their view, the situation with regard to eastern and western interests. They wanted to allow more eastern pollution in the name of protecting jobs but come down hard on any new pollution in the West. EPA officials were willing to talk explicitly about trade-offs in assessing pollution versus alleged loss of jobs if pollution controls were strictly implemented. (For one such example involving a high-sulfur coal plant in Ohio—a notoriously dirty state among coal-burning areas—see the *New York Times*, October 18, 1979.)

5. *Legal intervention.* Those opposed to EPA activities had money to hire good lawyers and they did so. In the timeless tradition of American lawyers they undertook a series of legal maneuvers that dramatically slowed down implementation. For example, water pollution permits were contested by over 2,000 companies, and each of those contested permits required an adjudicatory proceeding in which an EPA lawyer had to show up to do battle with the lawyers for the companies. At the same time the companies brought over 150 lawsuits against the general guidelines for allowable effluents into water. All of this took time. A particularly large case involving the Du Pont Company, and the definition of a requirement that the "best practicable technology" available be used took five years from the time the case was started until the Supreme Court issued a final ruling.

Redirection: 1976–1980. Beginning in the mid-1970s, as the national economy slumped, both the Ford and Carter administrations began pushing EPA to be more flexible. They wanted EPA to look favorably at the industry side of disputes more frequently and to worry more about costs to industry that were presumed to be damping economic growth. Congress also added its voice on the side of the industries with a number of specific provisions in the 1977 Clean Air Act amendments.

EPA responded formally by recognizing the limits it could not avoid that were clearly set out in the new provisions of the law and informally by becoming more solicitous of industry interests. It also responded by experimenting with different ways of looking at pollution control, especially in terms of market incentives and disincentives. Thus, for example:

Some plants were assessed on the basis of the *total* pollution they emitted rather than on a source-by-source basis. The plant managers could make the best economic trade-offs for their own companies.

Some plants were allowed to open with a certain level of pollution if they were willing to close down or restrict neighboring facilities of their own.

Some plants were allowed to open relatively dirty operations if they bought and closed or restricted neighboring plants owned by someone else. Some of those neighboring plants were in a totally different business.

Some plants were allowed to open dirty operations if other industries in the vicinity willingly offset the new pollution by reducing their own level of pollution.

In short, EPA was responding to some of the new realities surrounding the implementation of the laws governing its life by experimenting with new concepts. The command and control mode of proceeding had produced some genuine improvement in some environmental areas but it had also produced political opposition that would not tolerate continued unadulterated command and control stances replete with firm timetable, and unbending standards.

SUMMARY AND CONCLUSIONS

1. Protective regulatory implementation is inherently volatile. It is controversial, and it is highly visible both to those who feel cramped by it and to consumer and environmental groups that also view themselves as guardians of zealous implementation. The volatility is evidenced by shifting alliances, bursts of vigorous activity on the part of various actors followed by relative calm, and shifting policies at the level of statutes and regulations.

2. Routines are hard to establish in implementation in this field because of the volatility and controversial nature of what is being implemented. When routines do appear there are almost always constant pressures to alter them. The only exceptions to this generalization are examples like the Federal Maritime Commission—a backwater that no one cares much about that is allowed to slumber without making a dent on involved interests.

3. Deregulation has a different meaning in the area of protective regulation compared to competitive regulation. The natural alternative to competitive regulation of entry is a fairly straightforward reliance on market forces and economic incentives and disincentives presumably generated by those forces. But in the protective regulatory area some use of economic incentives and disincentives is only one option. Politically, deregulation in protective areas usually means the triumph, at least partially and perhaps temporarily, of the regulated interests over those they consider their antagonists. Thus business groups hostile to the Federal Trade Commission can view some of the provisions of

the 1980 statute as deregulatory, although the ultimate form of deregulation, killing the agency, did not occur.

4. Congress seems likely to be involved in this area of policy implementation. Its role will be sporadic, but some bursts of activity will surely be intense and relatively long-lasting. The stakes in implementation in the protective regulatory area are large enough to excite that kind of congressional attention.

5. The protective regulatory area is also one that seems to have relatively high potential for attracting personal presidential attention to implementation questions on a sporadic basis. This is probably, as with Congress, a result of controversy and the political power of the interests that get involved and agitated.

6. Implementers—in the form of federal bureaucrats in the regulatory agencies—must be directly involved in implementation efforts if implementation is to succeed. But this involvement in details and enforcement on the part of the implementers helps create and magnify pressures on the agency to cut back its efforts and to reshape them in a more reasonable (that is, less threatening) direction. At the same time, pro-enforcement forces push in the opposite direction. Like the Gilbert and Sullivan policeman, the lot of the protective regulatory implementer is, no doubt, not a happy one.

CHAPTER 7

The Implementation of Redistributive Programs

REDISTRIBUTIVE PROGRAMS AND POLICIES: INTRODUCTORY CONSIDERATIONS

Redistributive policy implementation is an area characterized by a high degree of conflict and disagreement, by a proliferation of specific programs professing redistributive aims, by somewhat restricted, although far from absent, congressional involvement, and by a very high degree of state and local involvement. Redistributive policy often has aspects of protective regulation mingled with it; almost always there are a number of pressures working to transform it into distributive policy. This introductory section will elaborate on these characteristics. The remainder of the chapter will examine four substantive areas of redistributive policy and discuss the implementation of specific programs to achieve broad goals in each area: economic development, employment and training, education, and equal rights. All of these programs are targeted for people identified as having special disadvantages and therefore in need of redistribution in their favor.

Conflict

There is a high degree of conflict over the formulation and legitimation of redistributive policy (see, for example, Ripley and Franklin, 1984:chapter 6), and that controversy carries over into implementation processes.

The reason for the conflict-prone nature of this policy area is reasonably simple: the policy involves either the reality or at least the appearance of transferring (that is, redistributing) something of value from one group of people to some other group of people. Politically, not all transfers are seen as redistributive, however. Only redistribution from relatively well-off groups to relatively less well-off groups excites much political debate during implementation. Thus we use *redistribution* only in the politically meaningful sense of rich to poor.

Conflict in the realm of redistribution has at least two results. First, it makes smooth implementation extremely difficult to achieve. Second, it puts pressures on the involved politicians and bureaucrats to shift the program away from strict redistribution to the less well-off and to make it a program that serves a broader clientele or one that, in effect, becomes distributive. Such changes offer advantages for many groups, including those who are politically more influential and for whom, therefore, help is less controversial.

Many Programs

The War on Poverty, created legislatively by the Equal Opportunity Act of 1964, was typical of redistributive efforts in that it contained many specific programs all aimed loosely at the same end. There were, among others, a community action program that aimed at increasing the participation of the poor in creating local efforts to fight local poverty; a Head Start program that involved preschool training for disadvantaged children; a Job Corps and a Neighborhood Youth Corps, both for job training and work experience; a legal services program; an Upward Bound program for college preparation; and a Green Thumb program for elderly workers.

The usual scenario in redistributive policy is that a general goal, often vague and containing internal contradictions, is endorsed by the president and Congress and is then given reality in a proliferation of specific programs authorized by statutes. These programs are embellished and proliferated even further by bureaucratic action during implementation because the statutes creating specific enterprises are often quite general.

The result in the typical redistributive area is that there are programs that, analyzed logically, appear to be redundant and often confusing. In some ways, programs proliferate on the basis of what seems to be primarily legislative and bureaucratic imperatives, not on the basis of objective analysis of a problem and careful design of means to meet the problem.

Congressional Involvement

Congress is heavily involved in the formulation and legitimation debates and actions for redistributive programs. Congress and its members, however, are not as likely to get involved in implementation details in this arena as they are in some of the other arenas. They tend to limit their intervention to two major kinds of cases.

First, members tend to view the implementation of redistributive programs through the lens of distribution. That is, they want to make sure their states or districts and the eligible constituents therein get the maximum allowable benefits. Thus if federal bureaucratic decisions or regulations spelling out the statutory directives in more detail threaten the benefits going to certain constituencies, the senators and representatives from those constituencies then have powerful incentives to intervene.

Second, at some point—and depending on the relative conservatism or liberalism of Congress at any given time—Congress or some part of it is likely to intervene in implementation if budgetary costs seem to be getting out of hand. For example, one of the motivations, although not the only one, for increasing congressional attention to implementation of the food stamp program was the rapidly escalating costs of the program.

A third occasion for after-the-fact congressional attention to implementation is assessment of program results. In large part most congressional committees and subcommittees either avoid asking serious evaluative questions about what these programs achieved or, if the questions are asked, are usually satisfied with a few anecdotes. And, for the most part, bureaucrats are content to present primarily anecdotes to Congress. The bureaucrats only rarely attempt to present more rigorous evaluation, even if such evaluation has been conducted. Congress rarely uses program evaluation information as a basis for adjusting and reshaping agency implementation routines.

Federalism

The redistributive arena involves state and local bureaucracies and also private bureaucracies at the local level that receive subcontracts allocating public money to provide services. By both design and necessity federalism and federalistic implementation are hallmarks of many redistributive programs. This fact means that local political and social systems that predate federal program interventions are very important in shaping and constraining what the federal programs can achieve. As was stated in one study of three federal programs, one of which was centrally redistributive (Model Cities), one of which was a mix of distribution and redistribution (Community Development Block Grants), and one of which was primarily distributive (General Revenue Sharing) (Browning, Marshall and Tabb, 1980:617): "The federal grant programs were seen...as instances in a long series of external interventions into local systems which develop partly according to their own internal evolutionary dynamic and partly by adapting to interventions."

There is good evidence that the federal government cannot have redistributive impact simply by mandating it (see, for example, Clinton, 1979). There is also good evidence that if the federal government, usually in the form of its bureaucrats in a variety of field offices, tries to intervene in all aspects of a program they will succeed only in alienating the state and local officials and private bureaucrats who, ultimately, will have the largest role in making the program succeed or fail (see Van Horn, 1978). There is also evidence, however, that *selective* federal intervention can make a difference. For example, federal law and regulations aimed at delivering benefits only to a targeted population of the relatively most needy, when pursued by federal enforcement activities, can make a difference in who actually gets served. Such was the case with Model Cities (see Browning, Marshall, and Tabb, 1980).

Relations to Other Types of Policies

As already indicated, there are pressures on many redistributive programs to move them into a more distributive mode during implementation. Frequently, what begins as a program to help disadvantaged people becomes a program designed to maximize the smooth flow of money to local governments and organizations to sustain their life and activities. Serving the disadvantaged becomes secondary and a matter of trickle down. We will see such pressures at work in the areas of economic development, employment and training, and education, which are discussed below. There are sometimes pressures running in the opposite direction too—that is, to keep the redistributive program pure during implementation—but those forces are usually weaker than those pushing for a more distributive form of implementation.

The standards for success in programs that are being pushed out of the pure redistributive mode into a more distributive mode also change. Standards for success in the latter case inevitably revolve around measures of how much money gets spent. Standards for success of redistributive programs revolve around who gets helped in what way, how quickly, and with what effect. It is much easier to prove that money gets spent (any half-competent auditor can do that) than to prove that an educational program for disadvantaged children really helps them make up their deficiencies in comparison to more advantaged children. Thus it is almost inevitable that programs with a high distributive component, even though they may have started with redistributive ends, are relatively easy to pronounce successes. The most common judgments about redistributive programs defined more narrowly are that they are failures. The distributive components are successes if they have spent all of their money at the end of every fiscal year. The redistributive components are failures unless they have profoundly altered human behavior at the end of the year. Naturally, the alterations sought are likely to take decades and are very difficult to measure at any point in a long evolution.

Some programs that are redistributive in intent also begin to look like protective regulation during implementation. Such is the case with a number of the equal rights and equal opportunity programs discussed below. Politically, these programs suffer from the disadvantages of protective regulatory programs (see

Chapter 6) *in addition to* the conflict inherent in redistributive programs.

ECONOMIC DEVELOPMENT

Three specific programs, all aiming at some form of compensatory, economic development for the most disadvantaged geographic areas and the disadvantaged residents of those areas, provide illustrations of some implementation activities and patterns in the redistributive arena.

New Towns in Town

In August 1967 President Johnson had an idea, and within a week a new federal program had been announced (Derthick, 1972). The essence of his idea was that the federal government could create new housing in central cities, largely for the poor, by selling the cities surplus federally owned land in such locations at very cheap prices. The idea required no new legislation. In principle, it could be directed from the White House and pieces of the federal bureaucracy under its control.

The implementation planning was first entrusted to an interagency task force chaired by the administrator of the General Services Administration and overseen by one of the president's personal assistants. After the initial planning period the responsibility for federal implementation came to reside in the Department of Housing and Urban Development.

What happened to this seemingly simple and creative idea during its implementation? The program began with personal presidential involvement; no necessity of going to Congress for new laws; no threat to local citizens of being relocated because the land was vacant or contained only federal buildings that could be razed; and little monetary cost, since the federal government already owned the land and wanted to sell it to cities at prices well below its market value. It ended basically as a failure: after four years only 120 units of housing had been built in one city; small developments were still possible in only three other cities.

Why did the program flop? A central reason was that the federal government ignored serious problems at the local level. Federal officials seemed to assume that the localities would support the program eagerly because of its advantages: cheap land and no relocation. However, local problems arose that proved to be fatal in many cases. Consultation by federal officials with local officials was minimal from start to finish. Even when such consultation took place, it came too late in the process to save the project. There was local opposition to providing central-city housing for the poor; a reluctance of local officials to ignore or oppose that opposition; no particular local support; and the normal desire of local officials to develop land so as to produce more taxes in the future, a desire that was incompatible with low-income housing. There was little positive local interest in the program, considerable local opposition, and no concerted federal effort to develop local support or at least neutralize local opposition. In short, the federal government was insensitive to local political factors standing in the way of successful implementation.

There were also serious implementation problems at the national level. There was, for example, a very loose administrative structure. Interagency task forces are usually weak administrative arrangements. When day-to-day operational responsibilities were finally located in the Department of Housing and Urban Development (HUD), that department added a number of its own goals to the program. In some cases, those goals were not consonant with the original presidential goals.

HUD also faced additional administrative roadblocks. It had to coordinate with other federal agencies that also had a programmatic stake in the program. These included the Department of Defense (the owner of the land that was to be declared surplus and put up for sale), the General Services Administration (which had a role to play in pricing the land for sale), and the Justice Department (which was concerned about racial integration in the housing that would finally be constructed on the land).

HUD also had to keep its own administrative house in order. Major HUD subunits in Washington were, in effect, expected to use some money and people that had been programmed for other purposes to accomplish the objectives of the new towns in town program. There is a natural bureaucratic resistance to such transfers. There was also tension between HUD headquarters in Washington and the HUD field establishment. Some of the HUD regional administrators were hostile to or at least profoundly skeptical about the new program.

HUD's relations with Congress were less than smooth. HUD had decided not to involve individual members of Congress in decisions about specific cities. That decision was a mistake. It also assumed that there was no need to approach Congress as a whole to request legislation. This assumption turned out to be false, as the land surplus disposal laws required modification if the program were to proceed as originally designed. Given the involvement of most congressmen in local politics and local decision making—especially in any matter in which the federal government is involved—they can be valuable allies or potent foes of a federal agency that is seeking to achieve something. In this case, since they were not even informed let alone wooed, they could offer no help, and in some instances, they offered opposition. Congressmen could have been used to help move local politicians into positions of support for the program, but HUD ignored them, and in return it received either no support or opposition from them.

There were also complications surrounding acquisition of appropriate land. Less federal land in central cities could reasonably be called surplus than had been assumed initially. In many cases military commanders opposed having their facility declared surplus and eligible for sale. The laws governing the sale of surplus federal land at below market-value were not as flexible as had been thought at first. The support of Congress would have been needed to change those laws. A bill was drafted, but it was never forwarded to Congress.

Another problem was the lack of sustained presidential interest and support. Inevitably, matters of greater consequence crowded onto the presidential agenda, and when President Johnson announced in March 1968 that he would not run for reelection, this reduced further the incentive of the HUD bureaucrats to try to please him and the White House staff members who were following the new towns program.

Finally, as is the case with many federal programs, there was an initial overselling of what the program could accomplish. The program's goals were stated in grandiose terms, and its expected benefits were overstated. This kind of oversell virtually always results in a sense of failure. Such a mood has an adverse impact on the morale of individuals charged with implementation responsibility.

Community Development Block Grants

In 1974 after a debate of many years, Congress enacted a new Housing and Community Development Act. The community development portion of the act combined into a single block-grant program a number of existing federal categorical programs for urban renewal, neighborhood development, Model Cities, water and sewer facilities, neighborhood facilities, public facilities, open space, and rehabilitation. It also authorized the dispensing of $8.6 billion over a three-year period to units of local government to achieve some broad community development ends. Much of this money went by entitlement, based on a formula, to cities over 50,000 and urban counties over 200,000. The rest went to all kinds of local governments on a discretionary basis. The program had a largely distributive aspect to the local units receiving the funds.

The goals of the program were quite unclear. Community development was defined in the act only in terms of permissible activities, largely the same activities that were allowed under the previous categorical programs. Local recipients defined their own priorities. Although presumably the block grants were intended to revitalize American communities, the main goal of the program in its first few years of operation was to disperse the money in a timely and efficient fashion without worrying too much about how that money was used or with what effect.

Even at the level of simply producing the money for localities in a timely and efficient fashion, there were implementation problems. In general, the red tape of the categorical programs was reduced. However, recipients of discretionary funds often had to wait unexpectedly long periods of time and then received less money than they anticipated. This created problems in their planning and operations.

The Department of Housing and Urban Development demonstrated its preference for a minimal role. The statute and regulations were vague, and HUD could opt for a range of roles from relatively aggressive to quite passive. In general, HUD officials opted for passivity; monitoring was very loose, and as a result a very broad range of local activities and local responses to specific regulations was accepted as legitimate. HUD did not push redistributive aspects of the program on local recipients.

The bias in favor of local autonomy contained in at least some parts of the statute and reinforced by HUD's passive stance resulted in choices by localities that did not really constitute an attack on urban blight. Instead, local decision-making politics made a focus on development or construction easier to achieve. Often such a focus had little to do with the problems of the inner city. Typically, it aimed at suburban areas. Local choice and the latitude given local choice both by law and especially by HUD inactivity, therefore, favored suburban development goals rather than cleaning up the messes of the urban past.

Finally, the funding formula itself reinforced the problems of implementing the program in such a way as to alleviate existing urban blight. The funding formula was biased in favor of the suburban areas, and in effect it redirected money from the urban areas to the suburban areas.

Transformed by local politics in the implementation process CDBG became much more distributive in character than redistributive. Summarizing the available evidence Van Horn (1979a:20; see also Van Horn, 1979b:chapter 4; and Rosenfeld, 1979) concluded that "it is clear that a relatively small proportion of the program's funds go to the poorest geographical areas.... When all the evidence is weighed, the net result indicates a reduction in benefits for poor individuals due to a wider geographical dispersal of funds, reductions in social services, and concentration on physical development.... The shift from federally managed programs with narrow definitions of participation eligibility to locally implemented programs with broader eligibility standards has tended to produce more widely distributed benefits diluting benefits to the poor."

Economic Development Administration Programs

The Department of Commerce's Economic Development Administration (EDA) has always had dual purposes: to subsidize local development efforts in what is basically a distributive manner *and* to focus on areas of greatest need. The agency was created in 1965 when it inherited the personnel, property, and functions of its predecessor, the Area Redevelopment Administration. Since then the distributive aspects of its programs have driven out the redistributive ones because of pressures and expectations at both the local level and at the national level.

A classic case study of implementation at the local level focused on the EDA program in Oakland, California (Pressman and Wildavsky, 1984). The program was aimed at benefiting the poor and minorities specifically and the entire city in general. Environmental groups, minority (black) groups, and tenants of the port of Oakland were all active in seeking benefits as they defined them. A very large roster of actors were mandated to have a part in the planning of the Oakland project. Pressman and Wildavsky summarize the 13 major groups connected with the program, their perspective and major objectives, and their sense of urgency about the program. Their table is reproduced here as Table 7–1 because it provides such a complete illustration of the complexity of local implementation. Not only were there a very large number of actors, but they all had different connections with the program, and most important, they did not share objectives or perspectives and had very different senses of the importance of the program. Under these conditions it is perhaps not surprising that the genuinely redistributive parts of the program in Oakland—employment for minorities—moved very slowly or not at all and the more distributive parts—in this case, public works—moved much more swiftly.

At the national level it was clear that by the late 1970s the transformation of EDA into almost purely a distributive agency had occurred (see Stanfield, 1979b; and Miller, 1979a). For example, when the Carter administration sought to stimulate business development in decaying inner cities by creating an autonomous urban development bank, the resulting negative response forced the administration to redirect their efforts through existing (distributive) EDA programs. The revised Carter proposal went through easily. In fact, EDA was widely regarded in Washington as a successful agency in large part because success and efficiency were defined during political debate as being able to get dollars delivered quickly to the local level without much attention to the exact way in which those dollars would be spent and whose ends would be best served and whose would be less well served. The Reagan administration made EDA an early

TABLE 7-1 Participants and Perspectives in the Oakland EDA Program

Participant	Connection with Program	Perspective and Major Objectives	Sense of Urgency
EDA—national office leadership: Foley (EDA director); Bradford (special assistant to director); special task force	Designed program, set up project machinery in Oakland	Wanted to initiate, in a relatively short time, a program of economic development that would create jobs for unemployed minorities	Very High
EDA—Operating departments in Washington	Project implementation—construction, financial processing, etc.	Aimed for construction of facilities in an efficient and administratively proper manner	High (some resentment of special task force; insistence that process meet administrative standards)
EDA—national office leadership after Foley	Exercised authority over projects after fall 1966	Sought to salvage original employment goals in Oakland project	Moderate (not personally identified with program; secretary of commerce indicated lack of enthusiasm)
EDA—Seattle regional office	Unclear; processed paperwork, but no authority to commit funds	Attempted to gain larger administrative role in project	Moderate
EDA—Oakland office	Monitoring of projects at local level	Hoped to salvage initial employment goals and complete each project	Varied with each officeholder
U.S. General Accounting Office	Questioned EDA policy regarding grant loan ratio for Port projects	Concerned with standards for disbursement of federal funds	Low
U.S. Department of Health, Education, and Welfare	Joint control over manpower training funds for hangar project	Supported goal of job training in Oakland, but had commitment to established skills center	Low (East Bay Skills Center bypassed by airline training program)

Participant			
U.S. Department of Labor	Joint control over manpower training funds for hangar project	Main interest was in job training	Low
U.S. Navy	Objected to terminal construction because of effects on flight safety	Was chiefly concerned with effects of Port construction on operations of Alameda Naval Air Station	Low
City of Oakland (mayor)	Represented city in dealings with EDA; tried to build support for program	Strongly supported EDA goals of economic development and job creation	High
City of Oakland (administration)	Drew up public works applications for EDA funding (coliseum access road approved)	Saw EDA funding as potential support for city public works projects	Low (access road completed early; no other city-sponsored projects approved)
Port of Oakland	Local recipient of major public works projects	Viewed EDA program as vital support for Port building program, but annoyed by multiplicity of federal guidelines	Moderate (port is involved in building and operating numerous other facilities)
Oakland black leaders	Met by EDA national office leaders on early visits; some served on Employment Plan Review Board	Wanted job creation for minorities	High
Conservation groups	Protested Port of Oakland bay-fill activities	Strongly protested fill as damaging to bay and environs	Low
Port of Oakland tenants	If benefited from EDA financing, had to sign employment agreement	Wanted to operate successful business	Low

SOURCE: Adapted from J.L. Pressman and A. Wildavsky, *Implementation*, 2d ed., Berkeley: University of California Press, pp. 95–97.

target for extinction but as of mid-1985 it had survived, largely because of political support stemming from its distributive nature.

EMPLOYMENT AND TRAINING

Since the passage of the Manpower Development and Training Act of 1962, numerous federally sponsored and supported programs have emerged to provide employment and training opportunities for unemployed and disadvantaged people who are hard to employ. Categorical programs run directly by the federal government through subcontracts with local service deliverers proliferated in the late 1960s. This kind of proliferation is typical of the redistributive arena.

Gradually, pressures mounted for a new approach with greater coordination and better management: a block grant to local units of government to make specific program choices within some guidelines about what is acceptable and who can be served with what. A compromise between contending forces was engineered in late 1973, and the Comprehensive Employment and Training Act (CETA) was enacted. It contained six different titles and authorized a variety of programs and, in subsequent years, more titles and programs were added. The intent to decategorize various employment and training categorical programs was only partially achieved even in the 1973 act, and a substantial amount of *re*categorization took place in subsequent years. In general, the distributive aspects of the program—the pumping of money into state and local units of government, called prime sponsorships—far overshadowed the redistributive aspects. Intent to serve the most disadvantaged was diluted by pressures to serve the relatively less disadvantaged among the eligible population.

CETA was replaced by the Job Training Partnership Act in 1983, but an analysis of the CETA program (1973–83) is rich in lessons for a general study of implementation of redistributive programs (for major analyses of the program see Franklin and Ripley, 1984; Baumer and Van Horn, 1984; and Mirengoff and Rindler, 1978). After we make some general introductory points about CETA as a whole, we will examine three specific segments briefly: a veterans employment program called HIRE II, a program designed to increase the participation of private business called the Private Sector Initiatives Program, and a related employment tax credit called the Targeted Jobs Tax Credit.

Several general statements best characterize key aspects of the entire CETA experience:

1. CETA was a large program, annually spending billions of dollars and serving about 3 million participants. Throughout its history and in virtually all programs it funded, its natural tendency was to serve the relatively least disadvantaged part of the eligible population in most, but not all, localities. Local political decision-making commitments and procedures protected the most disadvantaged in some cases. But in most locales this segment of the eligible population lost services over time compared to pre-CETA programs and compared to the relative gains in service by more well-off clients. Remember that well-off is a relative term here. All legally enrolled CETA clients had some form of economic need.

2. In 1978 Congress tightened some of the eligibility requirements that did, in fact, have the desired effect at the local level and helped redirect service to the more needy.

3. Bureaucratic hostilities rapidly emerged between the different layers of bureaucrats involved—national Department of Labor, regional Department of Labor, and local government units.

4. Both Congress and the Department of Labor showed strong inclinations to placate vocal interest groups with their own special programs, funding, and categories of activity. For example, DOL and Congress simultaneously funded special interest groups representing or claiming to represent business, organized labor, blacks, hispanics, Indians, counties, cities, and states. In the area of community-based organizations alone DOL expanded direct funding from 3 major groups to 15 in just a few years. Support for the total CETA endeavor was sought by dividing up the action among a number of national groups, which often had very different and conflicting goals.

5. Some local prime sponsorships also sought a distributive solution to creating political support for the program by giving all competing groups at the local level some share of dollars.

6. The net result was not a reduction in the complexity of programs and involved actors but rather a reshuffling into

somewhat different relationships and positions for influencing outcomes. At the local level complexity and sometimes confusion was still the rule. For example, a report by the General Accounting Office on just one locality (a consortium of local government units in the Norfolk, Virginia, area) concluded that the alleged simplification of the federal jobs programs still left 44 specific local programs that involved five federal departments, three independent federal agencies, one federally sponsored regional council, 50 local administering agencies, and 26 other groups, including state agencies and national organizations. Reasonably enough, GAO concluded: "The result is a vast network of special emphasis program categories characterized by programs with similar goals and target groups... federal moneys that follow a variety of administrative channels... and a complex and confusing approach to helping individuals obtain training or become gainfully employed" (see General Accounting Office, 1979).

HIRE II

In 1977 the Department of Labor contracted with the National Alliance of Business to implement a program called HIRE I (HIRE stood for Help through Industry Retraining and Employment), which was targeted for certain categories of veterans defined to be disadvantaged in the job market. That program went nowhere for a variety of reasons. The Department of Labor then reorganized it and created HIRE II, putting implementation in the regular prime sponsorship structure. Participating prime sponsorships (the program was not mandatory and close to one third chose not to implement the program) were given a grant by formula. They were told to produce jobs for eligible veterans, usually by creating on-the-job training situations for which employers would be reimbursed for a period of time for part of the wages spent for the veterans newly hired.

HIRE II also did not do very well, and it is instructive to summarize the reasons why (the following discussion is based on Ripley and Smith, 1979).

First, prime sponsorships participated in the program primarily because the money was available. Few had client-oriented goals. Most viewed the program as unimportant because it represented only a small amount of money: about one percent of their total CETA funding.

Second, the program depended on the building of a local network of committed actors who would work together to identify job slots. Central to these networks were the local employment service offices (a federal-state agency), local business groups, local community-based organizations serving the disadvantaged, and local veterans' groups, especially of the nontraditional kind serving younger veterans from the Vietnam era. Either the local CETA staff or the local employment service office needed to take the lead in building the appropriate network tailored to the needs of each locality. The few areas that did this had reasonably successful programs; the majority who did not achieved little.

Third, national groups in Washington made grandiose claims to Congress and the Department of Labor about their positive influence. In fact, out in the boondocks in the various prime sponsorships these groups had no impact on implementation whatsoever. They were unable to help deliver job opportunities or find eligible applicants.

Private Sector Initiatives Program

In the spring of 1978 the White House made a splashy announcement about a new initiative they were proposing in CETA: a special Private Sector Initiatives Program (PSIP) aimed at getting local businesspersons more involved in designing employment and training programs at the local level and, therefore—so the theory went—more committed to hiring the graduates of the programs. In the autumn of 1978 Congress passed a bill adding a new Title to CETA and authorizing some money for it. The level of subsequent appropriations meant that about 5 percent of a prime sponsorship's total CETA funds were now earmarked for PSIP.

One of the key requirements in the new Title of CETA was the creation of a Private Industry Council (PIC) that had to approve the use of PSIP funds. This new council had to have a majority of its members from business and also had to have representatives from organized labor, education, and community-based organizations.

A number of features of implementation helps explain the enormously varying degree of progress made in individual prime sponsorships. Above all, a PIC that had active members and, in effect, built a network of supporting actors and neutralized potentially hostile actors was able to promote a local program that created job opportunities in the private sector for disadvantaged people. Successful PSIP programs were more likely where the PIC and the professional CETA staff established a cooperative working relationship. The institutions with which local implementers, including PIC, would have to deal to create a supportive network and to neutralize potential opposition were numerous and diverse. They included local business organizations such as the Chamber of Commerce or the dry cleaners' association or printers' association; local labor unions; the general CETA advisory council (also required by law, with largely different members and different functions from PIC); deliverers of CETA services under all of the titles of the act, especially community-based organizations; the local employment service office; local elected officials—mayors, county commissioners, city council members; organizations dealing with economic development, such as local economic development corporations; local schools with vocational training competence; and officials from the Department of Labor, especially in the relevant regional office.

The Targeted Jobs Tax Credit (TJTC)

In the autumn of 1978 Congress added a provision to the internal revenue code that allowed employers to claim up to $4,500 over two years as a tax credit for each employee falling in one of seven categories of people thought to be disadvantaged in the labor market. The intent of TJTC was to stimulate private hiring of these disadvantaged persons. To implement the tax credit, Congress, in effect, specified that local networks in all of the 475 prime sponsorships throughout the country should advertise the program to employers, encourage hiring of eligible applicants, and recruit eligible participants.

This is an odd case of implementation because the prime sponsorships that built the appropriate networks of actors did not do any better in terms of number of people hired than those who did not build the network. The major explanation of why nothing much happened anywhere (except for the windfall effect for employers who were permitted to claim the credit retroactively for people they had already hired in the normal course of business) was that the tax credit was not attractive to employers. They had generally negative views of the tax credit for several reasons: suspicion of government programs in general; the relatively small size of the credit involved; and an unwillingness to alter normal hiring practices to look for special categories of employees.

We mention this case as a reminder that programmatic success is not wholly dependent on implementation. In this case perfect implementation performance by the administering agencies would still not have achieved the desired results because of a badly flawed program design.

EDUCATION: TITLE I OF THE ELEMENTARY AND SECONDARY EDUCATION ACT OF 1965 (ESEA)

In 1965 President Johnson and Congress broke a 20-year logjam over a number of sticky issues and a very large federal aid to elementary and secondary education bill became law, with major programs in five separate titles.

What follows focuses on the implementation of Title I from its inception in 1965 through 1972 (Murphy, 1973; Murphy, 1971; Bailey and Mosher, 1968). The central purpose of Title I was to aid disadvantaged students. During 1965–72 the annual cost of that single title grew from about $1 billion to about $1.6 billion. Two very complicated formulas were used to distribute the money to recipient counties and school districts. Title I attempted to provide more money for the schools with the poorest and most disadvantaged children. The money was intended to fund specific projects aimed at compensatory education. The states had the responsibility for approving projects, although they were supposed to apply federal standards. The school districts, however, got their money automatically as a matter of right through the operations of the two allocation formulas. The U.S. Office of Education (USOE) was supposed to accept or reject local assurances that the law would be followed in spending the money and was supposed to offer guidance in the administration of the program at the state and local levels.

From 1965 until 1970 the general outcome of the program can best be described as one in which the money was allocated according to the formula, but very little effort was made to see that the money was spent in compensatory ways as provided in the statute. Audits of abuses, for example, were delayed or not carried out. In many ways the program was treated simply as general aid to elementary and secondary education, with local school districts having virtual autonomy in deciding on how the money should be spent. Some school districts may have made a genuine effort to focus on the most disadvantaged students, but that was almost a matter of chance, not of federal, state, or local policy. In 1970 and 1971 a flurry of activity in USOE directed at increasing compliance was promoted by a few concerned people outside the agency who were following up on a report that detailed the failure of the program to focus on disadvantaged students. But that activity subsided after the external pressures dissolved.

What happened during the implementation process that can explain outcomes disappointing to those who meant to help poor students get better educations and thus break the cycle of poverty?

The people who had helped produce what they assumed to be a reform of the educational system in the United States that would use federal dollars as the lever to gain more focus on the poor were not the people who were responsible for implementing the reform. There was virtually no overlap between these two sets of individuals. The reformers had come from Congress, from the higher echelons of the executive branch, and from a few leading interest groups. The federal implementers were housed in USOE, an old and small bureaucracy. That bureaucracy was expanded dramatically to handle the new implementation chores, but the critical implementers were longtime civil servants who had well-defined and long-held views about how to proceed, views that were hostile to the goals envisioned by the reformers.

It did not help matters that the goals of the program were murky. Some of the murkiness was the inevitable result of putting together the winning coalition for passing the bill. The necessities of coalition-building often bring together groups of people who have very different views of the purpose of the legislation they are passing. In this case some of the people in the winning coalition really wanted to focus on the disadvantaged; others were much more interested in getting what amounted to general federal aid to public secondary and elementary education.

The Office of Education was badly understaffed. The agency was very small, almost a century old, and had never done anything particularly innovative in its entire history. Now it was called on to implement a massive and potentially highly innovative program very quickly. Some valiant efforts were made, but past inadequacies continued to plague its implementation efforts. Likewise, the state education agencies, which had a critical role to play in implementation, were for the most part ill prepared to undertake anything requiring innovation or a relatively high degree of competence.

The basic distribution of administrative powers in the program created problems. Much authority was simply given to state education agencies and local school districts. But even the authority retained by the U.S. Office of Education was not used in any directive or forceful way. For example, the Office of Education was authorized to accept or reject assurances submitted by each state that the law would be followed. Rejection of a state's assurances meant that funds would be withheld from it. But the Office of Education always accepted the assurances, without assessing their meaning or sincerity. The authority to withhold money is likely to be politically dangerous if the authority is exercised. Any such action would bring immediate protests from members of the House and Senate, local government officials, and the national interest groups for state and local government officials.

The Office of Education was also given power to establish basic criteria that state and local administrations had to meet. Again the ultimate sanction of withholding funds was present. But during the process of passing the law a vociferous minority in Congress made it clear that they would look with disfavor on efforts by USOE to do anything concrete with this provision. In fact, USOE never tried very hard.

The norm of local autonomy in public education was so strongly entrenched throughout the educational system that it constantly militated against any direction of the system that would have given the program a focus on the poor and the disadvantaged. Both USOE and state agencies deferred in word and deed to the autonomy of local school districts. This meant that they were reluctant to monitor, to criticize, or to undertake any enforcement activities. Good relations among persons who all considered themselves professional educators required that none of them hassle the others and that the tradition of local autonomy be respected.

Finally, there was no strong, sustained pressure from representatives of the reformist, redistributive view that the Title I programs should focus explicitly on the poor. Such pressure might have kept USOE and state and local agencies moving toward that goal, even if slowly. The outburst of such pressure in 1970 and 1971 did have some impact, but that impact turned out to be temporary because the outburst itself was temporary.

Few would argue that the implementation of Title I of the Elementary and Secondary Education Act has done no good. Local school systems certainly received monetary resources that they would not have received otherwise. But whether the program was implemented in such a way as to maximize its impact on the poor, which was one congressional and presidential intent, is a different question. In the first seven years of implementation the answer to that question was negative.

EQUAL RIGHTS

Equal rights programs are often thought of as protective regulatory efforts. However, we think they should be treated along with other redistributive programs because their aim is to enlarge the political, economic, or social rights of persons whose rights are limited on the basis of some sort of racial, ethnic, or sex discrimination. Policymakers supporting such efforts do not feel they are taking rights from any other group. However, what counts in the politics of policy implementation is how those affected perceive matters, and it seems quite clear that a number of whites view equal rights and affirmative action programs as taking their rights from them in some sense in order to give them to minorities. Similarly, some seem to believe that equal rights for women infringe on men's rights.

In the sections that follow we first want to explore the general status of equal rights implementation in the 1980s during the Reagan administration. Then we will turn to specific cases involving Chicago public housing in the 1960s; the performance of the Office for Civil Rights in the Department of Health, Education, and Welfare; the performance of the Equal Employment Opportunity Commission; and the Voting Rights Act of 1965.

Equal Rights Implementation in the 1980s

In its second term the Reagan administration took for a theme the symbolic phrase "a new American Revolution." Traditional civil rights groups have reason to feel that with regard to enforcing civil rights laws, there has indeed been a revolution in America, and that they are on the losing side.

The principal features of the Reagan administration's approach to civil rights enforcement have been reducing federal aggressiveness and eliminating school busing and hiring quotas as remedies for discrimination. The Reagan team seems to believe that the problem of discrimination against blacks and other minorities in this country has been largely solved, and that the federal bureaucracy charged with enforcing civil rights laws is unwieldy, inflexible, and overbearing.

Agency managers, staff, and commission members sharing these beliefs have been appointed to the federal agencies that implement civil rights laws. Assistant Attorney General William Bradford Reynolds, head of the Civil Rights Division in the Department of Justice, has been the lightning rod for critics of administration policy, but like-minded men and women have taken important positions in other agencies enforcing civil rights (in addition to Justice, these include the Department of Labor's Office of Federal Contract Compliance Programs, the Office of Civil Rights in the Education Department, the Equal Employment Opportunity Commission (EEOC), the U.S. Civil Rights Commission, and agencies within the Departments of Housing and Urban Development (HUD), Treasury, and Health and Human Services).

Reagan's appointees contend that they are committed to "color blind" implementation of the laws, that they oppose discrimination against anyone, and that they wish to replace the heavy-handed federal intrusion and regulation that characterized the 1960s and 1970s with voluntary cooperation.

Despite such rhetorical assurances, the unescapable feature of the civil rights landscape since 1981 has been a reduction across the board of civil rights enforcement activities by the federal government in both scope and pace (Wines, 1982:536; Citizens Commission on Civil Rights, 1984). The multiple bureaucracies involved in implementing civil rights have moved or been shoved at different paces, but without question they have been redirected by the philosophy of the Reagan administration.

The tenor of the new commitment to civil rights enforcement was set in 1981 and 1982 by a series of controversial events:

- Reagan's nominations to the Civil Rights Commission were rejected by Congress; Reagan wanted to replace five of the six commissioners appointed by earlier presidents. (He ultimately got a Commission malleable to his views following a congressional struggle to renew the Commission.)
- Reagan advocated granting tax-exempt status to colleges (including Bob Jones University) that discriminated against blacks, contravening established policy of the Treasury Department, which for years had rejected such tax-exempt applications (the Supreme Court later upheld the Treasury policy).
- The president and the Justice Department withheld support for the extension of the Voting Rights Act. The president took no position until after congressional Republicans had already lined up behind the bill; he then advocated narrowing the scope of a key section of the bill. As the chairman of the House Judiciary Subcommittee on Civil and Constitutional Rights said, "We had to pass it in the House without any help from the Justice Department."(Quoted in Stanfield, 1983:1123). Despite the lack of presidential leadership, a 25 year extension won overwhelming support from Congress and was signed into law.
- Within the Department of Justice, lawyers from the Civil Rights Divisions were in barely concealed revolt against the restrictive policies favored by the new assistant attorney general; many professional staff left the agency in protest.
- The heads of 33 state advisory commissions dealing with civil rights issued a statement accusing the administration of dismantling civil rights enforcement machinery (*National Journal*, September 18, 1982:1611).
- The Washington Council of Lawyers issued a report condemning the slackened pace of enforcement within the Civil Rights Division. Statistics from the Division showed that in 20 months fewer than 10 new cases had been filed in housing discrimination, school desegregation, voting rights, and handicapped rights (*National Journal*, September 18, 1982:1611).

Actions from 1983 through early 1985 show that the initial trends continued, although perhaps with a little less visibility.

- Prior to being tamed by the administration through reconstitution and recomposition in late 1983, the Civil Rights Commission cited cuts in federal funding as responsible for weakening civil rights enforcement activities in six federal agencies (*National Journal*, October 15, 1983:2131).

• Even the Reagan-appointed chairman of the reconstituted Civil Rights Commission lost patience with the administration and made public his letters chiding the president for playing politics with civil rights (*New York Times*, July 3, 1984).

• Opposition to affirmative action through busing and hiring quotas from the highest levels of the executive branch continued in speeches made by the president, the Secretary of Housing and Urban Development (ironically, the only black person in the Reagan cabinet), and the head of the Civil Rights Division. Assistant Attorney General Reynolds in a speech to the Florida bar association extended his opposition to quotas to include voluntary hiring plans and predicted that the Supreme Court would rule against such mechanisms (*Washington Post*, February 9, 1985).

• The application of federal sanctions for violation of discrimination laws was restricted. In a very controversial decision, the Supreme Court ruled in February 1984 (in *Grove City College v. Bell*) that only the unit receiving federal financial assistance had to be free of discrimination; civil rights laws did not apply to the entire institution of which the unit was part. The Department of Justice had argued for this position, and had pressured the Education Department into adopting it in the suit (*Washington Post*, Sept. 12, 1983).

• The Justice Department reversed its historical position in court cases. For example, in 1984 the department challenged the city of Birmingham's voluntary hiring plan for its police and fire departments on the grounds that it discriminated against whites. Yet the department had worked with the city to establish that plan years earlier after bringing suit against the city in 1975. The mayor complained, "The Justice Department is changing sides on a decree that they helped fashion. The Reagan administration is joining the rather persistent attacks to undermine or completely undo our decree. They have reneged." (Quoted in *New York Times*, March 5, 1984). In another example, the Justice Department unilaterally intervened to challenge settlement of a four-year-old suit involving public housing in Brooklyn because it claimed the issue of quotas was not resolved in the settlement. All sides in the suit denounced the uninvited intrusion (*New York Times*, June 29, 1984).

- The Justice Department pushed vigorously for restricting enforcement of civil rights to actual victims of discrimination. This means that litigation is pursued on an individual-by-individual basis, rather than for groups or classes in broad challenges to patterns and practices of discrimination. The new Civil Rights Commission and the EEOC have also adopted this approach to litigation.

- The establishment of block grants for many social welfare programs under the Health and Human Services Department meant that allocation of funds for specific purposes, including enforcement, was made at the state and local level. Enforcement of civil rights is almost always a lower state priority than a program directly serving beneficiaries. In late September 1984 the administration announced a pilot plan to decontrol enforcement further by delegating civil rights enforcement to selected states, allowing states to investigate complaints filed against block grant programs (*New York Times*, September 30, 1984).

In this kind of context, the more positive steps taken by the administration to relieve discrimination against minorities are overshadowed. The Reagan Justice Department actively implemented the Voting Rights Act (described below) and the number of cases filed in police brutality issues increased. But the dominant result of implementation activity between 1981 and mid-1985 represents a retreat from the activist federal enforcement posture in the 1960s and 1970s.

The civil rights lobby and other watchdogs have been vocal critics of the federal government's redirection of enforcement. But because the issues of enforcement of specific laws for housing, voting rights, and employment opportunity are technical, complex, and difficult to understand, and because the frequency of publicized political gaffes such as the tax-exemption for schools like Bob Jones University has subsided, the level of visibility and journalistic attention to civil rights enforcement has declined. The cumulative effect of implementation activities after late 1980 has been disheartening and frustrating to supporters of a strong federal enforcement role. Their only consolation must be that the pace of the redirected implementation activity has been slow and equally frustrating to proponents of the new strategies.

Discrimination in Public Housing:
The Case of Chicago, 1963–1971

In the public housing program in the city of Chicago in the early 1950s local priorities overshadowed federal priorities on virtually all fronts. The federal agency served primarily as a funnel for money that the city used to do what it wanted to do in the housing field, including fostering increased or continued segregation in housing for blacks.

The 1960s were a time of civil rights ferment and some important national policy statements on civil rights. In the housing field an executive order issued in 1962 and provisions of major civil rights statutes enacted in 1964 and 1968 made it illegal for a local public housing agency operating with federal funds to practice racial discrimination; discrimination in private housing markets was also prohibited.

How did these provisions affect the implementation of public housing programs at the local level in Chicago? Basically, they did not (Lazin, 1973). Throughout the 1960s the city of Chicago used its federally funded public housing program to promote racial segregation. Chicago may have been atypical, it is certainly true that the visible national political clout of its mayor, Richard Daley, was greater than that of almost any other local official in the country. But in fact many problems in implementation helped create the outcome and probably would have promoted it no matter who the mayor had been. The basic patterns of local dominance over a presumably federal program continued and were reinforced by a number of federal actions. Thus it would be a mistake to view the federal government as struggling valiantly to uphold the law only to be thwarted by a crafty, determined, and politically savvy local government. In fact, the feds and the locals worked together to achieve the result of promoting racially segregated housing, despite formal legally binding statements to the contrary by the president and Congress.

The authority under which HUD could have pursued racial desegregation in housing was itself murky. The 1968 statute did not authorize an administrative enforcement mechanism within HUD. The executive order and the two civil rights acts prohibiting discrimination in housing avoided defining key terms such as *racial discrimination* and *affirmative action* in any operationally meaningful way. *Fair housing* and *unfair housing practices* are not clearly defined, nor are the steps identified that federal agencies should take to promote fair housing (Lamb, 1984:163).

Would-be implementers found no help from the regulations. Under Presidents Nixon and Ford, HUD delayed writing regulations for the fair housing law. The few regulations that did get written contained ambiguities and uncertain definitions (Lamb, 1984:179). Not until the end of the Carter presidency did a complete set of fair housing regulations get written, and they were quickly dumped by the Reagan administration (Citizens' Commission on Civil Rights, 1983:49; *New York Times*, April 13, 1983). More than 15 years after the law was passed, regulations to guide implementation and spell out congressional intent were still absent.

Both nationally and at the local level HUD operated under norms that stressed federal deference to local wishes, bargaining with local officials rather than enforcing regulations or laws, and maintaining good relations with local officials so that HUD would get important local support for a number of its other programs and for its existence in general. Ultimately, for example, HUD simply would not question formal local assurances that the city was doing all it could to eliminate racial discrimination and segregation in housing even when such assurances were obviously untrue.

There was no countervailing local group or coalition that took a different view from the official city view in dealing with HUD. Had there been well-organized and persistent local dissidents to appeal to the local and national HUD officials, the outcome might have been the same, but at least HUD could not have easily ignored what was happening.

The public housing program probably helped provide better housing for some poor people in Chicago and elsewhere. But despite national policy, it does not appear that the program helped reduce the amount of racial segregation in housing. In fact, at least in Chicago, the program was used to perpetuate and even increase segregated patterns of housing.

HUD's reluctant performance in relation to fair housing provisions underscores the importance of presidential leadership as a symbol of federal commitment to implementation. Both Nixon and Ford shied away from supporting fair housing goals, and

Carter's support was mixed. The Department of Justice under Reagan reduced the pace of litigation and stressed voluntary agreements with local real estate agents. Fair housing remains the most poorly implemented of all civil rights laws.

As a result of halfhearted enforcement, the impact of fair housing laws on reducing segregated housing has been painfully slow. The first nationwide study of racial residential patterns showed an average reduction of six points on a standard measure of segregation between 1970 and 1980. At that rate, it would take another 50 years before existing segregation would be reduced by one half (Citizens' Commission on Civil Rights, 1983).

The Office for Civil Rights of HEW

In 1964 Congress passed the Civil Rights Act, which included a Title VI that provided that "No person in the United States shall, on the basis of race, color, or national origin, be excluded from participation in, be denied the benefits of, or be subjected to discrimination under, any program or activity receiving federal financial assistance." Similar prohibitions were included to cover sex discrimination in education programs and activities (in Title IX of the Education Amendments of 1972) and discrimination against the handicapped "in any program or activity receiving federal financial assistance" (in Section 504 of the Rehabilitation Act of 1973).

In the first few years the major enforcement activities for Title VI came from the commissioner's office in the Office of Education (which was part of the Department of Health, Education, and Welfare). In 1967, however, a separate Office for Civil Rights (OCR) was created in HEW and was charged with enforcing Title VI for all HEW programs. Education aid programs were the principal focus of their activities. When Title VI and section 504 were added to the statute books OCR assumed enforcement responsibility for them (on OCR see Rabkin, 1980; and Bullock, 1980).

The OCR implementation record was mixed. It seemed to move well and successfully in dealing with racial segregation in public schools in the South. But in dealing with the same problems in the North and in dealing with issues of discrimination against women in education, segregation of hispanics, and discrimination against the handicapped its record was not impressive, to put it mildly. What follows will summarize very briefly the general tone of OCR implementation activities in the southern segregation cases and then in its other antidiscrimination activities. We will also indicate some of the reasons for the very different performances in the two areas.

Southern school segregation. From 1965 to 1967 the commissioner of education began to move swiftly to implement Title VI against southern school systems bent on noncompliance. OCR picked up these activities when it came into being, wrote broad regulations quickly, and moved swiftly to implement them. The target was clear. OCR did not need to rely on a field staff, as it conducted few on-site inspections. It simply let figures and past history suffice to prove noncompliance. It was supported by Congress and the president, or at least left alone in a benign fashion. Local school systems were often hostile, but the leverage of funds-cutoff threats was too much to resist. And aside from the schools themselves and diehard southern members of Congress, there was little political support for stalling.

The results of these activities are impressive. In 1964 more than 98 percent of black public school students in the South were attending what amounted to all black schools (defined as 90 percent or more black). By 1968 this figure had dropped to 68 percent and by 1972 it had dropped to less than 9 percent. Most of these changes can fairly be attributed to OCR activities.

Other targets. When other activities were undertaken by OCR the results were unimpressive. This is clearest in the case of school segregation, primarily of blacks in the North and of hispanics in the Southwest. Forward movement on behalf of women and the handicapped has also been slow.

In general, as it attacked these new targets in the 1970s, OCR proceeded with very broad claims and definitions on paper but very weak and sporadic enforcement. Its critics that did not want progress were outraged by the extravagant claims of authority. Its critics that wanted progress, such as civil rights groups, denounced its dismal enforcement record.

OCR in the 1970s pursued this self-defeating course for several reasons. At the level of sweeping claims it was dealing with very broad and vague statutes and did so in the absence of any further direction from Congress or from the White House. OCR was genuinely committed to the rhetoric of civil rights and thought it could satisfy its civil rights activist clients by making broad-gauged pronouncements in support of nondiscrimination.

However, politically it ran into tougher customers. Even before OCR existed, a foretaste of the problems was given the commissioner of education when he tried to move against the city of Chicago. At the behest of the mayor of Chicago the president personally intervened to quash HEW efforts and the commissioner of education quickly went on to other pursuits and, in fact, another job.

A comparison of the two efforts. At least six factors in the circumstances surrounding these two different OCR ventures help explain the very different outcomes.

1. In the southern case the target was quite clear and progress was easy to measure. All-black and all-white schools needed to be transformed into biracial schools. Given the legal history of segregation in the South, any substantial segregation could be assumed to be the continuing result of years of what had been subsequently defined as unconstitutional. In the nonsouthern cases, however, the targets were more diffuse because there were other minorities in addition to blacks, and the existence of de facto segregation was not automatically provable as illegal. Thus, much more field work and investigation was needed.

2. The mandate for OCR in the southern case was also clear. The law was broad, but OCR and its bureaucratic and legislative superiors were all willing and anxious to have it focus on the southern target. In the other cases the mandate from above became very fuzzy. The laws were broad, vague, and ambiguous about details of definition. What is discrimination, for example? At the same time, OCR was left alone to make its own definitions without any particular guidance from anywhere else.

3. In the southern case Congress and the presidency were supportive of OCR efforts. In the other cases important parts of Congress and the presidency were either hostile, or, at best, only occasionally and sporadically supportive of OCR efforts. Some high legislative and bureaucratic officials supported some efforts but were bitterly critical of others and neutral or unconcerned about most. No one was uniformly supportive.

4. The southern target was visible, consolidated, and an easy mark. OCR could rely on its Washington staff to do most of the

work. This meant that clarity of instructions to bureaucrats could be achieved relatively easily. It also meant that a relatively small number of people would be involved and could be selected by the office head on the basis of ability to undertake specific tasks. In the nonsouthern cases—because they were more numerous, national rather than limited to 17 southern states, and aimed at many targets (discrimination against all minorities, women, and the handicapped)—OCR had to create and then rely on a sizable field apparatus for enforcement. This staff was much less capable than the Washington staff in the early OCR years and also received inadequate direction and instruction from Washington on how to proceed.

5. OCR was clearly committed—both in word and deed—to southern desegregation. The commitment in nonsouthern cases was rhetorically strong but questionable in terms of actual activities.

6. In the southern cases local forces were isolated and could only put up short-term resistance. In the nonsouthern cases the opponents of action proved to be much more numerous and much stronger.

The Equal Employment Opportunity Commission

Title VII of the Civil Rights Act of 1964 prohibited discrimination in hiring on the basis of race, sex, or other characteristics unrelated to job qualifications. *President Johnson* created the Equal Employment Opportunity Commission to carry out the mandate of Title VII and to work for equal opportunity in employment. By 1977 EEOC had created a mess—few successes, a monstrous backlog of work, and no political support (Chapman, 1977).

The scope of the problem with performance can be captured in a few figures. By 1977 EEOC had a backlog of 130,000 individual complaints. Its rate of resolving complaints in terms of numbers each year was going down. The General Accounting Office discovered that an individual filing a complaint had only one chance in 33 of having it settled in the same year that it was filed. The average case took two years to settle; some went on for many more years. Some were simply dropped because the complaining parties saw no point to pursuing their complaints after a certain amount of time had passed. This miserable performance—just in terms of processing people and paper—was offset only slightly by some industrywide or companywide rulings that addressed problems for more than one or two people at a time.

The reasons for this performance are several:

1. There was no stability of leadership at the top of the agency. EEOC had 6 different chairpeople and 10 different executive directors (the top professional staff person) during the first 11 years.

2. The agency was split into factions and units that never interacted in Washington. The investigating unit and suit-filing unit, for example, never talked much even though the second unit proceeded on the basis of information developed by the first unit.

3. The field offices, in which most of the hands-on investigations took place, were not staffed with inspiring public servants. In addition to questionable competence they also behaved quite autonomously. As the general counsel of the agency said, "If I can get an investigator to do something, it's only because he wants to. Some of the district directors just tell us to go to hell."

4. EEOC was staffed on the expectation of about 2,000 individual complaints a year. By 1976, however, the number of complaints had grown to 100,000. No doubt many of them were filed for marginal or dubious or symbolic reasons only. But EEOC had no way of knowing that until it investigated them because no effective screening procedure was in place. The individual complaint activity, even if efficiently run, would probably have little net impact on hiring practices except for those few individuals whose complaints were upheld. But it took up three quarters of the funds of the agency and left little time and energy for litigating major suits aimed at large companies or entire industries. Minority groups and women's groups were alienated in two ways: specific complaints were not being processed efficiently, and little effort was being put into the potentially more meaningful activity of pursuing the large cases. There was no identifiable, positive constituency for the agency because of its performance. Some civil rights groups were quite hostile to it.

5. The agency also had another potentially negative constituency in the form of businesses. As long as it pursued primarily individual complaints, especially inefficiently, business hostility was not likely to be highly mobilized. However, if and as it

pursued the larger cases, business could be expected to react negatively. It did. Thus the constituency problem was compounded. The potential positive constituency of civil rights' and women's groups had been alienated by incompetence. One way to regain some of their support was to pursue larger cases. Yet that route would immediately create a negative constituency in the form of powerful businesses and would not guarantee positive support from the civil rights' and women's groups. They would surely remain skeptical for a while until some improvement in performance was apparent.

In 1977 a new chairperson, Eleanor Holmes Norton, began cleaning up the mess at EEOC. She adopted administrative changes to improve case-handling procedures. The backlog gradually began to decline, and the length of time to process an individual complaint was reduced (Sheppard, 1979). Slowly, EEOC began to look like a respectable enforcement agency.

The opposition of the Reagan administration toward affirmative action threatened EEOC's status as a viable agency. Although the agency was initially not included in the undercutting of civil rights enforcement characteristic in the Justice Department, nonetheless the ideological net gradually included it. Staff morale suffered when a hostile General Counsel was appointed who reorganized staff, eliminated positions, and transferred top lawyers to different cities (Citizens Commission on Civil Rights, 1984:97). The position of chairperson was left unfilled for 15 months, as were three vacancies on the commission.

Leaderless and lacking a quorum for business meetings, enforcement activities drooped. The dismissal of cases increased (from 23 percent in fiscal 1980 to 41 percent in fiscal 1983). The number of new cases filed by the agency declined (from 358 in fiscal 1980 to 200 in fiscal 1983). Successful settlements also decreased (from 50 percent in fiscal 1980 to 38 percent in fiscal 1983) (see *Washington Post*, March 12, 1984). The only positive development was a reduction to 500 of the backlog of pending cases (*Washington Post*, March 14, 1984), although critics claimed the reduction had come at the expense of thorough reviews of cases.

Perhaps most significant for the redress of discriminatory practices was the trend away from filing broad class action litigation. Of the 358 new cases filed in fiscal 1980, one sixth attacked broad patterns of discrimination. Only 5 percent of the new cases filed in fiscal 1983 fit the same description.

The practice of focusing on individuals instead of classes or groups of people mirrored a policy in the Justice Department set by the Assistant Attorney General for Civil Rights. EEOC formally adopted the policy in early 1985 in a policy statement from Clarence Thomas, the chairman of the commission, who said "we are going to go all-out for anybody that was wronged...by litigating cases where there is a finding of discrimination. That is what this agency should be doing."(Quoted in *Washington Post*, February 13, 1985.)

The implication of the change is that cases prosecuted affect only those individuals who have the time, courage, and money to pursue their grievance actively in person. In addition to limits placed by time and money, the outcomes of such cases are limited to individuals, and do not contain remedies for other persons in similar situations who did not file a suit. The effect is to redefine, none too subtly, affirmative action to a meaning more compatible to the administration. Employers will merely have to discontinue discrimination against an individual rather than actively adopt remedial employment hiring goals, timetables, and ratios to correct past patterns and practices of discrimination.

Implementation of the Voting Rights Act

Introduction. The Voting Rights Act, passed in 1965 and renewed in 1970, 1975, and 1982, is generally viewed as the most successful and least controversial of the nation's civil rights laws. There is no serious or effective opposition to it at the national level, and local officials' efforts to thwart implementation are isolated and random.

The goals of the original act and its later versions have been reasonably clear. Progress was ascertainable through concrete measures of registration and voting rates. Although the ability of the Justice Department to monitor compliance physically at the local level has been limited, this has not substantially impeded goal achievement. The Department of Justice, under the watchful eye of Congress, continues to make administrative changes to improve handling of cases and ensure that election practices in states and localities are not discriminatory.

When does voting discrimination exist: renewing the law. The Supreme Court in 1980 ruled that the intent to discriminate had to be proven in civil rights cases—the effects of discrimination were insufficient to indicate a violation of civil rights was present. This standard was narrower and more difficult to prosecute.

Debate on the extension of the Voting Rights Act in 1981 and 1982 addressed the ruling of the Court. The chairman of the House Judiciary Committee, *Peter Rodino* (D-N.J.), summarized the position of the advocates of a results test clearly: "Efforts to find a 'smoking gun' to establish racial discriminatory purpose or intent are not only futile but irrelevant to the consideration whether discrimination has resulted from such election practices." (Quoted in *National Journal*, April 3, 1982:5931.) The House included a results provision in both its 1981 and 1982 bills. The Attorney General argued against it, but after the Senate passed the bill with the results test included, President Reagan did not object. The bill was signed into law on June 29, 1982.

The president waited until the last minute to support the extension effort, despite widespread bipartisan support in Congress for renewal. His personal role offended civil rights groups, especially when he endorsed the restrictive intent test contained in the Court decision.

Just days after the Voting Rights Act was extended, the Supreme Court overturned its 1980 decision, and ruled that evidence of discrimination was sufficient to demonstrate intentional voting rights discrimination (*National Journal*, July 10, 1982:1230). This outcome underscored the validity of the position adopted by Congress in the reauthorization of the act.

Voting rights enforcement. The 1965 act strengthened judicial remedies and added direct federal intervention as a new mechanism for enforcing the provisions of the law. Prior to 1965, statutes affecting voting relied on courts alone to counter discrimination. The new act gave implementation responsibility to the attorney general and introduced new enforcement tools. The attorney general could send federal examiners and observers to supervise local registration and elections. Also, states whose voting records met certain criteria were automatically subject to federal oversight of any changes in their election rules; preclearance by the national government was mandatory. The 25-year extension approved in 1982 contained a new provision that permitted states to be excused from federal supervision of electoral practices if they could demonstrate to a federal district court in Washington D.C. that their election practices for the preceding 10 years had been free of discrimination.

Federal examiners were used to ensure that blacks were registered without impediment while federal observers attended elections to make sure blacks were permitted to vote and that their votes were fairly counted. Attorney General Katzenbach preferred to promote voluntary compliance, believing that effective local organization and support, not a swarm of federal officials, were essential to register blacks successfully and get them to vote.

The desire to achieve the goals of the legislation through cooperation did not preclude a federal presence, however. Scher and Button (1984:41) report that most examiners were used during the first two years of implementation. Examiners were sent to only 60 to 533 covered jurisdictions, although additional localities were designated to have examiners. Often just the threat of federal intervention was sufficient to stimulate local activity. Federal observers, over 12,000 of them, were sent to monitor elections in nine covered states. The use of observers, like examiners, was greatest in the two years immediately following passage of the act.

The *preclearance* requirement automatically compelled states and localities meeting certain criteria to seek prior approval of the Department of Justice before implementing any change in their election laws. The preclearance mechanism was added in order to prevent states from substituting one set of discriminatory practices for another. Coverage was automatic if certain electoral practices had been present in the past (the essential test was whether the locality had used some test or device as a condition for voting or registration and whether less than 50 percent of its eligible population had registered or voted; see General Accounting Office, 1983:4–5).

The volume of preclearance activity started slowly but swelled to about 35,000 cases through 1980. Of these, fewer than 3 percent were rejected by the Justice Department (U.S. Commission on Civil Rights, 1981:68).

As Scher and Button (1984:34) observed, the focus of pre-clearance activity has shifted over twenty years. Originally it dealt with the removal of barriers to the physical act of voting. As localities sought to dilute the impact of black votes more subtly through annexation and gerrymandering, preclearance reviews shifted to keep pace; the effect has been to assure equality of both opportunity and results.

Preclearance enforcement problems. The major difficulty with enforcement of the Section 5 (preclearance) provisions has been and remains the absence of incentives or sanctions to encourage states and localities to comply. There were no rewards, financial or otherwise, nor, until the 1982 extension, did states have any hope of escaping from supervision.

Further, the Justice Department lacks a systematic independent mechanism for collecting information on compliance violations. The department has depended since 1965 on the watchdog role played by local civil rights groups, relying on them to report cases of local changes being implemented without prior approval by the department and cases of local implementation of changes objected to by the department. Even when such violations are discovered, the department has only the option of undertaking a lengthy lawsuit. The General Accounting Office review of enforcement activity found this limitation to be a significant problem in ensuring that states were complying with the act. GAO recommended that the department implement a selective screening and review of compliance on its own, rather than depending exclusively on information brought to it by local groups (General Accounting Office, 1983).

Other implementation difficulties sound familiar: shortage of staff and budget; expanding scope of responsibilities while resources remain constant or shrink; shifting priorities within the department. After 1968 the emphasis in the Justice department moved northward. Although unable to put a quantitative measure on the impact, Ball, Krane, and Lauth (1980) suggest that norms within the Civil Rights Division led attorneys there to shun an actively aggressive stance towards enforcement in favor of a conciliatory, negotiating stance.

Conclusion. The Voting Rights Act has without doubt achieved its goal of increasing black and minority participation in elections. In 1940 only 5 percent of the eligible black population was registered to vote in 11 southern states, and by 1964 only 38 percent was registered. This figure jumped to 62 percent by 1968. Actual voting rates followed a similar pattern of a large increase immediately following the 1965 act, with a levelling off a few years later (1968). Studies of disparities in black and white voting rates indicate that the differences result from socio-economic factors rather than continued disenfranchisement techniques directed at minorities (Wolfinger and Rosenstone, 1980:90–92; Verba and Nie, 1972:170–171).

Studies by academics and the General Accounting Office have not examined voting in states not covered by the preclearance requirement. The assumption behind preclearance is that in excluded states the level of discrimination is nonexistent or so limited that the payoff of investigation would be marginal at best. The bailout provision adopted in 1982 may permit some of the currently covered states to be excused from federal supervision if they can demonstrate a record of good behavior. But there is nothing to suggest the Voting Rights Act will not continue to be implemented fairly. Even in the unhospitable civil rights atmosphere created by the Reagan administration described earlier in this chapter, implementation of the Voting Rights Act has not suffered.

SUMMARY AND CONCLUSIONS

We have now inspected many separate instances and examples of implementation of redistributive policies and programs. A number of themes emerge from these investigations coupled with our observations in the opening of the chapter.

1. Redistributive policy is conceived during ideological debate and disagreement over what amount to issues of class or race, or both. Predictable coalitions that retain stability over time are typically engaged in the debate over whether to enact redistributive policy at all (see Ripley and Franklin, 1984:chapter 6). These same characteristics follow redistributive policy into its implementation phase as long as the implementation pursues or attempts to pursue or appears to be pursuing redistributive ends. Ideological debate continues. Political coalitions of a fairly predictable ideological character both for and against the programs

appear and often conduct the debate, when rhetoric is stripped away, in terms of protecting existing distribution of benefits and values on a class or racial basis or promoting a redistribution of them on that basis.

2. During implementation, political opposition to pursuing redistributive ends is often very strong and well organized. The interests that feel threatened mobilize, coalesce, and put considerable pressure on the bureaucratic implementers both directly and, when they can, indirectly through appealing to Congress or even to the White House. The mayor of Chicago's successful intervention in direct fashion with the president of the United States to block an OCR suit in Chicago is an exaggerated instance of such appeals. But other forms of it go on in other areas and are sometimes successful. The case of HUD and Chicago in relation to discrimination in public housing suggests that sometimes the bureaucrats themselves cave in.

3. The substance of policy excites both opposition and support. Often the opponents of the substance of the policy can attack the processes by which it is being implemented, complaining that they are unfair, awkward, inefficient, and harassing. Thus they do not have to oppose benefits to the poor or minorities directly, but they can attack the stupidity of the bureaucracy in developing poor implementation processes. For example, in criticizing CETA programs of training for the disadvantaged in general, opponents often focused on fraud and abuse that were allowed by deficient management processes. Or in opposing the goals presumably sought by OCR or EEOC, the opponents could, with some reason, point out that the agencies relied on poor procedures.

Genuinely redistributive programs often invent and use new procedures. And there is a considerable amount of ad hoc innovation in devising implementation procedures. Then these procedures become overlaid with bureaucratic language, habits, and proclivities, and the results are—even to the proponents of the redistributive ends—often disappointing and sometimes downright shocking. Virtually all redistributive programs rely on a direct hands-on contact with the recipients and sometimes the restricted clients. This feature inevitably rouses suspicion and criticism, sometimes just, of the processes for determining and applying eligibility criteria. Only a program like social security pensions, which primarily involves direct mailing of checks to recipients, can defuse these kinds of procedural criticisms. A voucher system for benefits, in which recipients are given a piece of paper with which to go shopping for housing, education, or a job, has some appeal. But even here the verification processes for eligibility are likely to be criticized.

4. Good management of redistributive programs cannot eliminate all of the complaints about process, but it can certainly minimize such complaints and can at least focus the debate on the substance of the policy goals. Bad management makes it virtually impossible for an agency to move beyond procedural debate and even get to the task of pursuing its substantive ends.

5. In addition to direct capitulation to opposition by implementing bureaucrats, a favorite means for reducing conflict over implementation of redistributive policy is for the whole program to move into a more distributive mode. Standards for success move from helping the disadvantaged to rapid, efficient, and geographically fair dispersal of money. Many CETA programs, community development programs, EDA programs, and aid to elementary and secondary education programs changed so that they became perceived in largely distributive terms. This change muted the debate over redistribution, but inevitably, the price was that genuine redistributive goals were also largely diluted.

6. As is evident by now, achieving genuine redistribution in the implementation process is extremely difficult. The path to such outcomes is fraught with perils, both political and managerial. A major consistent complicating factor is that a very large number of actors are involved in trying to implement redistributive policy. Where programs seem likely to have a chance of success, almost inevitably someone—probably at the local level—has taken the lead in building a *network* of supporting actors and institutions and simultaneously in neutralizing much of the potential opposition. The presence of such a network or its absence goes far in explaining relative progress or lack of it in most of our examples. Positive networks are, no doubt, always helpful in implementation of any kind of policy, but—given both the large number of actors and the likelihood of ideological positions being taken and maintained unless there are pressures pushing in another direction—such network-building is essential in the redistributive arena. A positive network cannot guarantee programmatic progress, but it at least increases the possibility of such progress.

CHAPTER 8

The Politics of Implementation

In this chapter we seek to weave a number of conceptual points with a number of points stemming from the empirical examinations of implementation in different policy areas. Some of the conceptual points have been made—at least in partial form—in earlier chapters. In this chapter we want to make a more complete assessment of the nature of implementation and its place in the policy process in the United States. We deliberately choose the words *more complete assessment* rather than *final assessment* because there is a great deal more to be learned about implementation processes and politics and the relationships of those processes and politics to program outcomes and results. We explicitly view the conclusions in this chapter as tentative. They represent our assessments at present; but we hope many scholars will find out a good deal more in future examinations and reexaminations.

Implementation depends, in large part, on a set of bureaucratic processes. Implementation involves a highly politicized set of interactions and interrelationships on the part of many actors. In the American setting there is no contradiction between these two general characteristics because, in fact, American bureaucracies are highly politicized actors in both the policy formulation process and in the program implementation process.

In this chapter we want to address three broad topics: (1) a summary characterization of the general shape of implementation; (2) a comparative review of the patterns of implementation for the four basic types of domestic policy; and (3) a short discussion of the nature of successful implementation.

THE GENERAL SHAPE OF IMPLEMENTATION

Implementation of all different kinds of policies and programs has some features that seem to apply across the board. All of these features result in complicated processes, confusing patterns of interaction, and—at minimum—delays for implementation. And each individual feature, although it can be broken out separately for analytical purposes, interacts with the others to compound the complexity.

First, bureaucracies are omnipresent during implementation processes, but they are not omnipotent. Note that we use the plural—*bureaucracies.* This indicates that most policies have several different governmental bureaucracies involved—different units in the same federal agency, field units as well as central units, and nonfederal units as well as federal units. While they are the most ubiquitous participants in implementation they do not control it. They bargain for influence just like other actors although they have a head start in some cases because of numbers and prior possession of information. They also have legal authority—but even that is subject to constant challenge, partly because congressional delegations of authority are often so vague and ambiguous.

Second, federalism is not omnipresent, but it is often a factor in implementation. Many federal policies and supposedly national goals in fact rely on units of state and local government and some nongovernmental units for critical aspects of implementation.

Third, bargaining is omnipresent. Government in the United States is rarely a matter of command from the center, control by the center, and obedience by those commanded and controlled. It is assumed that policies are malleable; they are never really in final form. It is also assumed that at all stages of the policy process various groups and individuals should have access to policymakers and policy implementers to try to influence what they do and how they proceed. Even protective regulatory policies, which represent the clearest case of what, in theory, should look like command and control often turn into situations with large elements of bargaining involved.

Some argue that even more bargaining should deliberately be injected (see, for example, Schuck, 1979). Others object strenuously to the nonauthoritative character of American law and to the prevalence of bargaining and what Lowi (1979) has called "interest group liberalism": the inclusion of interest groups *by design* in all sorts of decision-making and implementation activities. Strong normative arguments can be made in support of Lowi's position. But, like it or not, interest group liberalism does, in fact, characterize the world of implementation in the American policy process.

Fourth, given the pervasiveness of these three features—a strong but not dominant role for multiple governmental bureaucracies; federalism that multiplies the numbers of actors and the access points for influence; and the bargaining norm, in which almost everything is considered to be negotiable and up for grabs almost all of the time—routines for the smooth and efficient implementation of policies and programs are very hard to establish and maintain. In both the distributive field and in those parts of the competitive regulatory field that have come to resemble distribution, some routines involving federal agencies are established some of the time and are supported by the beneficiaries or, in the case of competitive regulation, the regulated interests. However, even in these two areas routines can and do break down, and various complications can arise and introduce disturbances, even chaos, in their place. And in the field of protective regulation, routines are quite rare. In redistributive policy, if routines are established at all, they are usually in many localities, not at the national level.

Finally, the result of all of the above factors is that no single authority appears to be in charge of the implementation of any major single policy, let alone any clustering of policies. As we said in Chapter 1, in a very real sense there is no single government in the United States in control of implementing policies. There are instead many governments, and each of them may well have its own individual problems in trying to implement its own piece of the policy world. Bargaining, coalition-building, and flux characterize these governments during implementation. In this situation many programs have either beneficiaries or theoretically restricted clients in very important decision-making positions during implementation. The bureaucrats will still be present, but they are hardly autonomous or unchecked. The best bargainers with the most political support get more of what they want during implementation than other actors. The bureaucrats are themselves bargainers much of the time in this process.

In a situation with no single authority in charge, accountability for results or nonresults is diffuse and murky. Who should be praised or blamed? In many cases there is no satisfying answer to that question beyond making a *long* list. The lack of a single authority in charge also inevitably slows down implementation beyond what the policy formulators view as desirable. Those who view this general situation at least partially positively argue that program implementation becomes more democratic and more responsive to local needs through the access afforded such a large number of actors and through the passage of time.

VARIATIONS IN IMPLEMENTATION BY POLICY TYPE

We chose the fourfold scheme for categorizing policies because we thought there would be some systematic differences between the different policy areas as implementation occurred, and we have not been disappointed. Variations do in fact occur. Not all that we expected turned up with the clarity that we expected, and some variations were observed that we had not particularly expected. In most cases the patterns are not rigid, and there are overlaps in behavior between the different areas. But there are central tendencies that can be observed in looking at the implementation patterns in the four different areas.

The Nature of Processes and Conflicts

Individual points of variation. 1. As indicated above, the likelihood of achieving smooth implementation through establishing stable routines that are widely accepted varies by policy area. It is most likely to occur in distributive implementation, although complications and disruptions can and do occur. It is also possible in competitive regulatory implementation, although complications and disruptions also happen with some frequency. Routines are very hard to establish and maintain in protective regulatory implementation. In redistributive policy federal routines are hard to establish and maintain, except where much of the federal action amounts to the mailing of checks, as with social security benefits that have some redistributive impact. The critical routines are often at the local level in redistributive policy, and these are also hard to establish and maintain.

2. The degree of stability or instability in the identity and working relationships of the principal actors varies from area to area. In general, the actors are fairly stable and retain the same kinds of relationships with each other in both distributive and redistributive policy. There is much more volatility and less stability in the identity and relationships of actors in the two regulatory fields.

3. The degree of conflict and controversy over implementation decisions and activities also varies by arena. Distributive implementation is an area of relatively low conflict. There is considerably more conflict surrounding the implementation of competitive regulatory policy, although its largely distributive nature mutes it in some cases. The implementation of both protective regulation and redistribution involves a high degree of conflict.

4. The presence and strength of opposition to the efforts of the bureaucrats to implement varies directly with the amount of controversy. In the distributive arena there is only sporadic opposition to bureaucratic implementation. The main pressures are to continue and expand the implementation, since it delivers tangible benefits that are coveted.

In the competitive regulatory arena there is some opposition to bureaucratic implementation, usually mounted by temporary coalitions. There is continuing pressure from some quarters to transform the competitive regulatory policies into distributive policies during the course of implementation.

In the protective regulatory arena there is a good deal of opposition to bureaucratic implementation, again mounted by shifting coalitions of opponents. The pressure from these opposing coalitions is basically aimed at eliminating all or most of the regulation, since transforming it into distribution is not feasible in all but a few isolated cases.

In the redistributive arena there tend to be strong, stable coalitions that oppose bureaucratic implementation. The pressures are aimed both at restricting or eliminating the flow of benefits to the targeted beneficiaries (the disadvantaged) and, in some cases, at transforming the programs in a more distributive direction by means such as defining broader eligibility criteria for individuals or mandating wider geographical distribution.

5. The ideological or nonideological content of the debate over implementation also varies by policy type. To the extent it occurs, debate over distributive implementation is usually highly pragmatic and nonideological. Considerable ideology—especially about the merits of deregulation or continued regulation—enters the debates about competitive regulatory implementation. There is even more ideology in the debates over protective regulation— with a small government-deregulation point of view opposed to an active government-regulation-for-the-public-interest point of view. Much of the debate over the implementation of redistributive policy is either openly or implicitly ideological, with issues of class, race, equality, reward for merit, and differing conceptions of justice in dispute.

Some of the ideological debates also focus on processes and advance competing conceptions of fairness, due process, and the meaning of a free government. This is particularly true in the case of protective regulatory policies and also occurs a fair amount of the time in both redistributive and competitive regulatory debates.

6. The nature of the drive for smaller government, less bureaucracy, and deregulation varies among the four policy areas. In the distributive arena there is not much genuine interest in smaller government except at the rhetorical level. Very few interests want their own benefits cut, although some are willing to see others' benefits cut.

In the competitive regulatory arena there have been significant coalitions working for deregulation. These coalitions have had considerable success, particularly in transportation (airlines, railroads, trucking, pipelines). While some implementing agencies are willing to support deregulation, some of the regulated interests resist it because they fear the chaos that the marketplace might bring to their enterprises.

In the protective regulatory arena the smaller government drive is usually aimed at restricting or even eliminating the activity in the name of deregulation. The regulated interests are almost always in the vanguard in pushing for less intrusive governmental activity. The chief officials of many agencies in the Reagan administration have sided primarily with the regulated interests.

In the redistributive arena the drive for smaller government is basically aimed at severely restricting or eliminating the programs under scrutiny.

Summary: Patterns of processes and conflicts. Table 8–1 summarizes the six points discussed above. Taken together they portray the distributive arena during implementation as one of high stability and low conflict. The competitive regulatory implementation arena appears as one of moderate-to-low stability and moderate-to-high conflict. The protective regulatory arena is one of low stability and uniformly high conflict. The redistributive arena appears as one of mixed stability and high conflict.

Actors and Influence

The bureaucracy. There are different layers of bureaucracy involved in the different policy areas. The central federal bureaucracy is present in all four kinds of implementation but is most dominant in competitive regulatory policy and protective regulatory policy. It is active in distributive policy. It is least active, although present, in redistributive policy. Federal field offices are particularly active in both distributive and redistributive policy and have some importance in protective regulatory policy. Depending on the exact design of individual programs, state and local bureaucracies are particularly important in both distributive and redistributive policy.

The chief bureaucrat (the president) and his immediate staff rarely get directly involved in detailed questions of implementation. When they do it seems most likely to happen in cases of protective regulation, but even in that arena, it is rare. This is very different, of course, from the presidential role in policy formulation and legitimation, in which he and his immediate staff are often quite visible, active, and influential. Ronald Reagan's closest advisers and staff were more involved in implementation than the advisers and staffs of his predecessors because the Reagan administration was especially anxious to use all of the policy levers at its disposal to make dramatic changes in the substance of American national policy.

Nongovernmental actors. There is also a different mix of private sector involvement in the different policy areas. In

TABLE 8–1 The Nature of Processes, Relations, and Conflict in Implementation of Different Policy Types

Type of Policy	Likelihood of Generally Accepted Stable Implementation Routines	Degree of Stability of Identity of Principal Actors and the Nature of Their Relationships	Degree of Conflict and Controversy Over Implementation	Degree of Opposition to Bureaucratic Implementation Decisions	Degree of Ideology in Debate Over Implementation	Degree of Pressure for Less Government Activity
Distributive	High	High	Low	Low	Low	Low
Competitive regulatory	Moderate	Low	Moderate	Moderate	Moderate to high	Moderate to high
Protective regulatory	Low	Low	High	High	High	High
Redistributive	Low	High	High	High	Very high	High

distributive policy the most visible and active are the beneficiaries that are receiving the goodies. Usually there are no active participants opposing that distribution at the level of implementation (there may, of course, be debate during policy formulation and legitimation that raises such questions, although even that is relatively rare).

In competitive regulatory policy the regulated interests are the most active private participants. A few consumer groups get involved occasionally.

In the implementation of protective regulation, again the regulated interests are highly visible and influential participants. Consumer groups, environmental groups, and public-interest organizations are also fairly active and visible.

In redistributive policy the recipients—what we earlier characterized as dependent classes and minorities—show some activity in organizing themselves to push for favorable implementation decisions. There is also usually a coalition of private-sector actors opposing implementation decisions they consider to be too favorable to the beneficiaries.

Congress. Congressional involvement in all kinds of implementation is sporadic, but the frequency varies. Even infrequent congressional interventions can be important. Such interventions are fairly frequent in distributive matters, including the distributive aspects of redistributive programs. They come sporadically on a case-by-case basis in both kinds of regulatory policy. Congress is fairly shy about intervening in redistributive implementation *except* to lend its hand to redefine those policies to be more distributive, an intervention it frequently makes. In general, Congress is likely to intervene under two conditions: (1) if tangible benefits going to influential constituents are at stake, and (2) if the federal bureaucrats engage in a hands on relationship with congressional constituents.

Patterns of Influence by Policy Type

Figures 8–1, 8–2, 8–3, and 8–4 summarize the typical influential relationships that are constant and predictable in decision making during the implementation of federal programs. Not every program will exhibit these relationships all of the time. But we think the diagrams accurately represent the large majority of cases.

Figure 8–1 portrays the influential relationships in the implementation of distributive policy. The actors are multiple layers of federal, state, and local bureaucracies, the beneficiaries of the programs (defined as producer interests in the broad way that we have used the term), and Congress. The beneficiaries and the bureaucracies have a close relationship in which influence flows both ways between them in making detailed decisions about implementation. The beneficiaries also have some influence on Congress relative to implementation decisions. And Congress and the bureaucracy interact sporadically and usually mutually influence each other when they do interact.

Figure 8–2 portrays the influence of relationships in the implementation of competitive regulatory policies. The major actors are the central federal bureaucracy in Washington, the regulated interests, Congress, and, occasionally, presumed beneficiaries in the form of general consumer groups. The principal two-way relationship with a good deal of mutual influence is between the bureaucrats and the regulated interests. This does not necessarily imply capture. It implies simply that the regulators and the regulated begin to develop mutually defined interests, although they also disagree on some matters. Secondary relationships exist between the regulated interests and Congress—with the former exerting some influence over the latter on implementation matters—and between Congress and the bureaucracy, with a two-way exchange of influence. The general consumer groups representing presumed beneficiaries are only sporadically active and have some limited influence on Congress and a modest two-way relationship with the bureaucracy.

Figure 8–3 portrays the influence relationships in the implementation of protective regulatory policy. The actors are the federal bureaucracy—both in Washington and in field offices—the regulated interests, Congress, and consumer groups representing presumed beneficiaries of the policies. Here the most important relationships are within the bureaucracy itself. The bureaucracy proceeds in a much less cozy relationship with the regulated interests than is the case in competitive regulatory policy. There is an important two-way relationship between the bureaucratic cluster of actors and the regulated interests, although hostility rather than cooperation may characterize the content of that relationship. The regulated interests also have considerable

FIGURE 8–1 Patterns of Influence in Implementation of Distributive
Policies

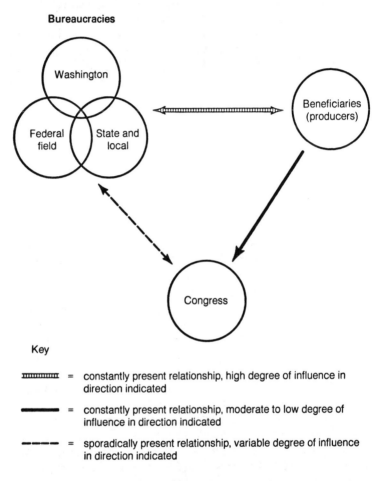

influence over Congress. Congress, in turn, engages in a sporadic
two-way relationship with the bureaucrats. The consumer groups
have a moderately strong two-way relationship with the bureaucrats and sporadically influence congress. Contending forces—regulated interests typically against vigorous implementation and
consumer forces typically for it—both have moderately strong
influence and continuing access to the regulating bureaucracies.

FIGURE 8–2   Patterns of Influence in Implementation of Competitive
Regulatory Policies

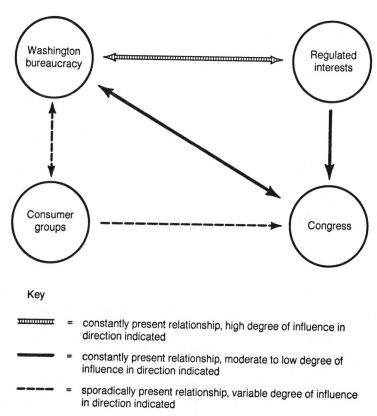

Key

━━━━━━   = constantly present relationship, high degree of influence in
direction indicated

━━━━━━   = constantly present relationship, moderate to low degree of
influence in direction indicated

━ ━ ━ ━   = sporadically present relationship, variable degree of influence
in direction indicated

They also both have ties to Congress as an indirect channel to the
bureaucracy, although the regulated interests' ties to Congress
tend to be stronger. Thus a system of competition is set up. This
competition pushes and pulls the bureaucracy in different directions at once. In a sense, it also gives the bureaucracy more
latitude than in the distributive and competitive regulatory arenas.

Figure 8–4 portrays the influence relationships in the implementation of redistributive programs. The actors are multiple
bureaucracies (federal agencies in Washington, federal agencies
in the field, and a host of state and local agencies); the beneficiary

FIGURE 8–3 Patterns of Influence in Implementation of Protective Regulatory Policies

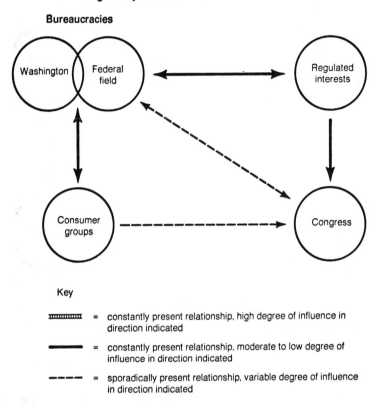

Bureaucracies

Key

▨▨▨▨▨ = constantly present relationship, high degree of influence in direction indicated

■■■■ = constantly present relationship, moderate to low degree of influence in direction indicated

– – – – = sporadically present relationship, variable degree of influence in direction indicated

groups and organizations representing them; ideological opponents of the program; and Congress. Again the bureaucracies, particularly at the local level, have considerable latitude. As in protective regulation there are no consistently cozy mutually beneficial two-way relationships. But the beneficiaries, *if organized,* have a fairly strong two-way relationship with implementing bureaucracies. Opponents have a strong one-way relationship: they put pressure on the bureaucracies to restrict the programs or to change them into distributive programs. They also put the

FIGURE 8–4   Patterns of Influence in Implementation of Redistributive
Policies

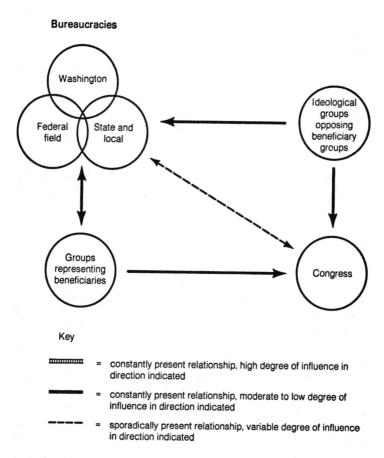

Bureaucracies

Key

███████ = constantly present relationship, high degree of influence in
direction indicated

▬▬▬▬ = constantly present relationship, moderate to low degree of
influence in direction indicated

- - - - = sporadically present relationship, variable degree of influence
in direction indicated

same kind of pressure on Congress. Beneficiary groups also have
access to Congress, however, and thus compete for congressional
attention. Congress, in turn, intervenes in bureaucratic activity at
the federal level only sporadically and primarily to push the
programs into a more distributive mode.

SUCCESSFUL IMPLEMENTATION—WHAT IS IT AND HOW DO YOU KNOW IT?

Recall that in the preceding chapters we looked at implementation results in terms of efficiency of operations, which is, we believe, the dominant working definition of success used by bureaucrats. That definition had three components: general productivity of a program as judged by the various standards of the bureaucrats themselves, no excessive time lags in forward movement, and a relative lack of controversy.

Now we want to consider the question of success in implementation again and do not want to be bound by the dominant views of the implementing bureaucrats. However, we must warn you we have no simple, absolute standard of successful implementation. As this book has made abundantly clear, implementation is complex. There is no reason to expect that judging relative success is less complex.

Three Conceptions

The notion of success in implementation has no single widely accepted definition. Different analysts and different actors have very different meanings in mind when they talk about or think about successful implementation. (For good discussions of assessing implementation see Nakamura and Smallwood, 1980: Chapter 8; and Bullock, 1984). There are three dominant ways of thinking about successful implementation.

First, some argue that success should be measured by the degree of *compliance* on the part of bureaucratic underlings to their bureaucratic superiors or by the degree of compliance on the part of bureaucracies in general with specific mandates contained in the statute. The compliance perspective merely speaks to the question of bureaucratic behavior. While bureaucratic behavior may be interesting to students of organizational theory it has little interest, in its narrow sense, to students of politics or to participants or citizens trying to make sense out of the confusion and complexity of public policies and programs.

A second perspective argues that successful implementation is characterized by smoothly functioning routines and the absence of problems. Accepting the *smoothness-lack of disruption* perspective would mean, given what we have observed about policy implementation, that successful implementation would generally be possible only in the distributive and competitive regulatory arenas. By definition, almost no instances of protective regulatory or redistributive policy could be successful. Conflict is not, in our view, necessarily bad. When passions run high, as they do most of the time in protective regulatory and redistributive questions, politics is a perfectly natural way for actors to pursue their conflicting ends. American policymaking and policy implementation is heavily politicized at all points. Since such politicization is a basic feature of our system, to say that implementation is less successful to the extent it exhibits conflictual politics makes little sense. To be sure, the outcome of the politics may make a hash of any specific program, but that is a separate question.

We think that these two conceptions of success are too narrow and have limited political interest. Therefore, we advance a third perspective, which is that successful implementation *leads to desired performance in and impacts from* whatever program is being analyzed. This perspective is the most appealing to us—despite problems we will discuss below—because governmental implementation activity is valuable only if it achieves something. Of what problems should the student of implementation be aware if this perspective is adopted?

First, there is no way around the fact that *desirable* is not an objective, neutral concept. The *desirability* relates to values held by one or more people. In some cases virtually all of the concerned parties may agree on the nature of desirable performance and impact. In more cases the actors are likely to disagree. The analyst of implementation must, when there are value conflicts, be aware of and take account of them. This means that the analyst may judge success from several different value perspectives (including his or her own, as long as it is clearly labeled) at the same time. And, depending on the content of those perspectives, the implementation of same program may be labeled a success from one perspective and a failure from another.

Second, programmatic impact is a very complicated concept. There are different levels of impact, and many impacts take a very long time to emerge. Consider a construction program for local health centers, for example. Usage or nonusage of the center by patients can be measured, but that is only one, direct, first-order impact. Additional longer-range impacts include reduction in time lost from work or school because of illness, increased productivity at school or work because of good health, and improvement in the rates of morbidity (illness) and mortality. But such effects take a long time to observe.

Even if important long-term impacts are measured, can they be attributed to the program? Determining causality is very difficult to do. For example, if the aggregate number of sick leave hours reported by workers in the area served by the health center is lower six years after the center was built and employment productivity is higher, have these changes been caused by the presence of the health center and the improved health care available there? Or are they due to other factors, such as changes in size and composition of the population, or changes in the type of employment and the reliance on automation? There are no pat answers.

Causality is problematic in another sense. How can it be proved that the attributes of implementation itself did or did not have anything to do with those impacts? Some programs may be so attractive and the incentives so compelling (unemployment compensation might be a good example) that it will implement itself even if the administering bureaucracy is filled with bumbling idiots. Clients will still draw their unemployment checks and spend them for food and shelter (the intended impacts) even if they have to wait six hours in line to get the checks. They will grumble about the half-witted bureaucrats involved, but, in fact, the half-witted bureaucrats cannot really sabotage the program fatally.

On the other hand, there are also programs whose design is so poor or whose goals are so far beyond the capacity of anyone to achieve them that not even the most intelligent and conscientious implementation decisions will be able to produce the desired impact.

Furthermore, the phenomenon of overselling a program at the time of policy formulation and legitimation is well-known and, in fact, characterizes much of policymaking in the United States (see, for many examples, Ripley and Franklin, 1984). Expectations created about what programs can achieve are often unrealistically high and, therefore, disappointment with the results is almost automatic. Jones (1979:119) makes the same general point when he observes that when actors perceive what they think is a crisis in some substantive field they typically react by making both "organizational and substantive changes...that are frequently quite beyond the capacity of government to absorb. 'Policy beyond capability' is typically proposed as a response to perceived failure in the existing system."

Even if one is willing to let the political actors' judgments about success of the implementation-impact linkage serve as the final judgments, serious problems immediately arise. Oversight by political actors of program impact is quite weak. Congress usually contents itself with a few anecdotes if it asks serious questions at all. Many bureaucratic agencies content themselves with the same fare, and that is all they are required to pass on to Congress.

Attention to implementation as a separate phenomenon is not a high priority for most political actors. Congress usually focuses on what amount to questions of secondary importance. One focus typically is on fraud and abuse—also the customary focus of the General Accounting Office, an arm of Congress. A second focus is on matters even more minute and less important—"why did you fire the secretary for the program director in my district?" for example. In short, the major congressional concern having to do with implementation is simply seeing that money is spent and that it is done so in timely fashion (defined inevitably in terms of the end of fiscal years) and without inordinate theft.

Only a few bureaucracies occasionally try to assess the impacts of implementation in any sophisticated way beyond concern with the minutiae of literal compliance.

The Bottom Line

Where does the preceding discussion leave us? We hardly need to repeat that implementation is complex and that any simple, single standard for judging success is highly inappropriate. We have already indicated that we find the perspective that links implementation success to program success the most satisfying, despite its numerous theoretical and practical problems. A successful program is, centrally, that which achieves both short-run performance in accord with its objectives *and* longer-run impacts in accord with objectives. (See Chapter 1 for the definitions of performance and impacts.) It is also one that does not have deleterious unintended consequences, although it may have beneficial unintended consequences. The critical questions about implementation processes are whether, in the final analysis, they helped or hindered a program achieve the kind of performance and impact sketched above. Assessing implementation and reaching judgments about its relative success ideally involves judgments about the program itself *and* judgments about the *facilitative or nonfacilitative consequences* of implementation activities in relation to program performance and impact.

Inevitably, by the above definition, final or summative judgments cannot be made about the degree of implementation success until some convincing evidence on program performance and impact can also be gathered and analyzed. This often takes years. But, of course, the actors responsible for implementing programs want to make judgments about implementation *during* the process itself and before performance data or impact data are available. Can outside analysts help make such timely judgments? The answer is a qualified yes. They can help because their guesses about the ultimate facilitating or nonfacilitating effect of various implementation options can be more informed and more grounded in an understanding of abstract principles and a wide range of empirical experience than the guesses of the actors themselves. Analysts have a broader perspective but they do not have a magic formula with which to judge implementation while it is taking place. Evaluations and assessments will, by definition, be partial, tentative, and formative instead of summative. Only later—after the program can be assessed—can more definitive judgments be made about implementation success. Those later, more definitive judgments are also important because, although they are generally too late to be of use in the program itself, they help build the stock of both theoretical and empirical knowledge about implementation in general.

Note that we do not dismiss political benefits of certain kinds of implementation as irrelevant. For example, if implementation processes help produce a satisfied clientele or greater political support, those developments can ultimately lead to increased achievement of program performance and impact goals. But we do not think that political benefits and political harmony should be the primary, and certainly not the only, criteria for judging implementation success. Similarly, criteria of simple efficiency can be relevant in helping promote a productive linkage between implementation and performance and impact.

Although we have used the words *success* and *successful* throughout this book in talking about implementation, we would have no objection if the word *facilitative* were substituted for *successful*. For us, successful implementation is that which facilitates desired program performance and impact.

Although we want you to remember all of the complexities and problems we have discussed in the preceding pages and throughout the book, we are also willing to offer the following summary statements for your consideration:

1. Successful implementation facilitates desired program performance and impact.
2. Assessment of *current* implementation activities by nonparticipant analysts is formative and involves informed *projections* of the degree of facilitation being generated by the activities in relation to *projected* performance and impact results.
3. Assessment of *past* implementation activities by nonparticipant analysts can be summative, although probably not definitive, through focusing on the degree of facilitation generated by the activities in relation to some known performance and impact results.

References and Bibliography

ABERBACH, J. D., R. D. PUTNAM, and B. A. ROCKMAN [1981] *Bureaucrats and Politicians in Western Democracies.* Cambridge, Mass.: Harvard University Press.

ABERBACH, J. D., and B. A. ROCKMAN [1976] "Clashing Beliefs within the Executive Branch: The Nixon Administration Bureaucracy." *American Political Science Review* 70 (June): 456–68.

—— [1977] "The Overlapping Worlds of American Federal Executives and Congressmen." *British Journal of Political Science* 7 (January): 23–47.

—— [1978] "Bureaucrats and Clientele Groups: A View from Capitol Hill." *American Journal of Political Science* 22 (November): 818–32.

ADAMS, G. [1982] *The Politics of Defense Contracting: The Iron Triangle.* New Brunswick, N.J.: Transaction Books.

ADVISORY COMMISSION ON INTERGOVERNMENTAL RELATIONS [1979] *A Catalog of Federal Grant-In-Aid Programs to State and Local Governments: Grants Funded Fiscal Year 1978.* Washington, D.C.: U.S. Government Printing Office.

ARNOLD, R. D. [1979] *Congress and the Bureaucracy.* New Haven: Yale University Press.

BAILEY, S. K., and E. K. MOSHER [1968] *ESEA: The Office of Education Administers a Law.* Syracuse, N.Y.: Syracuse University Press.

BALL, B. P. [1976] "Water Pollution and Compliance Decision Making." In *Public Policy Making in a Federal System,* edited by C. O. Jones and R. D. Thomas. Beverly Hills, Calif.: Sage.

BALL, H., D. KRANE, and T. P. LAUTH, JR. [1980] "Accountability and Discretion in a Federal System: The Politics of Compliance with the 1965 Voting Rights Act." Presentation at Symposium on Southern Politics, Charleston, S.C. (March 27–29).

BALZANO, M. [1979] "Putting the Skids to Meals on Wheels." *Regulation* (September/October): 52–54.

BARDACH, E. [1977] *The Implementation Game: What Happens After a Bill Becomes a Law.* Cambridge, Mass.: MIT Press.

BARRETT, S. and C. FUDGE, eds. [1981] *Policy and Action: Essays on the Implementation of Public Policy.* London: Methuen.

BAUMER, D. C. and C. E. VAN HORN [1984] *The Politics of Unemployment.* Washington: Congressional Quarterly Press.

BEAM, D. R. [1979] "The Accidental Leviathan: Was the Growth of Government a Mistake?" *Intergovernmental Perspective* 5 (Fall): 12–19.

BEHRMAN, B. [1980] "Civil Aeronautics Board." In *The Politics of Regulation,* edited by J. Q. Wilson. New York: Basic Books.

BERMAN, P. [1978] "The Study of Macro- and Micro-Implementation." *Public Policy* 26 (Spring): 157–84.

BERNSTEIN, M. [1980] "Dayton's I–675: The Washington, D.C., Horror Story." *Ohio Magazine* (March): 69–71.

BERRY, J. M. [1979] "Rivals Forced to Supply Oil to Ashland." *Washington Post* (December 31).

BROWNING, R. P., D. R. MARSHALL, and D. H. TABB [1980] "Implementation and Political Change: Sources of Local Variations in Federal Social Programs." *Policy Studies Journal* 8 (Special Issue 2): 616–32.

BRUNNER, R. D. [1980] "Decentralized Energy Policies." *Public Policy* 28 (Winter): 71–91.

BULLOCK, C. S., III [1980] "The Office for Civil Rights and Implementation of Desegregation Programs in the Public Schools." *Policy Studies Journal* 8 (Special Issue 2): 597–616.

——— [1984] "Conditions Associated with Policy Implementation." In *Implementation of Civil Rights Policy,* edited by C. S. Bullock III and C. M. Lamb. Monterey, Calif.: Brooks/Cole.

BULLOCK, C. S. III and C. M. LAMB, eds. [1984] *Implementation of Civil Rights Policy.* Monterey, Calif.: Brooks/Cole.

CALIFANO, J. A., Jr. [1978] *Remarks before the Economic Club of Chicago* (April 20).

CARSON, D. C. [1980] "Mesa Mint Battle May Mean Months of Building Delay." *San Diego Union* (March 25).

CHAPMAN, W. [1977] "An Agency in Shambles." *Washington Post* (February 6).

CHASE, G. [1979] "Implementing a Human Services Program: How Hard Will It Be?" *Public Policy* 27 (Fall): 385–435.

CHUBB, J. E. [1983] *Interest Groups and the Bureaucracy: The Politics of Energy.* Stanford, Calif.: Stanford University Press.

CITIZENS' COMMISSION ON CIVIL RIGHTS [1983] "A Decent Home." Washington, D.C.: Center for National Policy Review, Catholic University (April).

—— [1984] "Affirmative Action to Open the Doors of Job Opportunity." Washington, D.C. Center for National Policy Review, Catholic University (June).

CLARK, T. B. [1979a] "The Power Vacuum Outside the Oval Office." *National Journal* (January 24): 296–300.

—— [1979b] "New Approaches to Regulatory Reform—Letting the Market Do the Job." *National Journal* (August 11): 1316–22.

—— [1980] "The Public and the Private Sectors—The Old Distinctions Grow Fuzzy." *National Journal* (January 19): 99–104.

CLINTON, C. A. [1979] *Local Success and Federal Failure: A Study of Community Development and Educational Change in the Rural South.* Cambridge, Mass.: Abt Books.

COLE, R. L., and D. A. CAPUTO [1979] "Presidential Control of the Senior Civil Service: Assessing the Strategies of the Nixon Years." *American Political Science Review* 73 (June): 399–413.

COLELLA, C. C. [1979] "The Creation, Care and Feeding of Leviathan: Who and What Makes Government Grow." *Intergovernmental Perspective* 5 (Fall): 6–11.

CORSON, J. J., and R. S. PAUL [1966] *Men Near the Top.* Baltimore: Johns Hopkins University Press.

CURRY, B. [1977] "Product Safety Commission: An Agency Tied Up in Knots." *Washington Post* (May 16).

DAHL, R. A., and C. E. LINDBLOM [1953] *Politics, Economics, and Welfare.* New York: Harper & Row.

DERTHICK, M. [1972] *New Towns In-Town.* Washington, D.C.: Urban Institute.

DOMMEL, P. R. and Associates [1982] *Decentralizing Urban Policy: Case Studies in Community Development.* Washington, D.C.: Brookings Institution.

DOWNS, A. [1967] *Inside Bureaucracy.* Boston: Little, Brown.

DREW, E. B. [1967] "Is the FCC Dead?" *Atlantic* (July): 29–36.

—— [1970] "Dam Outrage: The Story of the Army Engineers." *Atlantic* (April): 51–62.

DUHL, R. [1979] "Carter Issues an Order, But Is Anybody Listening?" *National Journal* (July 14).

EDWARDS, G. C. III [1980] *Implementing Public Policy.* Washington: Congressional Quarterly Press.

ELMORE, R. F. [1978] "Organizational Models of Social Program Implementation." *Public Policy* 26 (Spring): 185–228.

FIORINA, M. P. [1977] *Congress: Keystone of the Washington Establishment.* New Haven: Yale University Press.

FRANKLIN, G. A. and R. B. RIPLEY [1984] *CETA: Politics and Policy, 1973–1982.* Knoxville, Tenn.: University of Tennessee Press.

FROMAN, L. A., JR. [1968] "The Categorization of Policy Contents," in *Political Science and Public Policy,* edited by A. Ranney. Chicago: Markham.

GANSLER, J. S. [1980] *The Defense Industry.* Cambridge, Mass.: MIT Press.

GELLHORN, E. [1980] "The Wages of Zealotry: the FTC under Siege." *Regulation* (January/February): 33–40.

GENERAL ACCOUNTING OFFICE [1979] "Federally Assisted Employment and Training: A Myriad of Programs Should Be Simplified." Report to the Congress (May 8).

——— [1983] "Justice Can Further Improve Its Monitoring of Changes in State/Local Voting Laws." Report to the Congress (December 19).

GORMLEY, W. T., JR. [1979] "A Test of the Revolving Door Hypothesis at the FCC." *American Journal of Political Science* (November): 665–83.

GRINDLE, M. S., ed. [1980] *Politics and Policy Implementation in the Third World.* Princeton, N.J.: Princeton University Press.

HARDEN, B. [1980] "Oil and Timber Firms Battle Environmentalists for Forest." *Washington Post* (May 27). © The Washington Post.

HARGROVE, E. C. [1975] *The Missing Link: The Study of the Implementation of Social Policy.* Washington, D.C.: The Urban Institute.

HARRIS, R. J., JR. [1980] "Tuna Fishermen See a Threat in Changes of Rules Concerning Killing of Porpoises." *The Wall Street Journal* (April 4).

HAYES, M. T. [1978] "The Semi-Sovereign Pressure Groups: A Critique of Current Theory and an Alternative Typology." *Journal of Politics* 40 (February): 134–61.

HECLO, H. [1977] *A Government of Strangers: Executive Politics in Washington.* Washington, D.C.: Brookings Institution.

HOLSENDOLPH, E. [1979] "TV Licensees Grow Anxious." *New York Times* (February 7). © 1979 by the New York Times Company.

———— [1980] "Black Mover Wins National License." *New York Times* (February 6).

HOROWITZ, D. L. [1977] *The Courts and Social Policy.* Washington, D.C.: Brookings Institution.

HUGHES, G. P. [1980] "Congressional Influence in Weapons Procurement: The Case of Lightweight Fighter Commonality." *Public Policy* 28 (Fall): 415–449.

INGRAM, H. [1977] "Policy Implementation through Bargaining: The Case of Federal Grants-in-Aid." *Public Policy* 25 (Fall): 499–526.

JANOWITZ, M. [1978] *The Last Half-Century: Societal Change and Politics in America.* Chicago: University of Chicago Press.

JANTSCHER, G. R. [1975] *Bread upon the Waters: Federal Aids to the Maritime Industries.* Washington, D.C.: Brookings Institution.

JOHNSON, H. [1977a] "Days of Endless Struggle, Drowning in a Sea of Paper." *Washington Post* (March 27). © The Washington Post.

———— [1977b] "Social Security: U.S. Umbilical Cord." *Washington Post* (March 28).

———— [1977c] "Government Gone Awry." *Washington Post* (March 29).

JONES, C. O. [1979] "American Politics and the Organization of Energy Decision Making." *Annual Review of Energy* 4: 99–121.

———— [1984] *An Introduction to the Study of Public Policy* (3d ed.). Monterey, Calif.: Brooks/Cole.

JONES, C. O., and R. D. THOMAS, eds. [1976] *Public Policy Making in a Federal System.* Beverly Hills, Calif.: Sage.

KATZ, D.; B. A. GUTEK; R. L. KAHN; and E. BARTON [1975] *Bureaucratic Encounters.* Ann Abor: Institute for Social Research, University of Michigan.

KATZMANN, R. A. [1980a] *Regulatory Bureaucracy: The Federal Trade Commission and Antitrust Policy.* Cambridge, Mass.: MIT Press.

———— [© 1980b] "Federal Trade Commission," in *The Politics of Regulation,* edited by J.Q. Wilson. New York: Basic Books.

KAUFMAN, H. [1960] *The Forest Ranger.* Baltimore: Johns Hopkins University Press.

———— [1976] *Are Government Organizations Immortal?* Washington, D.C.: Brookings Institution.

———— [1981] *The Administrative Behavior of Federal Bureau Chiefs.* Washington, D.C.: Brookings Institution.

KEISLING, P. [1982] "Old Soldiers Never Die: Can We Pay for the VA's Version of the Baby Boom?" *Washington Monthly* (March).

KETTL, D. F. [1983] *The Regulation of American Federalism.* Baton Rouge, La.: Louisiana State University Press.

KRAMER, L. [1979] "Oilman Says Energy Department Ruining Him, and It Agrees." *Washington Post* (August 24).

LAMB, C. M. [1984] "Equal Housing Opportunity." In *Implementation of Civil Rights Policy,* edited by C. S. Bullock III and C. M. Lamb. Monterey, Calif.: Brooks/Cole.

LAWRENCE, S. A. [1966] *United States Merchant Shipping Policies and Politics.* Washington, D.C.: Brookings Institution.

LAZIN, F. A. [1973] "The Failure of Federal Enforcement of Civil Rights Regulations in Public Housing, 1963–1971: The Co-optation of a Federal Agency by Its Local Constituency." *Policy Sciences* 4 (September): 263–73.

LEACH, R. H. [1970] *American Federalism.* New York: Norton.

LINDBLOM, C. E. [1965] *The Intelligence of Democracy.* New York: Free Press.

LIPSKY, M. [1980] *Street-Level Bureaucracy: Dilemmas of the Individual in Public Services.* New York: Russell Sage Foundation.

LOWI, T. J. [1964] "American Business, Public Policy, Case-Studies, and Political Theory." *World Politics* 16 (July): 677–715.

———— [1972] "Four Systems of Policy, Politics, and Choice." *Public Administration Review* 32 (July/August): 298–310.

———— [1979] *The End of Liberalism* (2d ed.). New York: W.W. Norton.

LYNN, N. B., and R. E. VADEN [1979] "Bureaucratic Response to Civil Service Reform." *Public Administration Review* 39 (July/August): 333–43.

MAASS, A. A. [1950] "Congress and Water Resources." *American Political Science Review* 44 (September): 576–93.

MANSFIELD, E. [1980] "Federal Maritime Commission," in *The Politics of Regulation,* edited by J.Q. Wilson. New York: Basic Books.

MARCUS, A. [1980] "Environmental Protection Agency," in *The Politics of Regulation,* edited by J.Q. Wilson. New York: Basic Books.

MAZMANIAN, D. A. and P. A. SABATIER [1983] *Implementation and Public Policy.* Glenview, Ill.: Scott, Foresman.

MCGREGOR, E. B., JR. [1982] "Public Service as Institution: The Conversation Continued." *Public Administration Review* 42 (July/August): 316–320.

MEAD, L. M. [1977] *Institutional Analysis: An Approach to Implementation Problems in Medicaid.* Washington, D.C.: Urban Institute.

MEIER, K. J. [1979] *Politics and the Bureaucracy.* North Scituate, Mass.: Duxbury.

——— [1985] *Regulation: Politics, Bureaucracy, and Economics.* New York: St. Martin's Press.

MEIER, K. J. and L. G. NIGRO [1976] "Representative Bureaucracy and Policy Preferences: A Study in the Attitudes of Federal Executives." *Public Administration Review* 36 (July/August): 458–69.

MENZEL, D. C. [1983] "Redirecting the Implementation of a Law: The Reagan Administration and Coal Surface Mining Regulation." *Public Administration Review* (September/October): 411–420.

MILLER, J. [1979a] "Using Public Dollars to Spur Private Development." *New York Times* (September 16).

——— [1979b] "Enforcer Unit Loses Support in S.E.C." *New York Times* (October 23).

MIRENGOFF, W., and L. RINDLER [1978] *CETA: Manpower Programs under Local Control.* Washington, D.C.: National Academy of Sciences.

MONTJOY, R. S. and L. J. O'TOOLE [1979] "Toward a Theory of Policy Implementation: An Organizational Perspective." *Public Administration Review* 39 (September/October): 465–76.

MOSHER, F. C. [1980] "The Changing Responsibilities and Tactics of the Federal Government." *Public Administration Review* 40 (November/December): 541–48.

MOSHER, L. [1980] "Water Politics as Usual May be Losing Ground in Congress." *National Journal* (July 19): 1187–90.

MOSSBERG, W. S. [1980] "The Energy Department Is a Flop." *The Wall Street Journal* (August 22).

MURPHY, J. T. [1971] "Title I of ESEA: The Politics of Implementing Federal Education Reform." *Harvard Educational Review* 41 (February): 35–63.

——— [1973] "The Education Bureaucracies Implement Novel Policy: The Politics of Title I of ESEA, 1965–72," in *Policy and Politics in America: Six Case Studies,* edited by A.P. Sindler. Boston: Little, Brown.

NAKAMURA, R. T., and F. SMALLWOOD [1980] *The Politics of Policy Implementation.* New York: St. Martin's Press.

NAVARRO, P. [1980] "The Politics of Air Pollution." *The Public Interest* (Spring): 36–44.

NEUSTADT, R. E. [1960] *Presidential Power.* New York: John Wiley & Sons.

———[1973] "Politicians and Bureaucrats," in *Congress and America's Future* (2d ed.), edited by D. B. Truman. Englewood Cliffs, N.J.: Prentice-Hall.

O'TOOLE, L. J., JR. and R. S. MONTJOY [1984] "Interorganizational Policy Implementation: A Theoretical Perspective." *Public Administration Review* 44 (November/December): 491–503.

PEIRCE, N. R. and R. GUSKIND [1985] "Reagan Budget Cutters Eye Community Block Grant Program on Its 10th Birthday." *National Journal* (January 5): 12–16.

PINCUS, W. [1980] "Deep Sea Mining Rules—Regulations U.S. and Business Wanted." *Washington Post* (December 1).

POOL, I. DES. [1979] "Protecting Human Subjects of Research: An Analysis on Proposed Amendments to HEW Policy." *PS* (Fall): 452–55.

PRESSMAN, J. L., and A. WILDAVSKY [1984] *Implementation* (3d ed.). Berkeley: University of California Press.

PRESTHUS, R. [1974] *Elites in the Policy Process.* New York: Cambridge University Press.

QUIRK, P. J. [1981] *Industry Influence in Regulatory Agencies.* Princeton, N.J.: Princeton University Press.

RABINOVITZ, F., J. PRESSMAN, and M. REIN [1976] "Guidelines: A Plethora of Forms, Authors, and Functions." *Policy Sciences* 7: 399–416.

RABKIN, J. [1980] "Office for Civil Rights," in *The Politics of Regulation,* edited by J. Q. Wilson. New York: Basic Books.

RADIN, B. A. [1977] *Implementation, Change, and the Federal Bureaucracy: School Desegregation Policy in H.E.W., 1964–1968.* New York: Teachers College Press.

RANDALL, R. [1979] "Presidential Power versus Bureaucratic Intransigence: The Influence of the Nixon Administration on Welfare Policy." *American Political Science Review* 73 (September): 795–810.

RANII, D. [1980] "Meals on Wheels: How to Turn Victory Into Defeat— and Back Into Victory." *National Journal* (March 29): 522–24.

REIN, M. and F. F. RABINOVITZ [1978] "Implementation: A Theoretical Perspective." In *American Politics and Public Policy,* edited by W. D. Burnham and M.W. Weinberg. Cambridge, Mass.: MIT Press.

RIPLEY, R. B. [1972] *The Politics of Economic and Human Resource Development.* Indianapolis: Bobbs-Merrill.

—— [1985] *Policy Analysis in Political Science.* Chicago: Nelson-Hall.

RIPLEY, R. B. and G. A. FRANKLIN [1984] *Congress, the Bureaucracy, and Public Policy* (3d ed.). Homewood, Ill.: Dorsey Press.

RIPLEY, R. B., and L. M. SMITH [1979] "The Implementation of HIRE II: Final Report," in *Hearing before the Committee on Veterans' Affairs, U.S. Senate, Oversight of Veterans' Employment Programs and Policies* (96th Congress, 1st Session, May 23): 720–97.

ROSENBAUM, W. [1979] "Public Participation: Now it's Required, But Is It Important?" *Citizen Participation* 1 (September/October): 12–13, 26.

ROSENFELD, R. A. [1979] "Local Implementation Decisions for Community Development Block Grants." *Public Administration Review* 39 (September/October): 448–57.

ROTHMAN, S. and S. R. LICHTER (1983) "How Liberal Are Bureaucrats?" *Regulation* (November/December): 16–22.

ROURKE, F. E. [1979] "Bureaucratic Autonomy and the Public Interest." *American Behavioral Scientist* 22 (May/June): 537–46.

SALAMON, L. M. [1980] "Rise of Third-Party Government..." *Washington Post* (June 29).

SALISBURY, R. H. [1968] "The Analysis of Public Policy: A Search for Theories and Roles," in *Political Science and Public Policy,* edited by A. Ranney. Chicago: Markham.

SARASOHN, J. [1980a] "Tentative Compromise Reached on Long-Stalled FTC Authorization Bill." *Congressional Quarterly Report* (April 26): 1148–49.

—— [1980b] "FTC Funded but Old Power Dispute Remains." *Congressional Quarterly Weekly Report* (May 3): 1167–68.

—— [1980c] "FTC Fund Bill with Legislative Veto Clears." *Congressional Quarterly Weekly Report* (May 24): 1407–9.

—— [1980d] "Congress Votes $49.7 Million for FTC but Not Before Agency Closed Two Days." *Congressional Quarterly Weekly Report* (June 7): 1573.

SAWYER, K. [1979a] "On the Chicken Line." *Washington Post* (September 2).

—— [© 1979b] "Schooling for Secretaries." *Washington Post* (October 14).

SCHER, R. and J. BUTTON [1984] "Voting Rights Act: Implementation and Impact." In *Implementation of Civil Rights Policy,* edited by C. S. Bullock III and C. M. Lamb. Monterey, Calif.: Brooks/Cole.

SCHUCK, P. H. [1979] "Litigation, Bargaining, and Regulation." *Regulation* (July/August): 26–34.

SCHWARTZ, T. [1980] "Debate on Broadcast Decontrol." *New York Times* (October 3).

SEIDMAN, H. [1980] *Politics, Position, and Power: The Dynamics of Federal Organization* (3d ed.). New York: Oxford University Press.

SEITZ, S. T. [1978] *Bureaucracy, Policy, and the Public.* St. Louis: Mosby.

SELZNICK, P.[1949] *TVA and the Grass Roots.* Berkeley: University of California Press.

SHABECOFF, P. [1980] "A 47-Year-Old Idea Renewed as the T.V.A. Tries Again." *New York Times* (March 2).

SHEPPARD, N., JR. [1979] "Fair-Employment Agency Cleans Up Its Backlog." *New York Times* (February 24).

SHIFRIN, C. [1979] "Freight Takeover for Rock Island Ordered by ICC." *Washington Post* (September 27).

SINGER, J. W. [1979a] "How the Renegotiation Board Went out of Business." *National Journal* (April 21): 642–45.

——— [1979b] "The Federal Trade Commission—Business's Government Enemy No. 1." *National Journal* (October 13): 1676–80.

STANFIELD, R. L. [1979a] "A New Breed of Mayors with a New View of Washington." *National Journal* (May 26): 866–70.

——— [1979b] "EDA's 'Revolutionary' Role." *National Journal* (August 18): 1377.

——— [1983] "Reagan Courting Women, Minorities, But It May Be Too Late to Win Them." *National Journal* (May 28): 1118–1123.

STANLEY, D. T., D. E. MANN, and J. W. DOIG [1967] *Men Who Govern.* Washington, D.C.: Brookings Institution.

SULLIVAN, J. F. [1979a] "Alexander Asserts Army Will Not Help Close Fort Dix." *New York Times* (September 25).

——— [1979b] "Fort Dix Gets a Reprieve for a Year to 18 Months." *New York Times* (October 11).

SULZBERGER, A. O., JR. [1980] "Cutting Red Tape in the U.S. Office of Goldstein." *New York Times* (July 6).

TALBOT, R. B., and D. F. HADWIGER [1968] *The Policy Process in American Agriculture.* San Francisco: Chandler.

THOMAS, J. [1967] "Performance of Consumer Agency Disappoints Its Early Supporters." *New York Times* (January 30).

TRUMAN, D. B. [1951] *The Governmental Process.* New York: Knopf.

UNITED STATES COMMISSION ON CIVIL RIGHTS [1981] "The Voting Rights Act: Unfulfilled Goals." Washington, D.C.: Government Printing Office.

VAN HORN, C. E. [1978] "Implementing CETA: The Federal Role." *Policy Analysis* 4 (Spring): 159–83.

———— [1979a] "Evaluating the New Federalism: National Goals and Local Implementors." *Public Administration Review* 39 (January/February): 17–22.

———— [1979b] *Policy Implementation in the Federal System: National Goals and Local Implementors.* Lexington, Mass.: Heath.

VAN HORN, C. E., and D. S. VAN METER [1976] "The Implementation of Inter-Governmental Policy," in *Public Policy Making in a Federal System,* edited by C. O. Jones and R. D. Thomas. Beverly Hills, California: Sage Publications.

VAN METER, D. S., and C. E. VAN HORN [1975] "The Policy Implementation Process: A Conceptual Framework." *Administration and Society* (February): 445–88.

VERBA, S. and N. H. NIE [1972] *Participation in America.* New York: Harper & Row.

WALKER, D.B. [1981] *Toward a Functioning Federalism.* Cambridge, Mass.: Winthrop.

WEIMER, D. L. [1980] "Federal Intervention in the Process of Innovation in Local Public Agencies: A Focus on Organizational Incentives." *Public Policy* 28 (Winter): 93–116.

WILDAVSKY, A. [1979] *The Politics of the Budgetary Process* (3d ed.). Boston: Little, Brown.

WILENSKY, H. L. [1967] *Organizational Intelligence.* New York: Basic Books.

WILSON, G. C. [1979] "Aircraft Engine Program Sparks Fierce Lobbying." *Washington Post* (March 12).

WILSON, J. Q. [1975] "The Rise of the Bureaucratic State." *The Public Interest,* no. 41 (Fall): 77–103.

———— [1980a] "The Politics of Regulation," in *The Politics of Regulation,* edited by J. Q. Wilson. New York: Basic Books: 357–94.

———— ed. [1980b] *The Politics of Regulation.* New York: Basic Books.

WINES, M. [1982] "Administration Says It Merely Seeks a 'Better Way' to Enforce Civil Rights." *National Journal* (March 27): 536–541.

—— [1983a] "Bewildering Battle on the High Seas—Some Carriers Seek an End to Subsidies." *National Journal* (April 16): 793–795.

—— [1983b] "FCC Ready to Act If Congress Fails to Approve TV Broadcast Deregulation." *National Journal* (July 30): 1592–1594.

WOLFINGER, R. E. and S. J. ROSENSTONE [1980] *Who Votes?* New Haven, Conn.: Yale University Press.

WOLL, P. [1977] *American Bureaucracy* (2d ed.). New York: Norton.

WRIGHT, D. S. [1978] *Understanding Intergovernmental Relations.* North Scituate, Mass.: Duxbury.

WYNIA, B. L. [1974] "Federal Bureaucrats' Attitudes toward a Democratic Ideology." *Public Administration Review* 34 (March/April): 156–62.

INDEX

About the Authors

Randall B. Ripley is Professor and chairperson of the Department of political Science and a Senior faculty Associate at the Mershon Center, The Ohio State University. He has written extensively on many aspects of U.S. politics and policy. He received his Ph.D. in political science from Harvard University and spent five years at the Brookings Institution in Washington, D.C., before moving to Ohio State in 1967.

Grace A. Franklin is a Research Associate at and Assistant Director of The Mershon Center of The Ohio State University. She has been affiliated with The Mershon Center since receiving her M.A. in political science at Ohio State in 1970. She has published a number of books and articles on politics and policy in the United States, including (with Ripley) *Congress, the Bureaucracy, and Public Policy,* a companion volume to 2Policy Implementation and Bureaucracy.

A Note on the Type

The text of this book was set in a photocomposition form of Times Roman, a face designed by Stanley Morison. Times Roman was first used by *The Times* (of London) in 1932. Part of Morison's special intent for Times Roman was to create a face that was editorially neutral. It is an especially compact, attractive, and legible typeface, which has come to be seen as the "most important type design of the twentieth century."

Composed by Publication Services, Champaign, Illinois.

Printed and bound by R. R. Donnelley & Sons, Crawfordsville, Indiana.